The Battle of Hampton Roads

The Battle of Hampton Roads

NEW PERSPECTIVES
ON THE
USS *Monitor* and CSS *Virginia*

EDITED BY

Harold Holzer

AND

Tim Mulligan

A special publication of
THE MARINERS' MUSEUM,
Newport News, Virginia

FORDHAM UNIVERSITY PRESS
New York • 2006

Copyright © 2006 Fordham University Press

All rights reserved. No part of this publication may be reproduced, stored in a retrieval system, or transmitted in any form or by any means—electronic, mechanical, photocopy, recording, or any other—except for brief quotations in printed reviews, without the prior permission of the publisher.

LIBRARY OF CONGRESS CATALOGING-IN-PUBLICATION DATA
The Battle of Hampton Roads : new perspectives on the USS Monitor and CSS Virginia / edited by Harold Holzer and Tim Mulligan.—1st ed.
    p. cm.
Includes bibliographical references and index.
ISBN 0-8232-2480-5 (hardcover) – ISBN 978-0-8232-2481-4 (pbk.)
1. Hampton Roads, Battle of, Va., 1862. 2. Monitor (Ironclad) 3. Virginia (Ironclad) 4. Virginia—History—Civil War, 1861–1865—Naval operations. 5. United States—History—Civil War, 1861–1865—Naval operations. I. Holzer, Harold, 1949-. II. Mulligan, Tim, 1938-
    E473.2.B38 2005
    973.7'52—dc22

                                                    2005018155

08 07 06   5 4 3 2 1
FIRST EDITION

To the brave men and women of the United States Navy and the National Oceanic and Atmospheric Administration (NOAA). Without them, there would be no USS Monitor *project.*

Contents

ACKNOWLEDGMENTS	ix
PREFACE *Harold Holzer*	xiii
INTRODUCTION *John Hightower*	xvii
1. The Battle of Hampton Roads *William C. Davis*	1
2. Building the Ironclads *Craig L. Symonds*	19
3. Iron Horse, Iron Coffin: Life Aboard the USS *Monitor* *David Mindell*	37
4. Sink Before Surrender: The Story of the CSS *Virginia* *John V. Quarstein*	57
5. Believe Only Half of What You Read about the Battle of Hampton Roads *Mabry Tyson*	85

6. Victory without Glory?
   The Battle of Hampton Roads in Art   111
   Harold Holzer

7. "This Country Now Occupies the Vantage Ground":
   Union Monitors vs. the British Navy   125
   Howard J. Fuller

8. Who Won the Battle of Hampton Roads?
   A Historians' Debate   141
   John V. Quarstein and Joseph Gutierrez

9. Discovery and Recovery—
   The Modern History of the USS *Monitor*:
   A Personal Memoir   155
   Jeff Johnston

PORTFOLIO: Highlights from the Monitor Center
   Collection   171

AFTERWORD: About The Mariners' Museum:
   The Collections   189

NOTES   193

CONTRIBUTORS   211

INDEX   215

Acknowledgments

FIRST AND FOREMOST, the editors are deeply grateful to the visionary John B. Hightower, President and CEO of The Mariners' Museum in Newport News, Virginia, for, among many other accomplishments, creating and generously supporting the institution's annual scholarly symposia. These events have become laboratories to engage both the general public and professional history community in an ongoing dialogue with the past. And they have spawned the kind of important, original scholarship that is reflected in this book.

At The Mariners' we have been privileged to work with a superb staff of professionals whose commitment to history is marked by enthusiasm and collegiality. We are especially appreciative of the support and friendship of Karen Grinnan, the Museum's former vice president for marketing, and Justin Lyons, public relations director. Their efforts have brought wide visibility and heartening audience support for the annual symposia, as well as great pleasure to those—like us—fortunate enough to work with them.

Anna Holloway, who helped organize that first symposium in her former role as the museum's director of education, continues to make important contributions from her essential new post as curator of the new USS *Monitor* Center. Marketing coordinator Ida Finifter has made every one of our visits to Newport News both useful and pleasant, and has made certain that visitors to the symposia are welcomed with the same level of enthusiasm and professionalism.

Claudia Jew, the Museum's manager of photographic services and licensing, was crucial in the demanding effort to research, secure, and organize the many images from the collection that illustrate this book. We are grateful indeed for her patient assistance in the wake of grueling deadline pressure. Thanks also go to her able colleague, Sidney Moore, coordinator of photographic services, for her valuable help as well.

The superb historians who participated in the very first Mariners' Museum symposium repaid our faith with brilliant presentations, many of which are featured on these pages, and we want very much again to acknowledge their hard work and faith in the institution as it launched this program. We owe a special debt of thanks to Craig L. Symonds, professor of history emeritus at the U.S. Naval Academy, and now official historian for the USS *Monitor* Center at The Mariners' Museum, for his wise counsel and memorable scholarly contribution.

Many corporate and community sponsors have supported these symposium programs, and The Mariners' Museum is particularly grateful to the two organizations that backed the initial event from which these chapters are drawn: The Lincoln Forum and the National Oceanic and Atmospheric Administration (NOAA). At The Lincoln Forum, we especially acknowledge Chief Justice Frank J. Williams, chairman; Charles D. Platt, Treasurer; and Annette Westerby, administrator, not to mention Linda Platt and Virginia Williams, who have lent their visible support to these events. From NOAA, Dr. John Broadwater has played a crucial leadership role, and Jeff Johnston ably communicated the excitement of historical discovery and recovery to an enthralled audience at Newport News.

Fordham University Press has been an enthusiastic partner in this publishing enterprise, and we particularly thank director Robert Oppedisano, former managing editor Chris Mohney, production manager Loomis Mayer, and marketing manager Kate O'Brien. Finally, we have greatly benefited from, and very much enjoyed working with, our copy editor Pat Cadigan.

Last but never least, the editors, together with Edith Holzer, who also worked to bring this project to fruition, gratefully acknowledge the advice, support, and priceless friendship of a man without whom neither the conference nor the book would have been remotely possible, or half as much fun: our public relations guru, overall eminence grise, and boon companion, John O'Keefe.

Harold Holzer and Tim Mulligan
New York
August 1, 2005

Preface
Harold Holzer

"THE OTHER DAY, there came...to see the President...a massive, vigorous, fine-looking man" to "show to the President, a model of a strange, altogether new sea-going war monster, devised by another man named Ericsson." So observed Abraham Lincoln's White House secretary, William O. Stoddard, on a momentous winter day in Washington in late 1861. Stoddard understood at once the importance of the visit—and of the "strange" vessel the visitor brought with him. And so did Lincoln.

Beset by unexpectedly strong Confederate military strength, frantically worried over reports of new and dangerous technological advancements in the South, the president desperately needed to shore up Union forces, on sea as well as on land. As Stoddard remembered: "Mr. Lincoln made a careful study of what was said to resemble a cheese-box on a raft, and he ordered a board of naval offices to get together and examine it.... There were adverse opinions from several other old salts, but Mr. Lincoln said he was like the fat girl when she put on her stockings—she thought there was something in it."[1] With that quintessentially Lincolnesque conclusion, work began on the USS *Monitor,* the ship that would change the course of the Civil War.

Nearly a century and a half later, on March 5, 2003—to commemorate the 141st anniversary of the battle that the ironclad went on to fight at Hampton Roads, Virginia—The Mariners' Museum in nearby Newport News hosted a scholarly symposium on the epochal duel that changed the history and technology of naval warfare in but a few hours: the meeting of the ironclads USS *Monitor* and CSS *Virginia*.

The conference, the first of three that have been hosted annually at the museum on the weekend closest to the battle date, brought together leading Civil War and military historians both to re-examine old theories about the *Monitor–Virginia* clash and to advance important new scholarship on the dramatic Hampton Bay encounter. The papers proved so stimulating that a number of people, including Mariners' Museum president John Hightower and Fordham University Press director Robert Oppedisano, devised the idea of bringing out a book that would preserve the scholarship and make it permanently available to a wider audience. This is the result.

To paraphrase Lincoln, it is "altogether fitting and proper" that the project was born—and enters a new phase—thanks to The Mariners' Museum, which is the official home of the remains of the USS *Monitor*, including its iconic gun turret, now rescued from the deep, undergoing restoration on the museum grounds, and awaiting permanent installation in a new Monitor Center being constructed adjacent to the existing building. Here, Civil War students, scholars, and visitors will be able to encounter what is left of the actual ship that so dramatically altered the momentum of the Civil War when it rode to the rescue of the federal fleet in March 1862.

"How can an admiral condescend to go to sea in an iron pot?" Nathaniel Hawthorne wondered when he first saw the *Monitor* a few weeks after the battle. "It could not be called a vessel at all; it was a machine... or for lack of a better similitude, it looked like a gigantic rat-trap. It was ugly, questionable, suspicious, evidently mischievous,—nay, I will allow myself to call it devilish; for this was the new war-fiend, destined, along with others of the same breed, to annihilate whole navies and batter down old supremacies."

"Yet even this," Hawthorne correctly predicted, "will not long be the last and most terrible improvement in the science of war."[2] But it was certainly one of the first. The editors and authors trust that the discussions on the pages that follow will open new windows onto its history—and that of its ironclad foe, the *Virginia*—so we may better understand not only the "terrible" technology they once symbolized, but also the human courage they once inspired.

Introduction
John Hightower

AS DIRECTOR OF The Mariners' Museum, I am delighted to be writing this Introduction that will, I hope, inaugurate a series of publications based on our annual symposia designed to explore the naval history of the Civil War in general and the Peninsula Campaign—on both land and sea—in particular.

We at The Mariners' Museum are immensely proud to have been chosen by the National Oceanic and Atmospheric Association (NOAA) on behalf of the United States Government as the permanent home of the USS *Monitor*. It seems more than appropriate, then, that we should host these symposia that will explore the history surrounding that iconic vessel and its influence and impact on both the Civil War and world history.

Almost immediately after that historic 1862 confrontation between the *Monitor* and the CSS *Virginia* at Hampton Roads, it was recognized around the world that something seminal had occurred. To cite only one instance, the English—who had seriously considered intervening in the war—quickly realized that, as one admiral put it, the introduction of the *Monitor* "renders the Americans practically unassailable in their own waters." No longer would there be any thought of taking on the United States.

Like the proverbial pebble dropped into the ocean, the ripples from the battle extended out from Hampton Roads influencing everything from ship construction to diplomacy. It is an endlessly fascinating subject, and one that I hope we will be exploring for many years to come.

At the same time, none of this could have taken place without the strong support of the Lincoln Forum, particularly its chairman, Frank Williams, and the advice and support of two historians renowned for their interest in and dedication to examining the Civil War and its meaning to our world. They are Craig Symonds of the United States Naval Academy, the leading authority on the Civil War navy, and Harold Holzer of The Metropolitan Museum of Art, the reigning expert on Civil War iconography. And we are particularly grateful to the NOAA for its heroic work in locating and rescuing the USS *Monitor* artifacts so they can be preserved and studied here at The Mariners' Museum—and ultimately displayed to the public in a brilliant new setting.

I'm sure you will enjoy the fascinating papers from this, our first symposiium, and I hope that I will soon have the pleasure of welcoming you to future Civil War symposia—and, beginning in 2007, to the new Monitor Center at The Mariners' Museum.

CHAPTER 1

The Battle of Hampton Roads
William C. Davis

THE BATTLE THAT TOOK PLACE BETWEEN THE TWO IRONclads on March 9, 1862, perhaps could only have happened in the 1860s. The timing was exactly right. Technology had been racing in ten-league boots for twenty or thirty years, and it all came together at Hampton Roads.

The *Monitor* and *Virginia* were not the first ironclads. Classical sources—that is, Greek and Latin sources—are not always reliable, but they tell us that in the third century B.C. the king of Syracuse built a merchant ship cased in lead. One wonders if it went down like a lead you-know-what. Obviously this was simply to protect the vessel from slings and arrows and outrageous fortune. But it is also known that the Vikings used their iron-rimmed shields lined along the gunnels of their vessels as a form of defense against arrows. In 1592, the famous Korean Admiral Yi apparently fought an engagement with a sort of plated vessel that was called the turtle boat or tortoise boat because it looked very much like a turtle. In the 1790s, Spain was already building floating batteries cased in iron. Iron-hulled merchant ships were being built in the 1840s in both Britain and the United States. Then, of course, in the

1850s, experiments began in making warships' armor, a development virtually forced by the introduction of the shell gun. On November 30, 1853, in the Crimean War, a Russian fleet armed with shell guns destroyed a Turkish fleet of wooden vessels. Clearly the day of the wooden warship was about over; only iron was going to be able to defend against iron. In 1859, France built the *Gloire*, protected by 4½ inches of armor, and by 1861 France had, according to some reports, as many as twenty more of these vessels on the way or completed.

Britain built the *Warrior* and the *Black Prince* in 1859, too, not just placing armor over a conventional wooden frame like the *Gloire*, but building the entire framework—the skeleton of the vessel—from iron. By 1861, Britain had nearly a dozen such vessels under construction, some boasting 6½ inches of armor. Thirty years earlier they wouldn't have had steam engines sufficiently powerful to drive these monsters. And, of course, the *Virginia* didn't in 1862. But developments in steam power were keeping up with, or catching up with, the added weight of the iron.

The United States was behind the rest, but not completely. In fact, the moment the Civil War began there were calls in the North for an ironclad fleet. Donald McKay, who was the nation's leading shipbuilder, the man who built all the great clipper ships, actually called for constructing a fleet of six hundred ironclads in one year, which would have been good business for him since he proposed that he should build them all himself. What happened, of course, is that events got ahead of North and South alike, and suddenly there was a war that neither side was prepared to fight on the rivers or on the seas. As a result, what otherwise might have taken years of slow technological development had to be dramatically compressed, and Hampton Roads was destined to be the technological turning point, not for the Civil War alone but for the world's industrial and naval history. It was a turning point that required months of frenzied development coming down to just a few hours on the proving ground, and, ultimately, to the eve of those hours of the final test in Hampton Roads.

The battle, of course, almost did not happen. The *Virginia*, as of March 7, had no powder, which is certainly a problem if you are going to be a battleship. The *Monitor* nearly went down on its trip south, which is also a problem unless you intend to be a submarine! But the *Virginia*'s prime target, the wooden Union fleet in Hampton Roads, was not going anywhere, and once her powder was on board, the Rebel behemoth steamed into the Roads on March 8 to comprehensively end the era of iron men in wooden ships in a single day. Suffice it to say that within just a few hours, and at a Confederate loss of just 27 men killed or wounded throughout the entire fleet, the USS *Cumberland* lay on the bottom, the USS *Congress* was ablaze and would explode in the night, and the USS *Minnesota* had run hard aground and offered a sitting target for the next day. So had the USS *St. Lawrence*, while the *Roanoke* was the only maneuverable Union warship left, and clearly no match for the *Virginia*, if or when she chose to come visiting again.

When the *Monitor* came into sight that night, in one of the best-timed entrances in world history, the scene before her was one of utter devastation, and with it came the realization that there would be a sleepless night ahead while her seamen prepared to hurl their own little vessel into the mouth of the monster that had just destroyed a fleet. It was not even dawn the next morning when the bosun's pipe awakened the sleeping crew of the *Virginia*. Dinwiddie Phillips, one of the officers, remembered that, "It seems as though we had scarcely been asleep." These men were still excited from the victory of the day before, and filled with anticipation of what they expected they were going to do again, that day. While the fife and the drum where still sounding to awaken the men, they hurriedly dressed and went to a hearty breakfast. For those who wanted it, the morning meal was rinsed down with two jiggers of whiskey per man (for the Confederate Navy never tried to abolish the grog ration).

Shortly after sunrise, about 6:30, they were ready to leave. Far off in the distance they could see dimly that the *Minnesota* still lay aground. She and any other Federal ships the Confederates might engage looked to be easy victories. Of course, the *Virginia*'s captain, Franklin Buchanan, had been put out of action by a wound suffered the day before, and his executive officer, Catesby Jones, had taken over. Jones got up steam, weighed anchor, and put out into Hampton Roads, which was still covered by the early morning fog, only now beginning to dissipate under the warm rays of the rising sun. It was going to be another unusually beautiful day. Off in the distance they could hear the signal gun at Fort Monroe awakening the garrison.

Accompanied by the Confederate ships *Patrick Henry*, *Jamestown*, and *Teaser*, Jones steamed the *Virginia* due north, directly toward the fort. Once again the banks along the Roads were lined with people and soldiers who had come early to get a good place to watch the show. This was the biggest spectator event of the Civil War. Thousands, maybe tens of thousands, of civilians were lining the bank to view what was happening.

Aboard the moving squadron, however, something else shortly came into view. As Jones steamed north into the Roads, he and his men saw that the *Minnesota* was no longer alone. There was an iron battery near her, Jones observed. Despite his later claims that he knew the *Monitor* had arrived, it is obvious that the appearance of Ericsson's ironclad took the Confederates quite by surprise. Looking out his gun port, George Eggleston, one of the men aboard the *Virginia*, thought her "the strangest looking craft we had ever seen before." "We could see nothing but the resemblance of a large cheese box," recalled another. Hunter Davidson at first exclaimed with glee that the *Minnesota*'s crew was "leaving her on a funny raft." Hardin Littlepage, another midshipman aboard, frankly admitted that, "we were taken wholly by surprise." At first he thought it was a raft on which they were removing the *Minnesota*'s engine and boilers to save them. The surprise extended to the other ships and those on shore as well. "We could not tell what the *Monitor* was," said one. Aboard the *Patrick Henry*, her executive officer, Lieutenant James Rochelle, saw next to the Federal frigate "such a craft as the eyes of a seaman never look upon before—an immense shingle floating in the water with a gigantic cheese box rising from its center. No sails, no wheels, no smokestack, no guns; what could it be?"

Some suspected that it was a water tank supplying the *Minnesota*. Others thought it was a floating magazine reloading her. "No words can express the surprise with which we beheld this strange craft," said an observer. Its appearance was tersely and graphically described by one as a tin can on a shingle.

"A few visionary observers," wrote Rochelle, "feebly intimated that it might be the *Monitor*," because the Confederates, of course, did know that the *Monitor* was being constructed. Once the surprise of seeing the *Monitor* was over, however, there were those aboard the *Virginia* who wondered what lay ahead. Lieutenant John Taylor Wood spoke for many: "She could not possibly have made her appearance at a more inopportune time for us." Those on the opposite shore might have disagreed. The Federals, this morning, had their first opportunity to view the *Monitor* as she lay at anchor near the *Minnesota*. Many were not impressed. "No one in our camp seemed to know what it was or how it came there," wrote a surgeon, "but at last it was conceded that it must be the strange new ironclad which we heard was being built in New York by Ericsson." Yet, he lamented, "She seemed so small and so trifling a thing that we feared she would only constitute additional prey for the *Leviathan*."

Another former sailor, aboard the now extinct *Congress*, confessed that, "to tell the truth, we didn't have much faith in the *Monitor*." Aboard the ship itself, those who had managed to get to sleep during the hectic night awakened and had a 7:00 A.M. breakfast, and no grog. Already the *Monitor* had her steam up. While some men ate, others raised the anchor. Slowly she steamed along the *Minnesota*'s side as it towered above her. Those on top of the turret looked up *Minnesota*'s sheer lofty side. Men were now leaving the ship, getting into small boats to go ashore. Some of the frigate's guns were being thrown overboard to prevent the enemy from getting them should there be a repeat today of what had happened the day before.

"Everything seemed in confusion," wrote Paymaster William Keeler aboard the *Monitor*. As an ominous reminder of the power of the *Virginia*, he and others in the turret could see the splintered holes made by the Confederate ironclad's shell where they penetrated the frigate's wooden side the day before. When the fog lifted, Keeler and others got their first glimpse of the *Virginia*, steaming north from Sewell's Point. It was nearly 8:00 A.M. by now. Some were still eating their breakfasts, but at the word that the ironclad was in sight, coffee was forgotten. Immediately the ironclad crew came to life, battening down the deck hatches, removing the smoke stacks and vent stacks, and putting stoppers on the deck lights. Every man went to his post. Lieutenant John Worden, with the pilot and Quartermaster Peter Williams to steer, would occupy the small and very exposed rectangular pilothouse toward the bow. Samuel Dana Greene, executive officer, would command the turret, with Alden Stimers and Louis Stodder helping to direct the two massive guns. Isaac Newton—a wonderful name for an engineer on an ironclad—would manage the engine of the boiler rooms. As Paymaster Keeler had no battle station, he remained on top of the turret, along with a few others. By now they could see the *Virginia* clearly. "There was no mistaking her slanting, rakish outline," said one. Then they saw a puff of white smoke jet out from her bow port and heard the howl of a shell as it passed over them and hit the *Minnesota*. The battle had begun.

Peeved at the foolishness of men staying exposed on the turret, Worden now came up and sternly said: "Gentlemen, that is the *Merrimack*. You had better go below." All raced down into the turret, Worden coming down last and shutting the heavy iron hatch behind him. The scene inside the turret now, and for the balance of the day, would be eerie and unforgettable. A few rays of sunlight filtered in through the gratings on top of the tower, while dim lanterns provided just enough additional illumination to cast misshapen shadows of men and gun on the turret interior.

The men mostly stood perfectly still, "almost like statues," thought Keeler. "The most profound silence reigned," he wrote, adding that "If there had been a coward heart there, its throb would have been audible, so intense was the stillness." The paymaster was baffled by the feelings he experienced; it was inexplicable. "We were enclosed in what we supposed to be an impenetrable armour. We knew that a powerful foe was about to meet us. Ours was an untried experiment and the enemy's first fire might make it a coffin for us all."

Making matters worse was the fact that with the gun port shutters closed no one in the turret could see the *Virginia*. They waited in the silent darkness, expecting every moment to hear a Rebel shell strike their untried iron. Keeler himself admitted that the suspense was awful. Soon they heard the firing of a gun, followed by two or three other shots, and then what sounded like a broadside from the *Minnesota* in reply. Unfortunately, the *Monitor*'s speaking tube wasn't working—yet another casualty of that trip south. So Lieutenant Greene sent Keeler forward to the pilothouse to ask Worden if he could open fire from the turret. "Tell Mr. Greene," said Worden, "not to fire until I give the word, to be cool and deliberate, to take sure aim and not to waste a shot."

Worden aimed his craft straight for the *Virginia*. Now he sent the word to Greene to commence firing. The engine stopped. Stodder laboriously turned the wheel that controlled the turret and the great lumbering iron tower began to revolve until its guns pointed at the enemy ship. Greene ordered a gun port stopper opened, ran out a gun, and pulled the lanyard. The quartermaster, William Trescott, peered out just after that first shot was fired to look at the *Virginia*. "You can see surprise on a ship the same as you can see it in a human being" he declared, "and there was surprise all over the *Merrimack*."

Indeed, the *Virginia* was surprised by the appearance of the

Monitor, but Catesby Jones did not change his original intention. He told his pilot to take the ship within a half-mile of the *Minnesota*, from which distance he could easily pulverize her. But the pilots would never get him any closer than a mile. He ordered the ironclad's first firing to commence when the enemy frigate was 1½ miles distant. Even when the Confederates saw the puff of smoke from the *Monitor*'s first shot, some still did not believe that it was an enemy ship. Littlepage, still thinking that the strange vessel was actually the frigate's boiler being removed for repairs, concluded that it had exploded. Jones knew what it was by now, but he decided at first to ignore the *Monitor* and keep trying to reach the *Minnesota*.

Only when it appeared that his pilots could not get him close enough to suit him did the lieutenant decide instead to try a fight with the enemy ironclad, which now peppered the *Virginia* repeatedly with its shells. It was about 8:45 A.M. For the next two hours these two iron monsters would give each other their undivided attention. At first they fired long range, but before long the ships closed to within 50 yards. They began circling each other in spirals, now opening the distance to 100 yards or more, and then closing until they almost touched. Thanks to her light draft and better engines, the *Monitor* moved about at will, steaming much faster and steering considerably better than the *Virginia*. Indeed, during the fight, Jones complained repeatedly that he couldn't bring his guns to bear on his antagonist because she presented such a relatively small target and was constantly moving and quickly maneuvering. As for the enemy's armament, Eggleston declared: "We never got sight of her guns, except when they were about to fire into us. As soon as the *Monitor*'s guns would fire, the turret revolved them out of view to reload." Jones marveled at how proper aim could be taken by the Yankee gunners when their guns stopped for such a short time on the target. Yet the sound of Yankee shells ricocheting off the *Virginia*'s side was proof that Greene was sending most of his shots true.

The *Virginia*'s gun deck took on the aspect of a scene from

Dante's *Inferno*, as the Confederates began battling the Yankee iron monster. All was dim light, figures bustling about in dense smoke, silence followed by deafening noise, men begrimed with sweat and soot, burnt powder flying everywhere, occasionally blood on the deck. Commands came from sometimes unseen officers, sternly putting the men through their tasks. It was a nightmare.

Below in the boiler room, the furnaces spewed fire and smoke while the firemen worked their controls to try to increase the heat to get more power. "The noise of the crackling, roaring fires, escaping steam with the loud and labored pulsations of the engines, together with the roar of battle above and the thud and vibration of the huge mass of iron being hurled against us, all together produced a scene and sound to be compared only with the poet's picture of the infernal regions," recalled one man about the ship.

The inside of the *Monitor*'s turret presented a scene far more calm, particularly after the first shots of the *Virginia* rebounded harmlessly off its side. When the first shots struck, a wave of consternation coursed over the men of the turret. They told Officer Greene where the shot had struck and showed him the indentation it had made in the iron. Green, in turn, reported this to engineer Alden Stimers, since he was better acquainted with the ship's construction. "Did the shot come through?" asked the engineer. "No, sir, it didn't come through," Richard Greene replied. "But it made a big dent—just look a there sir." "A big dent," exclaimed Stimers. "Of course it made a big dent—that's just what we expected. But what do you care about that, so long as it keeps out the shot." "Oh well it's all right, of course, sir," Greene replied. Stimers immediately sensed a feeling of relief in the turret as the men gained confidence in the vessels surrounding. It could withstand what the Confederates could throw at them.

As the heat from engines, boilers, and guns rose inside the turret, the men working the guns stripped to the waist. Powder and smoke soon turned their bodies black. Keeler could see the perspiration falling from them like rain. They loaded and fired the guns as fast as possible. Greene himself aimed and fired each gun personally. Because of a problem with the port stoppers, only one gun could be fired at a time. Then too, thanks to the closing of the ports as soon as the guns recoiled, no one could see what effect the shots were having; no one in the turret, that is, since the only way to see out at all was over the guns as they were being aimed. Consequently, after each shot, Greene would have to send Keeler forward to the pilothouse to ask Worden if they had hit anything. The situation, said Greene, was novel to say the least. Other problems soon reared up. The port stoppers had been designed with a little hole in them so that when the gun had been fired, and it had recoiled inside, the port stoppers then closed. There was very little distance between the muzzle of the gun and the port stopper. One could hardly get a rammer in there. So this little hole in the port stopper was used for running the rammer through outside the turret and then ramming things in it. This presented a very novel aspect, when these two guns were being loaded two poles stuck out—looking like chopsticks trying to get a grip on Asian food. The men finally just gave up. The port stoppers were so cumbersome and unwieldy to operate that they just left them open.

Then yet another difficulty arose. Much has been written about the problems the *Monitor* suffered during its trip south, including getting much of its machinery wet as well as the leather belts that helped to operate the machinery. Rust was already setting in on some of the gears and controls. This meant that it was only by the brute force involved in turning a very large wheel that they were able to stop and start the turret. Only Engineer Stimers was actually able to operate this thing. In the end, it became so difficult to stop the turret that instead they decided not to try, and for the balance of the battle, the *Monitor* turret was just slowly and constantly revolving, and the crew would take aim at the *Virginia* as it passed their sights on the fly.

The men, however, performed magnificently. During the previous forty-eight hours they had enjoyed little real rest and little food. Many had been hard at work during the night, and for breakfast had only some hard bread and coffee. Greene himself estimated that he had not slept in fifty-one hours. But after the first gun was fired, he forgot all the fatigue, hard work, and everything else, and went to work fighting.

Greene would have been pleased to know that the *Virginia* was operating under some severe handicaps as well. Among other problems, thanks to the loss of her ram the day before, she was now leaking badly and her pumps needed to be constantly in operation. With the added weight of water in her hull, she steered miserably. Her helm was sluggish and the men aboard could feel the lack of responsiveness in the way she jerked and vibrated under their feet when she tried to turn. It took nearly fifteen minutes for her to make a simple maneuver to turn her broadside toward the *Monitor*. Some men aboard thought she was actually close to sinking throughout the fight. Worse yet, her smokestack was so perforated by shot and shell from two days of fighting that it no longer served as a chimney to provide the necessary draft to draw in the fresh air needed to keep the fires going and the men's areas ventilated. Engineer Ramsey experienced a great deal of trouble just maintaining steam. "Our ship," he confirmed, "is working worse and worse."

But the Confederates could take comfort from the fact that the *Monitor*, so far, had done them very little damage, aside from a few cracked plates on the casemate. In fact, after nearly two hours of fighting, little damage had been done to either vessel. And clearly the fight was far from finished. Then, at about 10:30, when still far distant from the *Minnesota*, the rebel ironclad met calamity. Amidst all the circling and maneuvering her pilots became confused and allowed the *Virginia* to run aground in shoal water. She stuck fast. The situation seemed, for a time, critical. The engineers, in particular, were apprehensive. They did not think they had enough power in their engine to get the vessel back off of that sandbar. And then they saw the *Monitor* coming toward them, ready to deliver what might have been very telling blows, indeed. All the while the Confederates expended every effort to get their ship off the mud. "We had to take all chances," said Engineer Ramsey. They tied down the steam safety valves, which prevented the boiler from building up too much pressure. Ramsey wanted all the steam he could get, and safety was no longer a consideration. "It seemed impossible," he said, "that the boilers could stand any longer the pressure we were crowding upon them." Meanwhile, on the gun deck, the men were standing, awaiting their fate, unable to fire at the *Monitor* because she was out of view. But finally, seemingly miraculously, the *Virginia* built up enough steam and managed to shake herself loose.

And now, Catesby Jones revealed for the first time a new resolve. Never mind the *Monitor*'s guns, he declared. "We are going to ram her." Had his inspection of the *Virginia* the night before been more thorough he would have known that she no longer had her iron ram. He called Ramsey to him and ordered that the engines be reversed the second that they hit the *Monitor* so that he could back out and allow the Union ironclad to sink. Then he began a maneuver for position. But the *Virginia* required a mile of water just to get up headway. Jones gave short, sharp commands to the helmsman as he tried to turn the vessel into the *Monitor*'s midships. Aboard the Federal ironclad, of course, the Federals methodically kept up their fire and deduced what Jones and the *Virginia* were about to attempt. "Look out now," Greene, yelled to Keeler. "They are going to try to run us down."

Worden put the helm hard over, away from the *Virginia*, hoping the blow would strike obliquely and glance off. There was a moment of terrible suspense, and then a heavy jar that nearly threw them all to the floor. But the *Virginia* had struck only a glancing blow that dented the iron belt of armor around the vessel's hull but did no serious damage.

At first the Confederates thought they had done a great deal of damage. Then, of course, they realized that the *Monitor* was still afloat, and still fighting, and never did the firing from the *Monitor* stop. "The sounds of the conflict by this time," said Keeler, "were terrible." As yet, no one inside the turret had been injured. But several men had been bruised when nuts on the inside of the turret—they were connected to the bolts that held the iron plating—came free. When the bolt outside was hit by one of the *Virginia's* shells, it had the tendency to knock the nuts off the inside and send them flying around inside the turret, like deadly missiles. Had anybody been hit in the face or the eyes they would have been seriously, perhaps critically, injured. At one point, Alban Stimers, Louis Stodder, and another officer were conversing, all three of them foolishly leaning against the inside wall of the turret, at the moment a shot from the *Virginia* struck the outside almost opposite them. The impact knocked all three of them to the deck. Stimers, who only had his hand resting against the wall, sprang back up uninjured. Stodder, however, had rested his knee against it. "I was flung by the concussion clean over the guns to the floor of the turret," he recalled. Unconscious, he had to be taken below. The third man was the most seriously wounded of all; his head, while against the turret, was only inches from the point where the impact struck. "I dropped like a dead man," he recalled. Remarkably, he eventually regained full consciousness and was found to have suffered no permanent injury.

About that time Worden pulled the vessel out of the fight for more than half an hour. Ammunition was exhausted, and the crew needed to stop the turret in order to get further ammunition up from below. While this was happening, Jones took advantage of the opportunity to go after the *Minnesota* again, but the *Monitor* returned to the fight, and for the first and only time potential calamity struck the Union ship when one of the *Virginia's* shells hit the pilothouse just as John Worden was looking out through the viewing slit. No one on the rest of the vessel knew, at first, just what had happened. But, of course, what had happened was that the shell had exploded outside, nearly lifting the top of the pilothouse, and sending small needle-like shards of iron through the viewing slit, hitting Worden in the eyes. Others were hit as well and all the men inside the pilothouse were bleeding. All they saw was a flash of light and then darkness. Worden, himself, was heard to yell out: "My eyes—I am blind."

Greene had to take over. At first he wondered what to do, creating a brief, but understandable, loss of time, and some confusion on the *Monitor* as they transferred command. The *Monitor* also was running into shoal water, which meant the *Virginia* could not chase her. For all these reasons, there was a lull in the battle.

Jones was now of the opinion that the *Monitor* was not going to fight again, and, at first, concluded it was time to go back toward the *Minnesota*. Then Greene got the *Monitor* turned around and saw the *Virginia* steaming off toward Sewell's Point. By then, Jones had finally realized that he could not get to the *Minnesota* that day and he was simply going to go back to his berth. Aboard the *Monitor*, once it was returning to the fight, they saw the *Virginia* going home. Both commanders concluded that the other had given up. Thus an epic battle in American, and indeed, naval history, ended in a case of simultaneous, mutual misapprehension, with each side believing the other had thrown in the towel.

Shells were still flying, even while this was going on, and a little more damage was done, but then Greene, too, decided it was time to stop fighting. The *Monitor* had achieved its objective for the day. It had saved the *Minnesota*; it had saved the *Roanoke* and the *St. Lawrence*. The *Virginia* had apparently given up the fight and returned to her berth. So aboard the *Monitor* there was some jubilation. Aboard the *Virginia* going back home, there was jubilation, too. It had been a happy battle for everybody.

To the watching Federals on shore the battle seemed much the same. "The *Merrimack* and Ericsson's tiger battery fought like tigers for four hours," wrote one soldier at Fort Monroe, "in one of the greatest Naval engagements that has ever occurred since the beginning of the world." It had looked to some like David and Goliath afloat. Many men watched the fight from treetops or from riggings of the frigates. "To tell the truth, we didn't have much faith in the *Monitor*. We all expected to see the *Merrimack* destroy her," said one. What they saw instead was one of the grandest fights between two war vessels that the world had ever seen.

Of course, some did not see it that way. One survivor of the destroyed USS *Cumberland* viewed it from the *Roanoke*. "While the battle," he said, "was a notable affair, it seemed tame enough to me as seen from a distance of three or four miles." Perhaps so, but few were disappointed with the results.

It was a curious battle, bringing different results on different planes. In terms of the immediate mission of the two ships, it was certainly an unqualified victory for the *Monitor*. She had been ordered to protect the *Minnesota*, and protect her Worden did.

The *Virginia*'s objective was the destruction of that frigate and any other Federal warships she could engage. This she was not able to accomplish. Of course, the Confederacy claimed the *Monitor* had nothing to do with its failure to destroy the *Minnesota*; it had been prevented from doing so only by the fact that the water was too shallow for its ironclad to approach nearer than one mile from the frigate. But the argument falls down somewhat in the face of the damage the *Virginia* did do with the few shots it fired at the *Minnesota* that day.

From a tactical vantage point, in assessing the fighting itself, the verdict appears different. The *Virginia* left the fight in almost exactly the same condition in which she entered it—deplorable—but she wasn't any worse off than she had been that morning. Aside from some cracked plates—and those plates may have been cracked the previous day by shells from the *Congress* and the *Cumberland*—and a leak in her bow, she was relatively uninjured and reported no casualties other than a few walking wounded. Jones could have continued to fight had he wished, and according to his chief engineer, Jones actually intended first only to withdraw to Sewell's Point and then wait for the tide to come in so they could go back out and renew the attack. In terms of immediate tactical damage done, the *Virginia* probably emerged slightly the victor.

As for how the battle of the two iron monsters influenced the broad strategic picture in Virginia, for the moment it seemed a draw. The Federals still controlled Hampton Roads, the Confederates still held the James, the Nansemond, and the Elizabeth Rivers, and Norfolk. So long as the two ironclads remained afloat, the *Monitor* and her sister vessels stood no better chance of taking Norfolk by water and regaining the navy yard than did the *Virginia* and her consorts of escaping Hampton Roads to the Chesapeake and breaking the blockade.

The two ironclads would never meet again. The *Virginia* would be trapped and destroyed by her own crew on May 11. The *Monitor* lived on another seven months, patrolling the James up to Drewry's Bluff and then foundering in the pre-dawn darkness off Cape Hatteras on December 31. The aftermath was ram fever—North and South—the building of a host of classes of iron vessels and monitors. It is worth pointing out that in the end, even the Confederacy was planning to build a monitor as a more economical and more efficient design.

Neither lived up entirely to expectations. Confederate vessels were all too inadequately built from materials available and could seldom stand up to Union ironclads. They became floating batteries.

The Yankee monitors meanwhile could not stand the fire from fixed forts on land. And like the *Monitor* and the *Virginia* after March 9, they rarely ever met in action, but mainly stood and stared at each other, Rebel ironclads protecting harbors where possible, Union ships patrolling rivers and aiding in the blockade.

But just as a single pebble can create a ripple felt far away, so the local disturbance in the waters of Hampton Roads was felt around the globe. The full potential of the ironclad was only realized after the war, as all of the world's navies learned from the example of the *Monitor* and the *Virginia* and converted to iron and then steel. The day of the tall ship with the broadside was done. The only remaining constant "metal" would be the mettle of the men, and now women, who go to sea to fight. That has never changed. Nor will it.

CHAPTER 2

Building the Ironclads
Craig L. Symonds

MARCH 9, 1862, MARKED A TURNING POINT IN THE HISTORY OF modern warfare. The clash between the Confederate ironclad *Virginia* and the Federal *Monitor* was not merely an interesting curiosity of naval warfare, it was also symbolic of dramatic and fundamental changes in the nature of human conflict. Even before the Civil War began, it was evident that a revolution in naval technology was underway as the graceful frigates and sloops of the Age of Sail gave way to coal-fired steam ships. But it took the clash at Hampton Roads in March 1862, to demonstrate just how far that revolution had come.

Though the moment of recognition was jarring, the revolution itself had been long in the making. It began with the first practical application of steam propulsion to ships nearly a half century before the Battle at Hampton Roads, and in the fifty years since then, coal-fired steam engines became increasingly common on the warships of

---

Portions of this article are excerpted from Craig L. Symonds, *Decision at Sea: Five Naval Battles That Shaped American History* (New York: Oxford University Press, 2005).

the world's navies. Many had resisted the change, including most of the senior U.S. Navy officers. After all, coal was filthy stuff; its ubiquitous dust permeated everything on board, making it impossible to maintain the kind of spit-and-polish cleanliness that had long defined successful command at sea. Moreover, the wind was free, coal was expensive, and it was not available everywhere. A reliance on coal made warships operating thousands of miles from home dependent on foreign ports for fuel. Because of that, steam warships often spent most of their time under sail and were called "auxiliary steamers."

Many of these auxiliary steamers boasted large side-mounted paddlewheels to drive the ship through the water when under power. But paddlewheels not only masked as much as half of the ship's broadside, thus limiting its offensive potential, they also made an inviting target for the enemy. During the 1840s, paddlewheels gave way to the screw propeller, which proved more efficient. Even then, however, propellers were generally two-bladed rather than three-or four-bladed, so that when a ship was under sail, the propeller could be fixed in a vertical position to reduce its drag on the water. Many steam ships also had hinged crankshafts so that the propeller could be lifted out of the water altogether; others had hinged smokestacks that could be lowered to the deck. Practicality, as well as tradition, led naval architects to design the steam ships of the 1840s and '50s to look as much as possible like the ships that had fought in the American Revolution and the War of 1812.

Naval gunnery had changed, too. Naval guns in the 1860s still loaded from the muzzle, as they had for more than two hundred years, but the capacity of those guns was no longer measured by the weight of the shot they fired. In the War of 1812, sailors referred to 12-pounders and 18-pounders. What they meant was that the guns fired cannon balls that weighed 12 or 18 pounds. But by the 1850s, the weight of the shot had grown to more than 100 pounds, and the guns were now measured by the diameter of the muzzle, so that sailors began to speak of 5-inch guns or 7-inch guns. Once the Civil War began, the pace of change accelerated. Naval guns grew from 7 inches to 9 inches, to 11 inches, and finally to 15 inches—guns so large they dwarfed the human figures that served them.

Before the war was over, the Union Navy would forge a 20-inch gun that weighed over 10 tons, and though it never was deployed in battle, it was larger than the biggest naval guns of World War II.[1]

These guns not only were bigger, many of them were rifled—that is, they had grooves cut in a corkscrew pattern inside the barrel that put a spin on the projectile, enabling it to keep a true trajectory for a much longer distance—just as a football thrown in a perfect spiral keeps a truer trajectory than the proverbial "wounded duck." And the projectiles those guns fired were, more often than not, explosive shells rather than solid shot. When they did fire solid shot they fired what were called "bolts," some of which weighed 200 pounds.

In addition to these bigger and more dangerous naval guns, there were entirely new devices, including what Federal sailors called "infernal machines"—by which they meant underwater torpedoes, or what today would be called mines—as well as the first submarine, the *Hunley*, which successfully sank an enemy warship, albeit at the cost of its own destruction. And, above all, the war at sea featured the emergence of armored warships, commonly called ironclads. All of these innovations, even the submarine, offered an advantage to the Union states, for in a contest where the weapons of war required the application of iron smelters, rolling mills, and machine shops, the northern states had an overwhelming advantage, one the South would never be able to overcome.

Curiously, however, the North did not immediately take advantage of its overwhelming industrial superiority. Part of the reason was that, for once, the U.S. Navy found itself in the unfamiliar position of being the dominant naval power in a war, and consistent with the inherent conservatism of the superior power, its initial instinct was to rely on the time-tested weapons of naval warfare. Consequently, the North began the Civil War at sea by declaring a blockade—a blockade that was established and maintained by wooden-hulled vessels, most of them converted merchant ships. Some of them were sail driven, but it soon became evident that only steam ships were capable of the kind of sea-keeping necessary to maintain a blockade year round, and to pursue the steam-powered blockade runners that were their quarry. This required the North to establish coaling bases along the southern coast. Porous at first, the blockade became stronger month by month, and though it was never entirely effective, it eventually imposed genuine hardship on the struggling Confederacy.[2]

Bit by bit, southerners had to surrender large chunks of their coastline. Only in those few places where the Confederates were able to occupy existing forts built in the 1830s and '40s by the Army Corps of Engineers, such as Fort Sumter in Charleston Harbor, or Fort Morgan at the entrance to Mobile Bay, were they able to fend off repeated naval assaults. But where they had to depend instead on fortifications thrown up since the onset of war, such as at Hatteras Inlet in North Carolina, or Port Royal in South Carolina, the Union Navy generally had its way, blasting those dirt-and-log defenses into surrender within a matter of hours.[3]

To prevent the complete domination of the Southern coastline, Confederate Navy Secretary Stephen R. Mallory hoped to supplement the coastal forts by acquiring a few ships whose defensive characteristics were such that they could stand up to a whole squadron of conventional Union warships. "Knowing that the enemy could build one hundred ships to one of our own," he wrote to his wife, "my policy has been to make such ships so strong and invulnerable as would compensate for the inequality of numbers." In a word, he wanted ironclads. As early as May 8, less than a month after Fort Sumter, Mallory urged the Confederate Congress (which had not yet moved from Montgomery to Richmond), to authorize the construction of an ironclad warship. "I regard the possession of an iron-armored ship, as a matter of the first necessity," he wrote. "Such a vessel at this time could traverse the entire coast of the United States, prevent all blockades, and encounter, with a fair prospect of success, their entire Navy."[4]

The concept of iron-armored warships was not a new one. Robert Fulton had designed and built a self-powered floating battery (which he called the *Demologos*) for the defense of New York Harbor at the end of the War of 1812, though it never saw action. In 1854, the United States had experimented with a similar craft called the "Stevens Battery," but it was still unfinished in 1861 and had design flaws that made it unlikely it ever would be completed. In 1857, the French had initiated a program to build ten ironclad warships, thus stealing a nautical march (to use a mixed metaphor) on their British rivals, and the first of them, the *Gloire*, had been launched in 1859. Inspired, or rather provoked, by the French to reciprocate, the British had begun construction of an armored warship of their own, the *Warrior*.

Mallory's first thought was to try to buy the *Gloire* from the French outright. The French refused, however, not only because they were unwilling to relinquish the jewel of their fleet, but also because it would be an obvious violation of neutrality. If Mallory wanted armored warships for his new navy, he would have to find a way to build them at home.

His problem was that the Confederacy lacked the facilities (what today would be called the industrial infrastructure) necessary to build such a vessel from scratch and quickly. The design, fabrication, and construction of the engine plant alone was likely to take a year or more. Mallory therefore sought a shortcut, and he found one thanks mainly to the Federal commander of the Gosport Navy Yard near Norfolk, Virginia, Commodore Charles McCauley. Only days after Confederates fired the first shot of the war at Fort Sumter in Charleston Harbor and Virginia seceded from the Union, McCauley feared that a noisy mob of citizens outside the Navy Yard gate might try to storm the place. On April 20, 1861, he ordered that the yard be evacuated. Not only was his decision premature, the evacuation was also poorly coordinated and incompletely performed. Though McCauley ordered his men to destroy whatever could not be carried away, much of value was left behind, including repair facilities, machine shops, a huge granite dry dock, and the partially-burned hull of the U.S. Steam Frigate *Merrimack*.

Months later, long after the *Merrimack* had been transformed into the ironclad *Virginia* and won its first dramatic victories, an argument emerged over who deserved the credit for planning and building the South's first ironclad. One candidate is Confederate Navy Lieutenant John Mercer Brooke. On June 3, 1861, Brooke met with Mallory in Richmond to urge the construction of an iron-plated warship, and a week later he submitted a sketch of a casemate ironclad. For technical advice about the feasibility of the concept, Mallory sent for Chief Engineer William P. Williamson and Naval Contractor John L. Porter.

Porter is the other contender for credit as the designer of the CSS *Virginia*. He had no idea why Mallory had summoned him, but he had been thinking about an ironclad warship independently, and when he traveled to Richmond he brought with him a design of his own for just such a vessel. When he arrived there on June 23, he was surprised and pleased to discover that building an armored warship was the very project that Mallory had in mind. In fact, Brooke's drawing and Porter's model were strikingly similar. They both featured an iron fort or casemate with angled walls (Brooke's at a 45-degree angle, Porter's at 40 degrees), built atop a flat-bottomed hull. (After tests ashore, the walls of the casemate were eventually constructed at a 36-degree angle, slightly closer to Porter's initial proposal.)

The principal difference between the two designs was that in Porter's model the casemate covered the entire hull, whereas in Brooke's plan both the ship's pointed prow and its rounded stern extended beyond the casemate, partly to prevent the bow wave from washing up on the armored shield, and partly to increase buoyancy.

Porter agreed that this was a desirable feature, and volunteered to turn the rough sketch into a finished design.[5]

Both Porter and Brooke, along with Chief Engineer Williamson, then headed back to Norfolk to see if the hull of the partially-burned *Merrimack*, which had been raised from the bottom of the Elizabeth River and placed in the granite dry dock, would suit as a platform on which to construct their ironclad. Williamson thought it would, though both Brooke and Porter were dubious. They had each envisioned a flat-bottomed vessel, and with some justification they feared that using the *Merrimack*'s V-shaped hull would give the ship too great a draft for operations in coastal waters.[6] Nevertheless, they allowed themselves to be convinced since, as they put it in their letter to Mallory, "it would appear that this is our only chance to get a suitable vessel in a short time."[7]

By mid-July the work was under way. Porter supervised the refit of the hull itself as carpenters cut away the charred timbers on the *Merrimack* and began to erect a frame for the casemate, Williamson focused on repairing the cranky engines that had sent the *Merrimack* into the dockyard in the first place, and Brooke designed the rifled guns that would make up the ship's armament and took charge of procuring the iron plate that would constitute its armor shield.

In the end, it was the iron armor that proved to be the bottleneck. Tests conducted in October proved that 2-inch iron plate was dramatically more effective than 1-inch plate, even several layers of it. But there was only one facility in all the Confederacy that was capable of rolling 2-inch plate—the Tredegar Iron Works in Richmond—and covering the ship's casemate with two layers of 2-inch iron plate would require nearly 800 tons of iron. There was not that much iron available in the entire state of Virginia. Brooke scavenged scrap iron, old smoothbore cannon, even tools, all of which were melted down into iron plate, but he still came up well short. To make up the difference, the Confederacy began ripping up hundreds of miles of its own railroads, a measure of both its industrial weakness and its desperation. Even with crews working around the clock, production was limited and frustratingly slow. By October, only two tons of the 2-inch iron plate had reached Gosport—two of 800—and the last of it did not arrive until February 12, 1862. The Confederacy had begun with a considerable head start in the arms race to construct an ironclad warship, but as delay followed delay, the window of opportunity was swiftly closing.[8]

ONE HUNDRED MILES away in Washington, officials had known for some time what the Confederates were up to in Norfolk. The Union navy secretary, Gideon Welles, had even obtained a copy of Mallory's letter to the Confederate Congress claiming that one rebel ironclad vessel could "encounter, with a fair prospect of success," the entire U.S. Navy. At first, Welles did not take this boast seriously, his skepticism fed by the reaction of most of his senior naval officers, who scoffed at the notion. But all through May and June news of the rebel activity in Norfolk continued to reach him. In the middle of the nineteenth century there was no such thing as industrial secrecy, and Welles knew almost as soon as Mallory did when the *Merrimack's* hull was raised on May 30, when it was placed in dry dock, and when workmen began to reconfigure its superstructure. Southern newspapers proved a particularly valuable source of information and kept Welles up-to-date on the ship's progress, including the results of the ordnance testing against 1- and 2-inch iron plate.[9]

By the end of June, Welles decided that the Union Navy needed to develop a counterweapon, and on July 4 he asked Congress for an appropriation of $1.5 million to construct three experimental ironclad warships. To determine the appropriate design for these craft, that same legislation also authorized the creation of an Ironclad Board consisting of three serving naval officers, all of them captains. The bill worked its way through Congress, and President Lincoln signed it on August 4. Three days later, Welles issued a public solicitation of designs for an American warship. Thus by the late summer of 1861, Welles and Mallory were engaged in what amounted to a naval arms race.[10]

Despite that, events in Washington proceeded with a distinct lack of urgency. Fifteen proposals were submitted to the Ironclad Board, though only two of them received serious attention. One was a gunboat designed by Samuel Pook that was submitted by an enthusiastic entrepreneur named Cornelius Bushnell; the other was for a more-or-less conventional frigate with iron plating. The navy captains on the Ironclad Board, all veterans of the sailing era, were skeptical. Both designs called for the proposed vessels to carry a huge amount of iron plate above the waterline, and some board members openly expressed doubts that either ship would float. This is when Bushnell began to play a critical, if curious, role. Bushnell had a great deal invested—both financially and emotionally—in getting a contract, so he decided to verify his design with the man he had been told was the most reliable expert on maritime engineering in the country, the Swedish-born immigrant John Ericsson. Visiting Ericsson at his New York residence, Bushnell asked him to calculate the buoyancy of the two vessels under consideration. Ericsson did so, assuring Bushnell rather quickly that both ships would indeed float. But then Ericsson asked Bushnell if, as long as he was there, he would like to see a "floating battery" that Ericsson himself had designed, and the inventor brought out a model of a flat-bottomed vessel whose salient feature was a perfectly round rotating cylinder in the middle of its flat deck. Bushnell later claimed that he saw at once the potential of such a vessel, and he asked Ericsson if he could show it to Welles.[11]

From New York, Bushnell went straight to Welles's home in Hartford, Connecticut, where he declared somewhat melodramatically that "the country was safe because I had found a battery which would make us master of the situation as far as the ocean was concerned." Welles urged him to present the model to the Ironclad Board, but

Bushnell did more than that. He got William H. Seward to write him a letter of introduction to Abraham Lincoln, and he took Ericsson's model to the White House. Among his many other interests, Lincoln was fond of gadgets. Years earlier, when he had still been a prairie lawyer, he had obtained a patent for a device to float river steamers over sand bars, and during the war he was a frequent visitor to the Washington Navy Yard where he liked to observe ordnance tests. Intrigued by Ericsson's model, he agreed to accompany Bushnell to the next meeting of the Ironclad Board. At that meeting (on September 13), the members of the board remained skeptical, but Lincoln made his own feelings known in a characteristic way by remarking, "All I have to say is what the girl said when she put her foot into the stocking: 'It strikes me there's something in it.'"[12]

Even with that encouragement, the members of the board hesitated. Bushnell decided that the only man who could convince these skeptics of the little ship's technical feasibility was Ericsson himself. But Bushnell also knew that Ericsson would be less than eager to appear before the navy captains as a supplicant. With some justification, the Swedish inventor believed that he had been ill-treated by the navy ever since 1844, when a gun on board the USS *Princeton*, which Ericsson had helped design, had exploded, injuring a number of officials and dignitaries. Although the gun had not been designed by Ericsson but by Robert Stockton, much of the blame had attached itself to the Swede, and Ericsson had resolved never again to set foot in Washington. Aware of this, Bushnell was not completely honest with Ericsson about the reception the model had received in Washington. He told Ericsson that the board members had been impressed by the "genius" of the design, but that one member had asked some technical questions that Bushnell had not been able to answer. "Well," Ericsson replied, "I'll go—I'll go tonight." "From that moment," Bushnell wrote some years later, "I knew that the success of the affair was assured."[13]

Not quite. Both Bushnell and Welles knew that if the captains on the Ironclad Board greeted Ericsson coolly, the touchy inventor was likely to withdraw in a huff. Aware that time was running out, Welles urged Commodore Smith, the board's chairman, to give the inventor a fair and cordial hearing. Even then, the meeting was nearly disastrous. Ericsson was prepared for compliments, not criticism. He bristled from the start. But the mood in the room turned when, in responding to a question about the vessel's likely stability in a seaway, Ericsson became so involved in the answer that he delivered a lengthy and technically detailed dissertation that left the board members both subdued and impressed.

Impressed—but not yet convinced. It required another presentation in Welles's office to satisfy the board members. There, Ericsson declared that his ship could be built in ninety days. Welles asked him how much it would cost. "Two hundred and seventy five thousand dollars," Ericsson answered at once. That, of course, was only a fraction of what Welles had available. Welles then turned to face the board members and asked each of them one by one if a contract should be granted. Receiving an affirmative from each, Welles told Ericsson to go ahead and get started; a contract would be forthcoming in due time. It was the 15th of September. Down in Norfolk, the Confederates had already raised the *Merrimack*, cut away its charred scantlings, and redesigned and reconfigured it as an ironclad. On the other hand, the Tredegar Iron Works had begun only that month to produce the first sections of 2-inch iron plate for the vessel's armored shield. The arms race was still winnable, but only if Ericsson could make good on his promise to build the ship in ninety days.

ERICSSON SUBCONTRACTED VARIOUS parts of the ship to other companies (something his Confederate counterparts could not do), but he personally supervised the critical components: the engines, the assembly of the hull, and in, particular, the novel revolving turret. The ship's keel was laid on October 25, and the ship was launched ninety-three days later. At the launching, Ericsson was vindicated, and his critics silenced, when the vessel floated with exactly the draft that its designer had calculated.

For the command of this unusual vessel, Welles chose forty-three-year-old Lieutenant John L. Worden of New York, a twenty-seven-year navy veteran who had a reputation as a scientific officer rather than a warrior, and who had spent most of his career ashore at the Naval Observatory. There was more than a hint of skepticism in the orders he received from Commodore Smith, chairman of the Ironclad Board. "This vessel is an experiment," Smith wrote. "I believe you are the right officer to put in command of her."[14]

In receipt of these orders, Worden immediately went to the Brooklyn Navy Yard to view the infamous "Ericsson Battery," which Ericsson now decided should be called *Monitor*. Worden was less than overwhelmed by his first glimpse of the strange little craft, and he acknowledged his orders by cautiously expressing the hope that "she may prove a success." "At all events," he added gamely, "I am quite willing to be an agent in testing her capabilities."[15]

If Worden withheld judgment about the *Monitor*, the crew of the little vessel was equally dubious about their new commander. Worden's health was precarious, after having spent seven months in a Confederate prison, and he did not make much of an impression on the crew. He was thin, pale, and (in the opinion of at least one member of the wardroom) "effeminate looking." But Worden's appearance belied a fierce determination. For the next month, "everything was hurry and confusion" on the *Monitor* as Worden oversaw all the thousands of tiny details necessary to a ship's commissioning. The vessel was afloat, but it was not yet finished. As the final touches were added to the berthing spaces and officers' cabins, supplies of all kinds from dishware to chamber pots were loaded on board, including powder and shot for the vessel's two big 11-inch Dahlgren guns.[16]

Since the ship had only two guns, both Ericsson and Worden wanted the biggest caliber guns they could get. Indeed, Ericsson had specifically requested that the *Monitor* be armed with new 12-inch guns, but none were yet available. He therefore had to settle for two 11-inch guns, which were borrowed from other vessels in New York Harbor. Still, those 11-inch guns could each fire a 176-pound iron bolt as well as exploding shells as large as those of most battleships in World War I.

On the other hand, those guns came with a stipulation that no more than 15 pounds of powder be used in any single charge, a legacy of the explosion of Stockton's gun on the *Princeton* nearly twenty years before. If time had allowed, Worden might have been allowed to "proof" his guns by firing successive rounds from each one using progressively larger charges until it was clear that the weapon could bear the strain of larger loads without fracturing. But there was no time for such niceties in the current crisis, so Worden had to accept the 15-pound limit for his big guns.[17]

On February 27, the very day that the *Merrimack* was put into commission as the CSS *Virginia*, the *Monitor* embarked on its sea trial. It was nearly disastrous. The engines worked well enough, driving the ironclad through the water at a respectable seven or eight knots, but the helmsman called out that the ship would not answer the rudder. The vessel's great weight created such a powerful momentum that the tiller ropes connecting the wheel to the rudder had no effect. The *Monitor* ran back and forth across New York Harbor "like a drunken man on a sidewalk," as one crewman recalled, finally slamming into the Brooklyn dock near the city gas works with a jarring collision. Ignominiously, it had to be towed back to its berth in the Navy Yard. Notified of the problem, Ericsson went below and began to tinker with the lines and pulleys that transferred orders from the wheel to the rudder. By multiplying the ratio, he soon fixed the problem. But this incident reminded Worden, that, as Smith had warned him, "this vessel is an experiment."[18]

The *Monitor*'s departure from New York was delayed for a day due to bad weather, but finally, on March 6, it left the Brooklyn Navy

Yard bound for Hampton Roads. The journey itself was an adventure. In addition to relying on its own engines, the *Monitor* was also under tow, and it had an escort of two gunboats. Despite the predictions of the skeptics, the *Monitor* rode the water well, and the first day out, no new problems were identified. The engines clanked along satisfactorily, and from the top of the *Monitor*'s turret (the only part of the vessel where a man might stand while the ship was underway), Worden watched the tow line dipping in and out of the water between his vessel and the tug some 400 feet ahead. Off to each side were the escorting gunboats. So far, so good.[19]

The fifty-seven men who made up the *Monitor*'s crew were all volunteers. Rather than accept men arbitrarily assigned to him from the receiving ships in the harbor, Worden had asked for volunteers and was gratified that more men had responded than he needed. But if the men were enthusiastic, they were also mostly inexperienced. The ship's executive officer, Samuel Dana Greene, was only twenty-one and just three years out of the Academy; its paymaster was so innocent that he asked Worden if it was really necessary for him to buy a uniform: Couldn't he just continue to wear his civilian clothes on board? Besides Worden himself, only the ship's chief engineer, thirty-four-year-old Alban Stimers, was a veteran of long experience, and he was on board mainly to observe and report on how the *Monitor* functioned at sea. Of the ship's crew of fifty-seven, only nine had sufficient experience to be rated as ordinary seamen.[20]

Now that they were at sea, they discovered that living and working in the semi-submerged world of the *Monitor* was relatively comfortable—much more comfortable, one sailor wrote, than the receiving ship North Carolina had been. So far, it seemed, duty in an ironclad was not too bad. The only drawbacks seemed to be that the inside temperature was either too cold or, once the heat from the boilers was tapped, too hot, and the interior lighting was so dim below decks that it was difficult to see. Most compartments had small waterproof windows in the overhead to admit some natural light, but it remained dark in the narrow passageways, and when the ship was buttoned up for combat, it was almost pitch black.[21]

The good weather did not last. On the second day out, the barometer dropped and the wind increased. Heavy waves washed over the *Monitor*'s flat deck, foaming and sloshing against the turret. The officers in their staterooms looked up through the glass windows to see green water overhead. Save for the turret, the ship was, in effect, under water. From the tug, only the *Monitor*'s turret was visible above the waves, and occasionally even that was obscured by the rolling seas. Those seas also affected the ship's movement, especially under tow. Twenty-seven-year veteran that he was, Worden nevertheless felt the cold prickly sweat and rising nausea of seasickness. He had not fully recovered from his seven months in captivity, and the confined spaces, the hot oil smell from the engines, and the motion of an iron ship under tow, sent him rushing to the top of the turret where the bracing wind and sea provided only partial relief.

Despite his personal misery, his own comfort was not Worden's greatest worry. Ericsson had designed the *Monitor*'s turret to rest on a smooth brass ring embedded in the deck. He had calculated that the great weight of the 120-ton turret would press so securely on the ring that it would create a perfect waterproof seal. But just prior to the vessel's departure from New York, Stimers had placed a "plaited hemp rope" between the turret and the deck in order to provide what he thought would be a more perfect seal. Now, as the weather worsened, water began to work its way through this hempen seal, and soon water was dripping—and then cascading—down into the berthing spaces. The men below were not only seasick, many of them were now soaked, and Worden allowed his fellow sufferers to join him atop the ship's turret. There they lay flat on their backs atop the iron grating, shielded from the worst of the sea spray by a canvas tarpaulin.[22]

Then, at four o'clock, the ventilating fans in the engine room stopped working. So much water had sloshed down the blower pipes that the leather belts driving the blowers had stretched and lost their purchase on the pulleys. Smoke built up in the engine room, and sailors fought their way out coughing and wheezing. Rushing in to try to solve the problem, Stimers succumbed to the smoke and gas; and had to be dragged out unconscious and taken to the top of the now crowded turret top. Without a fire in the boiler, the pumps would not work, and Worden ordered the crew to man the hand pumps. The men went to work with a will, but the hand pumps were not powerful enough to force water all the way from the bilge to the top of the turret, which was the ship's only opening to the outside. Water began to build up below, and Worden ordered the ship's flag to be hoisted upside down as a signal of distress. In such a sea, however, there was nothing the escorting gunboats could do. Eventually, only the easing of the storm saved the ship. That allowed the engineers to restart the engines and re-engage the pumps.[23]

THE NEXT DAY was March 8. That morning, while the *Monitor* chugged southward along Maryland's outer banks, the CSS *Virginia* eased slowly down the Elizabeth River and out into Hampton Roads. At noon the *Virginia* aimed itself at the USS *Cumberland* anchored off Newport News Point. On board the *Monitor*, approaching the northern entrance to the Chesapeake Bay, Worden heard the sound of "heaving firing in the distance." Some thought it was only the guns of Fort Monroe "at practice," but Worden feared, correctly as it proved, that the *Merrimack* had at last come out and that he was too late. He ordered the ship cleared for action and asked for maximum speed. In spite of his eagerness, however, the ship would not be hurried. "Our iron hull crept slowly on," one officer wrote home later, "& the monotonous clank, clank, clank of the engine betokened no increase of its speed."[24]

It was evening by the time the *Monitor* and its escorts entered the Chesapeake Bay, and full dark before it entered the roadstead. The tow line was cast off and a pilot came on board. From him Worden learned that the *Merrimack* had indeed come out that morning, and that it had all but destroyed the Union fleet. The *Cumberland* had been sunk, the *Congress* had been pounded into a wreck and set afire with hot shot. Indeed, as the *Monitor* tied up alongside the damaged and grounded *Minnesota*, its way was lit by the reflected light of the burning *Congress*. Just past midnight the *Congress* exploded in a giant fireball. It was the final punctuation mark on the most disastrous defeat in the history of the U.S. Navy until the Japanese attack on Pearl Harbor eighty years later.

Worden agonized that he was too late. Or was he? Some twenty other U.S. Navy vessels lay at anchor in the roadstead, including the *Minnesota*. Without a doubt the Rebel ironclad would be back at it in the morning. When it was, Worden planned to interpose his little ironclad between the *Virginia* and the Union fleet. In fact, he had arrived quite literally in the nick of time.

It was a variety of circumstances that conspired to bring these two revolutionary ironclad vessels together at the same place and at the same time for them to meet in an historic confrontation the next day. The arrival of the *Monitor* on the evening of the very day that the *Virginia* made its first historic sortie set the stage for the great naval drama that would play out on March 9, 1862. But it would not have happened at all but for the policymakers who took a chance on an unproven technology, and the inventors and designers who made that technology a reality: Mallory, Brooke, Porter, and Williamson on one side; Lincoln, Welles, Bushnell, and Ericsson on the other.

CHAPTER 3

Iron Horse, Iron Coffin: Life Aboard the USS *Monitor*
David Mindell

THE *MONITOR* LEFT NEW YORK FOR HAMPTON ROADS ON March 6, 1862. On board was William Keeler, the most prolific and articulate of the crew members and its paymaster.

In a letter to his wife, Anna, Keeler wrote of that first day: "I've just returned from the top of the turret. The moon is shining bright, the water is smooth and everything seems favorable. The green lights of the gun boats are on our lead beam but a short distance off and the tug is pulling lustily on our big hawser (the *Monitor* was under tow). A number of sailboats are visible in different directions, their wide sails glistening in the moonlight. Not a sea has yet passed over our deck. It is as dry as when we left port."[1]

The next morning, Friday, March 7, he had found a slightly different situation: "When I awoke this morning, I found much more motion to the vessel and could see the green water through my deck light as the waves rolled across the deck." Keeler and the crew of the *Monitor* were, in fact, living in what was partly a submarine. The environment of iron and steam made the traditional human comforts—heat, air, shelter, dryness, and light—available below the surface of the ocean. If one looks at John Ericsson's famous drawing of the vessel, one can actually see a blown-up cutaway and that the *Monitor* consisted of two separate hulls. This was how Ericsson always described it. One hull is a wooden raft covered by iron armor; that's the deck, and it provides much of the buoyancy. The lower iron hull literally hangs underneath the upper hull. The gun crew (about twenty men) was above the water line, but the rest of the crew lived in the area below the water line. The *Monitor* had only about six inches of freeboard above the water in a calm sea, and most of the time the decks were actually awash. Inside the ship, it was comfortable—at least at first. As Keeler wrote his wife: "Perhaps you'd like to know how my room looks. I wish you could look into it and see it for yourself. All nice white wear with *Monitor* on each in gilt letters. Tapestry run on the floor. The birth draws and closets are all black walnut. The curtains are lace and damask or some imitation I suppose. I've seen no room as handsomely fitted up as ours." Keeler is living in a curiously stylish environment, especially stylish for a tool of war.

What was novel about this arrangement was that the *Monitor* surrounded the crew with water on four sides. Again, Keeler: "Now we scoop up a huge volume of water on one side of the deck, and as it rolls to the other with the motion of the vessel, it is met by a sea coming from the opposite direction. The accumulative weight seeming sufficient to bury us forever."

During the day, light would enter through skylights in the deck. These were holes both forward and aft of the turret, about six inches in diameter set with a thick glass in an iron frame. They often were covered by six to eight inches of water, but light could still penetrate through, and Keeler actually wrote his letters by light filtered through the ocean: "When the sun shines bright," he wrote, "it is sufficiently light to read and write without difficulty." The captain of one of the later monitors noted that sometimes the waves, when they washed over the skylights, would bring fish with them that would swim in the skylights for a few seconds before they were washed out by the next wave. The captain delighted in seeing the shadows of the fish on the floor of his stateroom.

In addition to the unusual lighting, the air also was unusual because it was processed through a machine. The ventilating system drew fresh air in through large blowers that rose above the deck and passed it into the crew spaces and engine room. This air flue actually kept the engine room at slightly above normal barometric pressure. In ideal circumstances, these conditions made the vessel quite comfortable for the crew, and they found it secure. Here is Keeler again: "The dash of the waves as they roll over our heads is the only audible sound that reaches us from the outer world. One would hardly suppose from the quiet stillness that pervades our submarine abode that a gale was ranging around us. Our life, I assure you, is getting monotonous enough." In that same letter he referred to his room as "my little snuggery." Anyone who has spent the night on a submarine knows that while it can be claustrophobic, it also can indeed be quite comfortable and snug. He also wrote: "Nothing would strike a stranger with more surprise after walking our cheerless, wave-washed iron deck than to go below and see our bright, cheerful, well lighted cozy wardroom with the officers grouped around the table reading, writing or talking. I went to sleep last night with a swash, swash, swash of the waves as they rolled over my head and the same monotonous sound will be my lullaby tonight."

George Geer, an enlisted man on the *Monitor* whose letters are at The Mariners' Museum, found the *Monitor* much more comfortable than his previous home, the receiving ship, *North Carolina*. "We lie much better here," he wrote to his wife, "than we did on that devilish hulk, the *North Carolina*."[2] The novelist Nathaniel Hawthorne visited the *Monitor* when it was in Hampton Roads.[3] He wrote that, "It was like finding a palace with all its conveniences under the sea. The members of the crew hermetically seal themselves and go below and until they see fit to reappear, there would seem to be no power given to men whereby they can be brought to light. A storm of cannon shot damages them no more than a handful of dried peas." Hawthorne's vision of the *Monitor* may recall the submarine environment of Jules Verne's *Nautilus*, also an elegantly appointed Victorian world encased in an aggressive iron shell. Echoes of the *Monitor*, in fact, appear in *20,000 Leagues Under the Sea*, which was published in 1867, five years after the *Monitor* appeared. Verne's narrator, on first hearing of the exploits of what they would later discover was the *Nautilus*, speculates that it might be a submarine monitor.

Throughout its career, themes of comfort and calm continue to appear in accounts of the *Monitor*, but they never quite regained this particular novelty and serenity that we find in the first few days at sea in March, 1862. The enclosing home also had a dark side, and the *Monitor* found it early in the first trip. Soon after leaving New York, the ship hit a gale that forced water through the blowers and hatches. The deck seals had not been caulked properly, and the water poured in around the base of the turret, the deck lights, and other of the various openings in the deck.

As Executive Officer Samuel Dana Greene wrote, "The water came down under the tower [the turret] like a waterfall. It would strike the pilot house and go over the tower in the most beautiful curves. The water came through the narrow eye holes in the pilot house with such force as to throw the helmsmen completely around from the wheel. Now seawater also entered the blowers that drew in the fresh air for the crew. It leaked onto the leather belts that drove the blowers and those belts stretched, causing the blowers to fail and, in turn, causing the engine room to fill up with noxious gases from the coal fires."[4]

In another account, Second Engineer Albert Campbell wrote: "We left New York on a beautiful day and the next afternoon we broke both our blower belts which spoiled the draft of our fires and drove all the gas into the engine room. This of course was rather inconvenient, for carbonic acid gas and hydrogen is not calculated to support animal life. I found myself getting weak and lost all consciousness and did not know any more until I found myself on top of the turret with a couple of engineers lying along side of me looking more dead than anything else. The water poured into the engine room and the smokestacks and ventilators like a miniature Niagara and it was doubtful whether we would float during the night."

To avert suffocation, the engineers opened the engine room doors, but then the entire *Monitor* filled with the noxious fumes. Keeler went below to investigate and met one of the engineers, pale, wet, and black, staggering along, gasping for breath. The engineers were caught in a bind here because, in order to make the ship habitable, they had to fix the machinery, but until the gas was evacuated, no one could go into the engine room to do so. The crew of the *Monitor* had stumbled on an unanticipated characteristic of their artificial environment: the very ability to support life depended on properly functioning machinery. Eventually they solved the problem by gathering all the engineers on the deck, giving each a specific instruction, and sending them down, one after the other, for short periods to perform a small part of the repair task before the fumes overcame them. By nightfall, the crew had reentered their quarters, but they were shaken, they were sick, and they had a new appreciation for the terrible potential of this enclosing home.

Upon hearing of this episode, John Ericsson wrote: "As to the imperfections in the structure [i.e., the leaks], I saw those a long time back but I also saw how to do them better next time. But, the insufficient height of the ventilating and smoke trunks—on that point you have floored me."[5] For all his vision and imagination, Ericsson had failed to account for the critical importance of the ventilating shafts. The *Monitor*'s life support systems were what we would call today a single point failure; when they stopped, the entire system broke down.

The dark side of the *Monitor*'s enclosed spaces was not just one of such immediate and acute danger. As early as March 18, just two weeks after leaving New York, Keeler lamented the dehumanizing nature of the surroundings: "I'd give a good pair of boots to read on something besides iron. I'm tired of everlasting iron. The clank, clank, clank while I'm writing this of the officer of the deck as he paces back and forth on the iron plates above my head, although suggestive of security, is not a good opiate."

The crew complained regularly about life within the *Monitor*'s cramped spaces, the leaky hull, the many problems with the machinery, and the hard mechanical environment. Frank Butts, for example, was a seaman who came aboard in October 1862. He was thrilled to be assigned to the famous vessel, but he soon found that, "In the opinion of the crew, a monitor was the worst craft for a man to live aboard that ever floated upon water." Quickly, Butts came to agree: "The life of a sailor aboard this vessel was the most laborious of any in the service. I will venture to say that my feet were not dry once in the entire time I was aboard the *Monitor*."

Even in port, George Geer observed that the slightest rough water would cause the deck to flood and the hatches to leak. During the summer, the conditions became even worse as the heat inside reached well over 100 degrees. Forced to sleep out on the deck that summer, George Geer complained that "iron is not very soft but better than the inside, for hell is an ice house aside of this ship." The enlisted men's quarters where Geer slept were less ventilated than those of the officers, and during the summer, men would frequently break down and have to be sent to the hospital. The captain reported to Secretary of the Navy Gideon Welles that "human endurance has a limit and it is impossible one should not become exhausted if confined for many days in such an atmosphere." In fact, living conditions repeatedly arose at the center of the debates about the effectiveness of the ironclad warship.

John Ericsson was a great calculator and a great draftsman, but his machine's suitability for supporting life was vague, unscientific, imprecise, immeasurable, and irreducibly human. John Ericsson had no purchase on these problems. He would only consider those that he could calculate and design around. In fact, he mocked the crew's complaints about excessive heat, stale air and the general stifling conditions as womanly weakness or worse, nostalgia for the old world of sailing ships. He wrote: "As to ventilation, old sailors who have been in these vessels night and day for two years have assured me that no other vessels of war can compare with them." I have never actually found any letters that he is referring to, but I have found accounts from numerous crew members, including, as I have mentioned, John Worden, William Frederick Keeler, Captain Jeffers, Frank Butts, Samuel Dana Greene, Isaac Newton, and George Geer—from all different aspects of the rank, all different sides of the debates, and all contradicting Ericsson's opinion. They consistently wrote of the misery below decks on the *Monitor*, especially during the summer. Anyone who had been to sea on the *Monitor* knew also that discomfort was not simply a matter of personal preference. Living aboard the *Monitor* could make a man sick and unable to fight. Nathaniel Hawthorne, as an outside observer, found the enclosure of the *Monitor* not only protecting but ominous. "In fact, the thing looked altogether too safe," he wrote in the *Atlantic Monthly*. "Though it may not prove quite an agreeable predicament to be thus boxed up in impenetrable iron, with the possibility one would imagine, of being sent to the bottom of the sea, and, even there, not drowned, but stifled."[6]

Several of the men emphasized that the heroism of the *Monitor* crew members lay not necessarily in their performance in battle but rather in their willingness to live in this strange and radically new environment. Wrote Keeler: "I think we get more credit for the fight than we deserve. Anyone could fight behind an impenetrable armor; after all, many have fought as well behind wooden walls or behind nothing at all. The credit, if any is due, is in daring to undertake the trip and to go into the fight in an untried experiment in our unprepared condition." Similarly, Captain Worden wrote, "Here was an unknown, untried vessel with all but a small portion of her below the water line. Her crew to live with the ocean beating over their heads; an iron, coffin-like ship of which the gloomiest predictions were made."[7] The phrase "iron coffin," by the way, reappears in the twentieth century as applied to submarines. With the *Monitor*'s crew shut out from sunlight and the air above the sea, depending entirely on artificial means to supply the air they breathed, a failure of the machinery would have been almost certain death for her men.

Hawthorne asked, "How can an admiral condescend to go to sea in an iron pot?" He was wondering about the fate of naval glory and traditional sailing vessels and their strutting, Nelsonian heroes. "What space and elbow-room can be found for the quarter-deck dignity in the cramped lookout of the *Monitor* or even in the twenty-feet diameter of her cheese-box?"[8] The crew found, and I think they were correct, that one answer to his question is that heroism lay as much in facing the machine as it did in facing the enemy. And this remains true today; just think about the large number of deaths related to accidents, with no enemy in sight. You begin to see that the dangers of the machine for the operator is a critical component of industrialized warfare.

As noted earlier, the living conditions were not just a matter of comfort or even of danger or physical health; they also affected the ability of the vessel to fight. Just to remind you of the structure of the *Monitor*, the captain, the pilot, and the helmsman were up front in the pilot house and the turret crew was amidships. A speaking tube connected the two, although every account says the speaking tube was out of commission during the fight in Hampton Bays. I have yet to figure out how a speaking tube can actually go out of commission, seeing as it's just a tube, but maybe archeology will help us there.

The gun crew was amazingly well protected by the turret. Look at the dents in the turret and think about what those explosions would do to a human being. This protection came at the cost of the gun crew's disconnection from the outside world and from their commander. The captain and the pilot could not communicate directly with the gunnery crew during the fight with the *Virginia*. The lieutenant in charge of the gun crews, Executive Officer Samuel Dana Greene, reported: "The effect of one shut up in a revolving drum is perplexing and it is not a simple matter to keep the bearings. White marks have been placed upon the stationary deck immediately below the turret to indicate the direction of the starboard and port sides and the bow and stern, but these marks were obliterated early in the action. I would continually ask the captain 'How does the *Merrimac* bear?' and he would reply 'On the starboard or on the port quarter' as the case might be. The difficulty then was to determine the direction of the starboard beam or the port quarter or any other bearing."[9] Remember, Greene and his crew were in the turret and the very large guns were sticking out the gun ports, and since the stoppers to the gun ports might well have been closed at any one time they could not really see out at all. Interestingly, the *Scientific American* article that published the design of the *Monitor,* while it was under construction, mentions a kind of periscope-like device installed in the turret, but I have never seen any textual evidence that it was actually there, and I assume they did not have time to put it in. So, Keeler and one of his aides would run back and forth between the captain and the gun crew exchanging messages about firing the guns.

Greene later recalled: "The drawbacks to the position of the pilothouse were soon realized. Keeler and Toffee [Keeler's clerk] passed the captain's orders and messages to me and my inquiries and answers to him. They performed their work with zeal and alacrity but our technical communications sometimes miscarried." In other words, this new command configuration created by the *Monitor*'s physical structure interrupted technical and command communication between the captain and the crew, leading ultimately toward the crisis of control in combat that ended the battle. This issue stood at the very heart of the debate over Hampton Roads. John Ericsson and Samuel Dana Greene blamed each other for what each considered to be losing the battle. Greene blamed the ship's structure. The situation was novel—a vessel of war was engaged in desperate combat with a powerful foe. The captain, commanding and guiding, was enclosed in one place and the executive officer, working and fighting the guns, was shut up in another, and communication between them was difficult and uncertain.

There is a caveat here: the best known and most complete account of fighting in the *Monitor* turret comes from Samuel Dana Greene, and it was written for *Century Illustrated Magazine* for the *Battles and Leaders of the Civil War* series in 1883. Greene was defending his own conduct and therefore had an interest in showing that he behaved heroically and appropriately when he took command from Ericsson. It is worth knowing that when he wrote this account for the *Century* to publish, he put it in the mail and the next day shot himself. It obviously was a deep issue for him and for many of the crew. Even taking Greene's account with a grain of salt, if we think of the *Monitor* as a living organism going into battle, it had intermittent and unreliable connections between its eyes, the captain; its brain, also the captain; and its fists, the gun crew.

Ericsson, curiously enough, admitted that this disconnection was a major drawback of the first monitor. Consider this remarkable statement, which he wrote in 1876. "Well informed naval officers are aware that Worden failed to sink the *Merrimack* at Hampton Roads because he could not personally control the firing and at the same time direct the steering of his vessel from a point enabling him to observe properly the movement of his antagonist. Accepting the omission to place the pilothouse on top of the turret, the original monitor was a perfect fighting machine." That is a remarkable statement because he is saying that, except for this fatal flaw that caused it to lose its most famous and critical battle, the machine was perfect—unusually imperfect logic for this very technical engineer. On all the later monitors, he moved the pilot house to the top of the turret.

After the battle of Hampton Roads, a part of the *Monitor*'s career began that is rarely written about. When I began writing my book, *War, Technology, and Experience Aboard the* USS *Monitor*, I never in my research found more than a paragraph about the many months between May 1862, when the *Virginia* was blown up, and the *Monitor*'s sinking on New Year's Eve, 1862. After the fall of Norfolk and the loss of the *Virginia*, the *Monitor* headed up the James River to support Union General George B. McClellan's failed Peninsula Campaign. Louis Goldsborough, the head of the Atlantic Blockade Squadron, gave the *Monitor* simple and totally unrealistic orders: "Proceed to Richmond... and shell the city into surrender."[10] He expected that task to take about two days.

During that summer, while the *Monitor* sat on the James River, the crew experienced not this single great, miraculous, amazing historical battle, but rather began to adjust to the monotonous and sometimes terrifying experience of war. The crew found the *Monitor* quite ill-suited for combat on rivers.

There was a new captain aboard, Captain William Jeffers, who led them in an ill-fated attempt to reach Richmond that was stopped at Drewry's Bluff, where living conditions played a critical role in the conflict. The crew from the *Virginia* and many of the guns from the *Virginia* occupied a high point. Below, the river was blockaded under water with sunken vessels. The *Monitor*, the *Galena*, and a few other smaller gun boats could not get through, and the *Monitor* was unable to elevate its guns high enough to head up on the banks. Yet the guns at Drewry's Bluff could easily fire downward, a very devastating type of fire, and the *Galena* was very roughly used in that encounter.

During the encounter at Drewry's Bluff, the *Monitor* eventually withdrew because it couldn't be effective. Simply staying below the decks during that encounter proved bad punishment for the crew. As Keeler wrote, "At times we were filled with powder and smoke below threatening suffocation to us all. Some of the heartiest looking men dropped, fainting at the guns." In the battle, the heat, of course, had practical consequences. Captain Jeffers reported: "I was obliged to discontinue the action for a quarter of an hour and take the men below to the forward part of the ship for purer air." The ship's log reported, "Several of our crew sick, going to the river water and foul air in the ship."

After withdrawing from Drewry's Bluff, the Union flotilla returned a bit down-river to await reinforcement and, indeed, the defenses at Drewry's Bluff would resist Union advances for the remainder of war. Now the *Monitor* stalled on the river. But the banks were occupied by Confederate forces, and the vessel was floating out in the middle of the river in hostile territory. Wrote Keeler: "Not a man could shove himself on the decks without a ball whizzing by him. One passed between my legs and another just over Lieutenant Greene's head." Confederate sharpshooters, of course, did not take long to figure out that all they had to do was shoot a little bit to confine the men to the inside of the ship and then convert the ironclad into a sweltering prison where their enemy would simply cook to death. Lieutenant Greene later wrote that "Probably no ship was ever devised which was so uncomfortable for her crew and certainly no sailor led a more disagreeable life than we did on the James River, suffocated with heat and bad air if we remained below and a target for sharpshooters if we came up on deck."

The *Monitor* spent late May and June of 1862 idle, further plagued by mechanical problems. Doing their best to survive in a combination of torrential rain and sweltering heat, the crew cooked on the deck and took refuge from the sun on the shady side of the turret. That is also an interesting irony—this enormous turret with eight inches of armor and all this incredibly powerful firepower was used for shade in the summer on the river. In a famous photograph made around this time, these men appear to be in bad shape. They are sunburned, dirty, and not happy-looking sailors. It is also interesting to note that in these pictures, the photographers go well out of their way to make sure that the dents in the turret are obvious—the crew is proud of those dents. Some of these men look as though they are anticipating later events; at least three of them drowned when the *Monitor* sank.

During this summer, one of the blower belts broke again and the temperature rose to 150 degrees in the galley, 125 degrees on the berth deck where the crew slept, and, with both blowers working, a more comfortable 132 degrees in the galley. These are actual entries in the ship's log. They start recording the temperature inside the ship and it becomes a remarkable text. Interestingly, early in the ship's career, the ship's log is written in a beautiful, neat, very horizontal handwriting. Then during the summer, it gradually drifts downward and you can barely read it. In the archives, you can see how the pages have been wet with the sweat of the people who actually wrote the log. That's true of Keeler's letters, too. He says that "all of my letters are bought at a very great expense of sweat," and the paper from the letters, which are in the United States Naval Academy library, indeed look as though they have been wetted.

The crew was forbidden to forage off the land and therefore had to keep their food aboard, making the quite serious, ominous war machine into something of a floating farmyard. "A portion of the iron deck has been converted into a stockyard," Keeler wrote to his wife, "containing just at present one home-sick lamb, one tough, combative old ram, a consumptive calf, one fine lean swine, an antediluvian rooster and his mate." Another day fire erupted in the galley and threatened the magazine before being quenched.

During the summer, Captain William Jeffers issued a report to the Navy Department about the *Monitor*'s capabilities. Unlike Worden, Jeffers was an ordnance expert, one of the new breed of scientifically trained officers. In his report to the Navy Department, Jeffers mentioned the control problems for the captain in the pilot house, the difficulty of accurately turning the turret, and the single point failure of the leather belts that drove the blowers. But he reserved for a special indictment the ventilation problems. When the weather was cold, he wrote, "it was quite warm below but no inconvenience was felt other than the impurity of the air passing through the turret. But with the heat of the last ten days, the air stood at 140 degrees in the turret when in action which, when added to the gases of the gun powder and smoke, bases from the fire room, smoke and heat of the illuminating lamps and emanations from the large number of persons stationed below, produced a most fetid atmosphere, causing an alarming degree of prostration. If the hatches were all closed, as they must be at sea, in this warm weather, the crew would be unable to live for 48 hours shut up. Quite one-third of the crew are now suffering from debility, there being no shelter on deck, they have to keep below to avoid sharpshooters."

More than the discomfort that Keeler complained of, Jeffers saw the bad air as a liability in combat, as it had been for him at Drewry's Bluff. "This vessel cannot go to sea until this defect is remedied," he wrote. He gave his recommendations for modifications to improve the *Monitor*, but ultimately Jeffers concluded that wooden ships, shell guns, and forts had not been superseded. Again, we need to take Jeffers's report with a little grain of salt because Jeffers failed to carry out his orders to shell Richmond into submission in two days. So while he is criticizing the living conditions on the *Monitor*, he also provides a convenient explanation for his own failure to take Drewry's Bluff. A dichotomy emerges: living conditions and imperfection of the actual design of the ship, versus mistakes and errors in judgment on the part of the crew. Jeffers left the command of the *Monitor* soon after making this report.

John Ericsson, for his part, read Jeffers's report and called it "a pernicious document."[11] He assured the navy that ventilation problems were already eliminated in the newer monitors. (Within a week after the battle of Hampton Roads, the navy ordered six new monitors from Ericsson.) At the end of August, the *Monitor* came down the James as McClellan retreated from the Peninsula. That fall, the mechanics at the Washington Navy Yard overhauled the vessel, adding new lifeboats and replacing the smokestacks and fresh-air intakes with higher ones that would remain above the water. The dents in the armor were patched over with iron plates marked Merrimac or Fort Darling (another name for Drewry's Bluff) to denote their origins. The two Dahlgren guns were engraved with the words "Ericsson"and "Worden." A new awning was installed above the turret, again improving the shade. A new blower engine was installed for the berth decks and workers added "many other conveniences which would have added greatly to our comfort last summer." New white paint, for example, made the officers' rooms brighter and more pleasant than before.

Then, only a few months after this overhaul, in December 1862, the crew's worst fears about their leaky, enclosing, threatening home became frighteningly real as the *Monitor* sank in a gale. Seaman Frank Butts, as he escaped the doomed vessel, heard the cook screaming at the frightened crew: "He congratulated them for being in a metallic coffin and that the devil would surely pick their bones as no shark could penetrate their graves."

Even after the loss of the *Monitor*, questions continued about living conditions on both the original *Monitor* and now on the new series of monitors that Ericsson was building. One month before the *Monitor*'s sinking, the second one, *Passaic*, was commissioned, and a writer from *Harper's Weekly* actually accompanied it on its maiden voyage. "Every wave broke over our low decks," he wrote, "and like a huge sea monster, the ship plunged through them, dripping and leaking in a matter unpleasantly suggestive." On New Year's Eve—that same New Year's Eve the original *Monitor* was lost—the *Passaic* barely survived the same storm. In the words of Captain Percival Drayton of the *Passaic*, "My crew as you may suppose have been very much overtasked and could scarcely have stood the fatigue they were necessarily subject to much longer and were fast breaking down from want of sleep and impure air, again the air." After the storm, Captain Drayton wrote to Secretary of the Navy Gideon Welles, "I think it will be a cause of disappointment if the vessels of this class are looked upon as more than steam batteries to be towed from one point to the other in fine weather."[12] The secretary, in turn, forwarded Drayton's comments to Ericsson, adding: "These reports require your very careful and serious attention and they invite your special attention to the weaknesses developed in the junction of the two vessels caused by the very great overhang." The overhang he mentions is where the two hulls, upper and lower, meet at a sharp angle, something that many people commented on and which may well have been a cause of the sinking of the original *Monitor*. In response, Ericsson called Drayton "utterly incompetent to decide on the merits of this vessel."

The debate raged for years in the *Army and Navy Journal*, a patriotic magazine that was published by Ericsson's friend and biographer, William Conant Church.[13] The first issue of the journal in 1863 printed a letter that criticized the living arrangements: "There must still remain objections to armored vessels which should exempt their opponents from the charge of unreasonable old fogyism." This was the charge that Ericsson leveled at everyone who opposed him. "While the protection of the *Monitor* as a fort is so complete that their officers and crew may escape the perils of battle, they are still forced to accept the alternative of the daily discomforts of a life in the confined and necessarily ill-ventilated apartments of a submerged vessel. If they escape untouched in life and limb, it is at the expense often of constitutions so shattered that they must bear through years of ill health and suffering the pain otherwise concentrated into a brief period of agony." Here was a very interesting approach—that without armor, the pain is immediate and very sharp, whereas the armor dissipates the pain into a long lifetime. This letter was published anonymously, but actually it was written by Isaac Newton, the chief engineer of the *Monitor* and good friend of John Ericsson.

By contrast, another letter from another anonymous respondent in the *Army and Navy Journal* criticized the officers of the old wooden navy for retaining a taste for comfort over combat. "Our seamen, however, have a noble object in view than mere personal convenience and comfort. Their ambition is fearlessly to do their duty. Believe me, old fogy, your days of canvass, wood, popguns and comfort is over." Another wrote in calling ironclads "perfect coffins for their occupants even when on a peaceful cruise." A group of monitor captains, including Percival Drayton and John Rogers (the latter Ericsson considered a hero), also criticized the vessel to the Navy Department. "We agree that the ventilation may be improved," they wrote. "At present the air from the birth deck has breathed by men, packed upon it and filled with their exhalations. Air from the water closets and from the galley is taken into the blowers and diluted with fresh air and redistributed for use again." So the debate over living conditions joined the debate about new versus old technology. Still, many of the officers who criticized the monitors belonged to the new generation of scientifically trained officers. The controversy would continue back and forth for months and, indeed, years.

Ericsson, for his part, tirelessly countered all this criticism and generated an impressive array of articles and letters that rebutted skeptics with engineering arguments. For him, the issue came down to expertise. "It has often given me pain," he wrote, "to think that our fighting machines are entrusted to officers who know nothing of mechanics and therefore have no confidence in their vessel." In a sense they were saying, "These things are uncomfortable; they make our men sick; we can't go into combat with them." Ericsson replied by saying, "You just don't understand how they work." The problems, in Ericsson's view, of the leaking from the turret and all the various ventilations were, in Ericsson's view, due to "disregard of my instructions and the adoption of a sailor expedient for sealing." Here he is referring to the question of whether the *Monitor* turret was indeed sealed with oakum, which may or may not have been a factor in its sinking. When Drayton criticized the leaking hull of the monitor *Passaic*, Ericsson replied that, "his reports show how necessary it is to receive with caution the statements made and inferences drawn even by experienced and impartial seamen in relation to our new system."[14] That is a key phrase—Ericsson truly believed that monitors were part of a whole new system of naval warfare that included many other types of inventions in which engineers would be the heroes, and not necessarily the line officers. For Ericsson, arguments born of experience of the vessels were to be countered by engineering logic: "I should rather trust the judgment of a skillful practical engineer after the real damage done by the heavy seas than to the opinion of the gallant commanders of these vessels, most of whom know nothing of mechanical matters."

The navy's line officers did, however, have one thing that Ericsson lacked. They might not have been engineers, they might not have been competent, they might even have been fools. But all of them had direct experience with the vessels. John Ericsson had never been out to sea in a monitor; he had never lived on one; he certainly never entered combat in one. In fact, he had never been in combat at sea at all. For Ericsson, the questions came down to a new era of technology. His grand vision would proceed according to the laws of machinery, and people would have to adapt no matter how uncomfortable or dangerous the arrangements. To quote him again: "I begged earnestly to call their [the officers'] attention to the fact that they have entered onto a new era and they are handling not ships but floating fighting machines and that however eminent their seamanship, they cannot afford to disregard the advice of the engineer." Of course, today we realize that the reverse is also true, the engineer can not afford to disregard the advice of the seaman.

One can criticize the living conditions aboard the *Monitor*, but that does not mean—and this writer does not mean to imply—that these comments diminish the historical significance of this fascinating and strange ship. These issues, and the way they played out, enhance the significance of the ship and make it relevant to the world today. Similar issues concerning living conditions and the matching of humans to machine reappear through the twentieth-century history of submarines, tanks, and even the robot planes and smart bombs and virtual environments.

As we know only too well from today's world of ergonomics, human factors, engineering, and all too many accident investigations, people must be matched to the machines. But the machine must also be matched to the people. Otherwise fatigue, stale air, and discomfort will generate not only complaints but also confusion, mistakes, and errors in judgment, often costing human lives. Perhaps, if John Ericsson had paid more attention to the human arrangements inside his remarkable vessel, we would not be debating whether or not its battle with the *Virginia* was a draw.

CHAPTER 4

Sink Before Surrender: The Story of the CSS *Virginia*

John V. Quarstein

WHEN THE CSS *VIRGINIA* SLOWLY STEAMED DOWN THE Elizabeth River on March 8, 1862, the tide of naval warfare turned from wooden sailing ships to armored, internally powered vessels. Little did the Confederate ironclad's crew realize that their makeshift warship would achieve the greatest Confederate naval victory of the entire war. The trip was thought by most of the crew to be simply a shakedown cruise. Instead, the aggressive nature of the *Virginia*'s commander, Franklin Buchanan, made the voyage a test by fire that proved the power of iron over wood, thereby setting the stage for navies of the future.

It is important to clarify the real name of this Confederate ironclad as her name is often inaccurately expressed and misspelled. The most common usage is *Merrimack*. Merrimack is a native American word meaning "swift water." Nevertheless, *Merrimack* was the name selected by John Lenthall, chief of the U.S. Bureau of Naval Construction on September 25, 1854, for the steam-powered, 40-gun frigate with a screw propeller then being built at Charlestown Navy Yard. The frigate was the first of a class of six frigates built during the 1850s, and each of the *Merrimack*'s sister ships was named for an American river: *Roanoke, Wabash, Colorado, Minnesota,* and *Niagara.*[1]

I also must correct the misconception about how to spell *Merrimack.* It always should be spelled with a *k.* President Franklin Pierce, a native of Concord, New Hampshire, the county seat of Merrimack County and located on the Merrimack River, signed the act approving the appropriation and ship names—including the *k*—on April 6, 1854. New Hampshire citizens use the *k.* When the river is in Massachusetts it is generally spelled without the *k.* This probably is why so many Civil War contemporaries spell it as *Merrimac.*

The USS *Merrimack* was destroyed by fire on the evening of April 20, 1861. But the Confederates raised the burned hull, reconfigured it into an ironclad, and christened it on February 17, 1862, as the CSS *Virginia.* Confederate Secretary of the Navy Stephen Russell Mallory and Flag Officer Franklin Buchanan, the ship's commander, both referred to the ironclad in all of their correspondence after this date as the *Virginia.* Consequently, from February, 1862, the ironclad should always be called the *Virginia.* Unfortunately, few recognized this, as even the ironclad's executive officer, Lieutenant Catesby ap Roger Jones, and chief engineer, H. Ashton Ramsay, wrote of the vessel as the *Merrimac.* Both of these men served on the frigate prior to the war, which may be the cause of their usage of the *Merrimac* name. The Southern newspapers usually referred to the vessel by its re-christened name, CSS *Virginia,* but Northern newspapers constantly used the name *Merrimac*—without the *k.*

Crew member William Norris perhaps clearly expressed why the Confederate ironclad that fought in Hampton Roads should be called the *Virginia* when he wrote: "And *Virginia* was her name, not *Merrimac,* which has a nasal twang equally abhorrent to sentiment and to melody, and meanly compares with the sonorous sweetness of Virginia. She fought under Confederate colors, and her fame belongs to all of us: but there was a peculiar fitness in the name we gave her.

In Virginia, *of* Virginia iron and wood, and *by* Virginians she was built, and *in* Virginia's waters, now made classic by her exploits, she made a record which shall live forever."[2]

The full story begins in 1854, when the USS *Merrimack*'s keel was laid at the Charlestown Navy Yard. The *Merrimack*'s most notable feature was the screw propeller. This propulsion method, ironically enough, was designed by John Ericsson. It enabled the frigate's engines to be installed below the waterline, thereby providing protection for the propulsion unit from enemy cannon fire. The USS *Merrimack* was quickly acclaimed as "a magnificent specimen of naval architecture."[3] Even though she was considered the "finest vessel of war of her class that had been ever constructed," the *Merrimack*'s engines were a constant problem, leading to an overhaul in 1857. She returned to service as the flagship of Commodore John Collins Long's Pacific Squadron. Still, the frigate's engines continued to be unreliable and were described as "exclusively auxiliary to her sails, and to be used only in going in and out of port...."[4] Accordingly, the *Merrimack* was ordered to Gosport Navy Yard near Norfolk and was placed in ordinary on February 6, 1860, joining over a dozen warships in Gosport's "rotten row" and including the USS *Pennsylvania*, (120 guns), the USS *Delaware* (74 guns) and the USS *Germantown*, (22 guns).[5]

When the secession crisis struck the nation, Gosport fell into "disorder and confusion." The problem was due to the yard's commandant, Flag Officer Charles Stewart McCauley. McCauley had served in the U.S. Navy from before the War of 1812, and his long career had included command of both the Pacific and South Atlantic Squadrons. But by 1860, the 67-year-old McCauley was rumored to have taken to drink and often was ridiculed as being too old for active command. During the tense days of April 1861, many would question his decision-making abilities.[6]

Following the fall of Fort Sumter, President Abraham Lincoln's call for 75,000 volunteers to suppress the southern rebellion prompted Virginia to secede from the Union on April 17, 1861. Hampton Roads immediately became a major flashpoint. Virginians clamored to secure Federal property there, which they believed to belong to the Commonwealth. Fort Monroe on Old Point Comfort, Fort Calhoun on the Rip Raps in the middle of Hampton Roads' entrance, and Gosport Navy Yard in Portsmouth were military assets that both the North and South wished to control. The two forts seemed out of Virginia's reach, but Gosport appeared ripe for conquest.

Union Secretary of the Navy Gideon Welles had already taken steps to retrieve the *Merrimack* from Gosport. On April 10, 1861, he ordered McCauley to get the *Merrimack* ready to steam to Philadelphia or, in case of danger from unlawful attempts to take possession of her, that she should be placed beyond their reach. Welles further advised that McCauley should "exercise...judgment in discharging the responsibility that rests upon you."[7] Gosport's commandant responded by telegram that it would take a month to revitalize the *Merrimack*'s dismantled engines. Welles replied by sending U.S. Navy Engineer-in-Chief Benjamin Franklin Isherwood to Portsmouth to repair the *Merrimack*'s engines. Isherwood arrived on April 14, and the *Merrimack* was ready to leave port on April 18. McCauley, however, refused to let the *Merrimack* leave Gosport because of his interpretation of Welles's order that there should be no steps taken to give needless alarm. His decisions, or lack thereof, were further influenced by the many pro-Southern officers on his staff; thirteen out of twenty would later serve the Confederacy. The bottom line was that McCauley found excuses for inaction everywhere and remained passive as events headed toward an explosive conclusion.[8]

As the Federals struggled with McCauley's procrastination, local Southern patriots were quickly organizing their own effort to secure Gosport Navy Yard. A Vigilant Committee was established as militia troops mustered in Norfolk and Portsmouth. Fort Norfolk was seized, and with it a vast store of gunpowder. Batteries were rapidly constructed along the Elizabeth River, and several ships were sunk in the channel off Sewell's Point to block Union access to the navy yard. The pro-Southern citizenry was in a bellicose mood and gathered outside the yard's gates demanding that Gosport should be handed over to the Commonwealth of Virginia. Several militia officers, including William Booth Taliaferro, Henry Heth, and William Mahone—all destined to become Confederate generals—arrived in Portsmouth and opened negotiations with Flag Officer McCauley. Taliaferro, a Mexican War veteran and member of the Virginia House of Delegates, advised McCauley that he planned to assume possession of Gosport Navy Yard on behalf of the Sovereign State of Virginia. When McCauley refused to concede, Mahone began running trains in and out of Portsmouth to give the impression that the Southern troops besieging Gosport were increasing by the hour.[9]

Meanwhile, when the *Merrimack* did not leave Gosport Navy Yard on April 18, Gideon Welles realized that more resolute action was required. Welles dispatched Flag Officer Hiram Paulding, a veteran of fifty years of naval service, on board the 8-gun steamer USS *Pawnee* with 100 marines to take command at Gosport and protect all United States property in the yard. Paulding reached Fort Monroe on the afternoon of April 20 and embarked 350 men of the 3rd Massachusetts Volunteer Regiment. He arrived at Gosport around 8:00 P.M., but Paulding was too late. McCauley had finally taken decisive action and had begun scuttling the warships at Gosport.

Paulding assumed command from a demoralized McCauley but quickly realized that there was little else he could do other than finish the job. The USS *Cumberland* and USS *Pawnee* were stationed in the river to protect the work of demolition crews. The local Southern patriots could only observe from afar the flames' destructive work. Paulding ordered his men to the ships at 4:20 P.M., believing that everything that could be done to destroy the yard's military value had been done.

When the Virginia volunteers entered Gosport Navy Yard the morning after the blaze, evidence of destruction was everywhere. Nevertheless, amongst all the rubble, scuttled ships, and charred buildings, the Confederacy was able to find the wherewithal to create a challenge to the U.S. Navy. The Federals left with such haste that their destructive work was far from complete. Over five warehouses filled with naval supplies survived the flames. The Federals had also abandoned a tremendous array of ordnance, including 1,085 heavy cannon and 250,000 pounds of powder. Numerous dwellings, including the foundry, machine shop, and several workshops remained untouched by the blaze. More importantly, the retreating Federals failed to destroy the infrastructure that would enable the Confederacy to construct vessels to challenge the Federal blockade. The Richmond press gloated over the abundance of equipment and supplies stating that "we have material enough to build a navy of iron-plated ships."[10]

Captain Robert Pegram of the Virginia State Navy assumed command of Gosport Navy Yard for the Commonwealth of Virginia on April 20, 1861. Pegram was replaced on April 22 by the fifty-year naval veteran Flag Officer French Forrest. Forrest was known as a "blusterer of the real old-tar school," and he energetically set himself to the immense task of reorganizing the yard, even sending divers to investigate several of the sunken hulls. It was quickly discovered that several ships were not total losses; the *Germantown*, for example, burned down only to her portside bulwark, while the *Plymouth* was lying scuttled beneath the waves. In addition, Forrest noted that the while the fire had burned the *Merrimack* down to her copperline, destroying the spar and gundecks and damaging the berth deck, the engines appeared undamaged because the *Merrimack* had her sea cocks pulled as she was burning. Flag Officer Forrest then contracted with the Baker Wrecking Company on May 18 to raise the *Merrimack*. On May 30 Forrest reported to General Robert E. Lee that "We have the *Merrimack* up and just pulling her in the dry dock." While questions were raised regarding what to do with this "burned and blackened hulk," Forrest also arranged to raise the two scuttled sloops of war, *Germantown* and *Plymouth*.[11]

Gosport Navy Yard's capture was a godsend for the agrarian South. Since the Union blockade strangled Southern trade, Gosport provided the Confederacy with the capability to build ships to challenge the Union fleet, thereby maintaining the crucial cotton-for-cannon trade with Europe. The man who truly recognized Gosport's ability to achieve this goal was Confederate Secretary of the Navy Stephen Russell Mallory. One of Jefferson Davis's better cabinet appointments, Mallory was elected senator from Florida in 1851 and in 1854 became chairman of the Committee of Naval Affairs, where he was successful in obtaining appropriations to construct new screw-propeller steam frigates and sloops of war that became the envy of European navies. His tenure as chairman of the Committee on Naval Affairs prepared him to assume the tremendous task of creating a navy from nothing.

Mallory immediately recognized upon assuming the duties of secretary of the navy that the Confederacy required a new type of warship to challenge the Union Navy. He advised the Confederate Congress:

> I regard the possession of an iron-armored ship as a matter of the first necessity. Such a vessel at this time could traverse the entire coast of the United States, prevent all blockades, and encounter, with a fair prospect of success, their entire Navy.[1]

Mallory wanted an ocean-going ironclad constructed in Europe. Since he recognized this would take time, he looked to create an ironclad using the weak Southern industrial infrastructure.

Mallory decided that converting the *Merrimack* appeared to be the best solution in implementing a Southern ironclad construction program. He therefore held a meeting in Richmond on June 23, 1861, to plan for the conversion. Lieutenant John Mercer Brooke, Naval Constructor John Luke Porter, and Chief Engineer William Price Williamson formed the ironclad development committee. Porter actually brought with him an iron-cased floating harbor-defense battery plan that he conceived in 1848, while Brooke provided drawings he had made at Mallory's request. Both designs featured an inclined casemate based on the Barnard principle, but Brooke's concept submerged the bow and stern of the vessel to enhance buoyancy and speed. Since Mallory—unrealistically—wanted an oceangoing armored warship, Brooke's design became the plan selected for the *Merrimack*'s conversion.

Porter noted during the conference that his model "was intended for harbor defense only, and was of light draft...."[13] Although Porter's concept was similar to the French iron-cased floating batteries that had served during the Crimean War, Brooke's ends were "shaped like those of any fast vessel, and in order to protect them from the enemy they were to be submerged 2 feet under the water, so that nothing could be seen afloat but the shield itself." Brooke's "novel plan of submerging the ends of the ship and the eaves of the casemate," according to Mallory was "the peculiar and distinctive feature.... It was never before adopted." Despite Brooke's fears "that Mr. P___ would, having an idea of his own, make objection to my plan but he did not regarding it as an improvement, "the committee accepted Brooke's concept of submerged ends 'by unanimous consent."[14]

Even before Mallory gained formal approval from the Confederate Congress, work commenced on the *Merrimack*'s reconfiguration. While Porter supervised the cutting away of the *Merrimack*'s charred timbers, Williamson sought to solve the power plant problems. He quickly learned that new engines provided by Tredegar Iron Works in Richmond would take too long to build and decided that the old, previously condemned, engines of the *Merrimack* could be reworked despite serious corrosion from the saltwater of the Elizabeth River. Williamson was fortunate in that he could rely on the services of Ashton Ramsay; Ramsay had served on the *Merrimack* before the war and knew "her every timber by heart."[15]

Mallory, an astute politician, presented his request for a project appropriation to the Confederate Congress and reported that reconstruction of the *Merrimack* as a frigate would cost $450,000, but that conversion to an armorclad would cost only $172,523. The ironclad project was approved. Despite that shrewd success, Mallory did err with his shipbuilding program by delegating responsibilities among several individuals: French Forrest retained administrative control as yard commandant, Chief Engineer William P. Williamson was given the task of machinery revitalization, and Naval Constructor John L. Porter was charged with supervising the actual construction. In addition, John Mercer Brooke managed the armor and armament for the ironclad as well as acted as Mallory's inspecting officer for the entire project. Friction arose immediately between Brooke and Porter as the projects overlapped. The acrimony began with the fact that both men claimed the vessel's design as their own.

Lieutenant John Mercer Brooke, an 1847 graduate of the U.S. Naval Academy at Annapolis, had one of the most inventive minds in the Confederate Navy, which led to a career filled with successes, including the invention of a bathometer, which won the Gold Medal of Science from the Academy of Berlin. But Naval Constructor John L. Porter would actually complete all the construction plans for the conversion. Porter was a Portsmouth native whose naval career had not been as successful as Brooke's. Nevertheless, he was the only naval constructor to join the Confederacy. Despite his faults and problems with Brooke, Porter immersed himself in his work on the *Merrimack*. Porter's plan called for a length of just over 262 feet and a draft of 21 feet. He supervised the removal of all of the upperworks, then cut the vessel on a straight line from bow to stern at the berth deck level. Soon the main gun deck was laid, and the casemate begun to take shape.

The casemate was the ironclad's most distinctive feature, 28 feet from the bow and extending aft 172 feet. The fantail continued another 56 feet. The sides were sloped upward at a 36-degree angle to deflect shot, but this acute slope allowed only 7 feet of head room and a beam of 30 feet. The roof was grated to provide ventilation to the gun deck, and the grating was manufactured of 2-inch iron bars supporting rafters of yellow pine and white oak. Three hatchways were constructed to enable access to the 14-foot-wide deck. At the front of the casemate was an iron conical pilothouse.

The casemate was constructed of 4 inches of oak laid horizontally, 8 inches of yellow pine laid vertically, and 12 inches of white pine laid horizontally. It was bolted together and then sheathed with 2-inch thick 2- by-6- inch iron plate laid horizontally. A second course of similar iron plate covered the first layer vertically. An additional course of 1-inch iron plate extended 3 feet from the deck to a depth of 3 feet around the vessel. The joining of the casemate to the hull was an obvious weak point. Porter had devised a displacement that would submerge the knuckle 2 feet below the waterline. The casemate eaves were also extended 2 feet to provide additional protection from shot aimed at the ironclad's hull.

Meanwhile, Brooke worked with Tredegar Iron Works on the production of rifled cannon as part of his effort to arm the *Merrimack*. He developed a brilliant system of converting old smoothbore cannon into rifles by forging bands over their breech to resist the greater pressure of firing rifled projectiles. Brooke invented special explosive shells and, more importantly, an elongated armor-piercing, wrought-iron bolt for both the 7-inch and 6.4-inch versions of his rifled cannon. Since Mallory wanted the *Merrimack* armed with the finest heavy cannon, Tredegar immediately forged ahead with the production of Brooke's rifles and projectiles. Thus, Brooke proposed that the *Merrimack* be armed with a broadside battery of six 9-inch Dahlgren smoothbores and two 6.4-inch rifles. Two of the Dahlgrens were hot shot guns, and a special furnace was installed in the engine room to prepare shot for these guns during combat. At each end of the casemate, three gun ports were pierced for the two 7-inch Brooke rifles, which served as pivot guns.

The stern and bow pivot guns were just one of the many disagreements that arose between Brooke and Porter. Porter had overlooked this opportunity to enhance the ironclad's field of fire, and Brooke demanded this improvement. The ram was another issue that only increased the animosity between the two men. Porter did not entirely approve of the 1,500-pound cast-iron ram and installed it only at Brooke's insistence. One flange securing the ram cracked during its mounting. Nothing was done to correct the problem. Nevertheless, the *Virginia*'s weaponry, the ram and guns capable of firing explosive shells and hot shot, made the Confederate ironclad a death knell for wooden warships.

John Mercer Brooke was also assigned the task of coordinating the production of the ironclad's armor. He stayed in Richmond to supervise the production of ironplate by Tredegar Iron Works. The initial contract, based on Porter's specifications, called for ironplate 1-inch thick and 8-feet long. Brooke, however, was uncertain that three courses of 1-inch plate would provide the casemate with adequate shot-proof qualities. Consequently, Brooke and Lieutenant Catesby ap Roger Jones conducted tests on Jamestown Island. Using rifled cannon and projectiles designed by Brooke, they penetrated the 3-inch plate test shield at 300 yards. This forced Tredegar to retool its plate-rolling capacity to produce the necessary 2-inch plate. Even when the plates were completed, there were difficulties and delays transporting the iron from Richmond to Gosport Navy Yard.

One area of great concern remained the *Merrimack*'s old engines. The *Merrimack* was selected to become the nucleus of the Confederacy's first ironclad fleet primarily because she already had a propulsion system. Despite the fire that had consumed her upper works, Chief Engineer William P. Williamson declared the "boiler and heavy and costly parts of the engine but little injured." Still, although the engines could be salvaged, a "more ill-contrived or unreliable pair of engines" could not be found anywhere else. Ashton Ramsay, who served as an assistant engineer on the USS *Merrimack* under Alban Stimers and was assigned as acting chief engineer of the ironclad, believed the engines to be "radically defective" and "that they can not be relied upon." Somehow Williamson and Ramsay were able to improve the power plant's operation; the engines remained temperamental and undependable.[16]

The *Merrimack's* conversion was scheduled for completion in late November, but the project fell far behind schedule. John Porter was depressed and stressed by the effort. Not only was he overworked from his responsibilities with the *Merrimack* but also from providing designs for other Confederate shipbuilding projects. "I received but little encouragement from anyone," Porter complained. "Hundreds—I may say thousands—asserted she would never float." Delays caused by construction problems, technical arrangements, and delivery of iron from Richmond plagued the conversion project. Many observers wondered if it ever would be completed; as Captain Sidney Smith Lee, the yard's executive officer asked, "Do you really think she will float?"[17]

The Confederates were in a rush to finish the ironclad. News of the construction of several ironclads in the North, particularly "Ericsson's Battery," meant that the South might lose its naval advantage if their ironclad was not quickly put into action. Each Federal squadron that arrived in Hampton Roads was reason for alarm. Many Confederates feared that Union troops would capture Norfolk. Mallory's concerns about construction delays prompted him to detail Lieutenant Catesby ap Roger Jones as the *Merrimack's* executive officer in November 1861. Jones was a noted U.S. Navy ordnance expert and had served aboard the USS *Merrimack* during the frigate's maiden voyage. Jones's early assignment to the *Merrimack* expedited construction, in part, by mitigating the disagreements between

Brooke and Porter. His further duties included mounting the ironclad's ordnance, mustering a crew, and preparing the vessel for sea.

Nevertheless, the overall *Merrimack* conversion did not move forward any faster. Although workmen labored seven days a week until 8:00 each evening, delays continued. A frustrated Jones stated to Brooke on January 24, 1862, "Someone ought to be hung." The ironclad's executive officer was especially dismayed over several critical errors made by Porter, which were discovered once the vessel was afloat. Porter had miscalculated the vessel's displacement, which caused the ship to ride too high in the water. Ballast was added to lower the ironclad into the water, but this did not satisfy Jones as he believed the *Merrimack* needed more armor along her hull.[18]

Jones also had difficulty obtaining an adequate crew to man the ironclad, although he was able to assemble an excellent group of officers, including Charles Carroll Simms, Robert Dabney Minor, Hunter Davidson, John Taylor Wood, and Henry Ashton Ramsay, among others. But most of the available seamen in the South had joined the Confederate Army at the war's beginning. Jones therefore detached Lieutenant John Taylor Wood, grandson of President Zachary Taylor and nephew by marriage of President Jefferson Davis, in January, 1862, to search for recruits from nearby army commands. Wood met with Major General John Bankhead Magruder, commander of the Army of the Peninsula, to obtain volunteers. Magruder, who needed more troops to man his Peninsula defensive lines, acquiesced to Wood's request and provided 200 volunteers. Wood selected 80, including Private Richard Curtis of the 32nd Virginia. Curtis, a veteran of the Battle of Big Bethel, worked before the war as a boatman. Several crew members, such as Charles Hasker, came from Flag Officer William Lynch's North Carolina "Mosquito Fleet" Squadron. While Charles Oliver, a Royal Navy veteran, and Albert Griswold had deserted the USS *Cumberland* as she left Gosport. Several units from Major General Benjamin Huger's Department of Norfolk command also volunteered to serve on the ironclad. But more men were needed to man the guns and operate the ironclad, and Captain Franklin Buchanan, head of the Office of Orders and Detail, was concerned about the lack of sufficient crew members. He wrote Mallory on February 10, 1862, that the "*Merrimack* has not yet received her crew, not withstanding all my efforts to procure them from the Army."[19] Only on March 6, when Captain Thomas Kevill and thirty-one men of the United Artillery mustered for "service aboard the ironclad steamer *Virginia*," did the ironclad finally fill her necessary complement of 320 men.[20]

The *Merrimack* needed a commander and Mallory selected Franklin Buchanan. The Maryland native was an excellent choice for command of the ironclad and "was hailed with great satisfaction" by the crew. A grandson of a signer of the Declaration of Independence, Buchanan was appointed midshipman in the U.S. Navy in 1815. Franklin Buchanan was the first superintendent of the U.S. Naval Academy at Annapolis and commanded the sloop-of-war *Germantown* during the Mexican War. He was commander of Matthew C. Perry's flagship, the USS *Susquehanna*, when Perry opened Japan to American trade. "A typical product of the old-time quarter deck," John Randolph Eggleston wrote of Buchanan, he was "as indomitably courageous as Nelson and as arbitrary."[21] Buchanan commanded the Washington Navy Yard when the Civil War erupted. When it appeared that Maryland would leave the Union following the April 19, 1861 Baltimore Riot, Buchanan resigned his commission. Since Maryland did not secede, Buchanan strove for reinstatement, only to be denied by Gideon Welles. Buchanan was then named a captain in the C.S. Navy and assigned to the Office of Orders and Details until detached on February 24, 1862, to prepare the Confederate ironclad for combat.

The ironclad was launched and commissioned as the CSS *Virginia* one week before Buchanan assumed command. The February 17, 1862, event was an unimpressive affair. Workmen were still feverishly completing the conversion, and the mood was one of desperation. On March 4, 1862, however, Buchanan reported that the ironclad was ready for combat. Mallory was overjoyed. He expected great things of both Buchanan and the *Virginia*. Mallory's orders to Buchanan included his hopes for the ironclad's use:

> The *Virginia* is a novelty in naval construction, is untried and her power unknown.... Her powers as a ram are regarded as formidable, and it is hoped that you may be able to test them. Like a bayonet charge of infantry, this mode of attack, while most distinctive, will commend itself to you in this present scarcity of ammunition.

The Confederate secretary of the navy also suggested that if the ironclad could "pass Old Point and make a dashing cruise on the Potomac as far as Washington, its effect upon the public mind would be important to our cause." Such a bold move could surely bring victory at a time when the Confederacy was reeling from defeats in Tennessee and along the North Carolina Sounds, and Mallory was convinced "that the opportunity and the means for striking a blow for our Navy are now for the first time presented, I congratulate you upon it, and know that your judgment and gallantry will meet all expectations." Mallory concluded his letter stating that, "Action, prompt and successful action—now would be of serious importance to our course."[22]

Mallory's orders for prompt action had not been lost on Franklin Buchanan. Buchanan sought to make the most of the tactical superiority that his ironclad would give the Confederacy by coordinating a joint attack against the Federal forces at Newport News Point with Major General John Bankhead Magruder's Army of the Peninsula. Buchanan envisioned such an attack dislodging the Union hold on Hampton Roads. Magruder refused to participate in the plan because of the bad weather, stating that "no one ship can produce such an impression upon the troops at Newport News Point as to cause them to evacuate the fort."²³ Buchanan was undaunted by Magruder's lack of interest. He had been assigned to the *Virginia* because of his aggressive nature, and he intended to take his ironclad into action as quickly as possible. A gale forced Buchanan to call off any attack on March 6 and 7, as the ironclad needed calm waters in which to operate.

On March 8, 1862, the weather cleared, and Buchanan prepared his ironclad for action. The casemate was coated with tallow (ship's grease): Catesby Jones noted that it would "increase the tendency of the projectiles to glance." Buchanan hoisted his flag officer pendant and ordered the workmen, who were still laboring on the *Virginia*'s armor, off the vessel. At 11:00 A.M. the *Virginia* cast off from the quay and began its trip down the Elizabeth River. Buchanan's aggressive intentions took most of the crew by surprise; he had told only one or two of his officers that he intended to attack the Union fleet that day. Lieutenant John Randolph Eggleston remembered that the crew thought "we were going on an ordinary trial trip."²⁴

As the *Virginia* steamed down the Elizabeth River, accompanied by her gunboat consorts CSS *Beaufort* and CSS *Raleigh,* both sides of the riverbank were "thronged with people." Ship surgeon Dinwiddie Phillips commented that, "most of them, perhaps, (were) attracted by our novel appearance, and desirous of witnessing our movements through the water." "Few, if any," Phillips added, "entertained an exalted idea of our efficiency, and many predicted a total failure."²⁵ Midshipman Hardin Littlepage remembered one man shouting, "Go on with your old metallic coffin! She will never amount to anything else!"²⁶ Others realized that this was the day, as Lieutenant William Parker of the *Beaufort* wrote, "that here was to be tried the great experiment of the ram and iron-clad in naval warfare."²⁷ Yet there still were problems on board the ironclad: "From the start we saw that she was slow, not over five knots," Lieutenant John Taylor Wood later commented. "She steered so badly that, with her great length it took thirty to forty minutes to turn. . . . She was as unmanageable as a water-logged vessel."[28] The huge ironclad's keel was running so close to the river bottom that the ship's rudder could not steer her. The *Virginia* took a towline from the *Beaufort* to help negotiate a bend in the river.

As the *Virginia* entered Hampton Roads, the crew could see the entire Federal fleet arrayed in a line that stretched from Newport News Point to Fort Monroe. Five major warships, USS *Cumberland* (26 guns), USS *Congress* (52 guns), USS *Minnesota* (47 guns), USS. *Roanoke* (42 guns), and USS *St. Lawrence* (50 guns), awaited the Confederate ironclad. Undaunted by such a force, Buchanan informed the crew:

> Sailors in a few minutes you will have the long awaited opportunity to show your devotion to your country and our cause. Remember that you are about to strike for your country and your homes, your wives, and your children. The Confederacy expects everyman to do his duty, beat to quarters! [29]

The flag officer reminded everyone that "many Confederates had complained that they were not taken near enough to the enemy" as Harden Littlepage remembered Buchanan's comments, "and assured us that there should be no complaint this time, for he intended to head directly for the *Cumberland.*"[30] Buchanan concluded his exhortations with the admonition that the "whole world is watching you today" and commanded them, "Those ships must be taken.... Go to your guns!"[31]

Even though the Federals knew all about the Confederate ironclad project, they were surprised by the *Virginia*'s appearance. Captain Henry Gershon Jacques Van Brunt, captain of the USS *Minnesota,* had written only a few days before, "The *Merrimac* is still invisible to us, but report says she is ready to come out. I sincerely wish she would; I am quite tired of hearing of her." Van Brunt added that "the sooner she gives us the opportunity to test her strength the better."[32] Nevertheless, the Federals were caught off guard when a crewmember of the USS *Congress* noted, "I believed that thing is a-comin' down at last."[33] To the Union sailors the *Virginia* appeared "like the roof of a very big barn belching forth smoke as from a chimney on fire." Very soon the Federals would recognize the *Virginia* to be "a huge, half-submerged crocodile intent on evil."[34]

For the next twenty-four hours the *Virginia* would be engaged in the Civil War's greatest naval battle. While she fought one ironclad, the *Monitor*, to a draw, the *Virginia* also inflicted upon the U.S. Navy a staggering defeat. The Union losses on March 8 included two capital warships sunk, one steam frigate damaged, one sailing frigate slightly damaged, two tugs damaged, three transports destroyed, and 247 men killed. "It was a great victory," recalled Robert Minor, "The IRON and the HEAVY GUNS did the work."[35] Catesby Jones was disappointed and viewed the two-day battle as only a partial success. Jones noted that the "destruction of those wooden vessels was a matter of course especially so, being at anchor, but in not capturing the ironclad, I feel as if we had done nothing. Give me that vessel," Jones added, "and I will sink this one in twenty minutes."[36]

Mallory's faith in the Confederate ironclad was vindicated by the *Virginia*'s actions on March 8 and 9, 1862. The Confederate secretary of the navy believed the *Virginia* had won "the most remarkable victory which naval annals record" and dreamed that the ironclad would "strike a blow from which the enemy could never recover"[37] by shelling and burning New York City. The *Virginia*'s officers, however, were not as ecstatic about their ironclad's performance. John Taylor Wood advised Mallory that in "the *Monitor* we had met our equal."[38] Buchanan believed that the *Virginia* was "by no means invulnerable" and also was unseaworthy, stating that should the ironclad "encounter a gale, or a very heavy swell, I think it more than probable she would founder."[39] The newly promoted admiral believed the *Virginia* should be used only to defend Norfolk.

The undefeated *Virginia*'s mere existence following the March 9 engagement defended Norfolk and blocked the entrance to the James River just at the point when Major General George B. McClellan decided to march toward Richmond by way of the Virginia Peninsula. McClellan's original plan entailed the use of both the James and York Rivers. Gunboats would guard his flanks, while steamers would transport supplies as McClellan's troops moved up the Peninsula. Now the entire concept was placed in jeopardy because of the Confederate ironclad; Brigadier General John G. Barnard, chief engineer of the Army of the Potomac, lamented that the Confederate ironclad "paralyzes the movement of this army."[40] In addition, many Union commanders were not sure of the USS *Monitor*'s ability to keep the Confederate ironclad in check. In fact, the *Virginia* mesmerized Flag Officer Louis Goldsborough, commander of the North Atlantic Blockading Squadron, and influenced the U.S. Navy's ability to support McClellan's campaign. "The James River was declared by the naval authorities closed to the operations of their vessels," McClellan noted, adding that the U.S. Navy's "highest and most imperative duty was to watch and neutralize the *Merrimac*...."[41] This situation caused Goldsborough (who was suffering from the dreaded disease known as "ram fever" or "*Merrimack* on the brain" that spring) to refuse to attack the Confederate water batteries at Yorktown and Gloucester Point, prompting McClellan to besiege the Confederate defenses and thereby delaying his march toward Richmond.

Since the *Virginia* was actually unfinished when it attacked the Union fleet on March 8, and had suffered significant damage during the two days of combat (primarily from her fight with the *Cumberland*), the ironclad was placed in dry dock for modification and repair immediately upon its return to Gosport Navy Yard. John Mercer Brooke recognized that the *Virginia*'s ordnance required improved armor-piercing shot, and by March 10 he already was at work producing wrought-iron, steel-tipped bolts for the 7- and 6.4-inch rifles.

A new ram also was required. Brooke designed a new 12-foot-long, steel-pointed iron ram that extended the ironclad's bow 14 feet, and the port shutters were finally fitted into the broadside gunports. Battle damage to the shield necessitated the replacement of several 2-inch plates. One shipyard worker noted that "shots had plowed up the roofing so that you could lay a large watermelon in the spot where the shot had struck."[42] Even greater attention was given to one of the *Virginia*'s primary flaws: lack of armor below the eaves of the casemate to protect the ironclad's knuckle, but time and available resources limited this effort. Eventually, only a band of 2-inch plates extending 3.5 feet below the eaves and covering 160 feet on both sides was installed.

The *Virginia* also needed a new commander to replace Franklin Buchanan, who had been wounded. Mallory appointed the sixty-seven-year-old Georgian Flag Officer Josiah Tattnall on March 21 to assume command of all naval forces in *Virginia*'s waters. Tattnall had joined the U.S. Navy in 1812 and fought in his first battle on Craney Island in 1813. Josiah Tattnall was known as the "beau ideal of a naval officer" and many believed that he "possessed all the traits found in heroic characters."[43] Almost 6 feet tall, with long arms and a protruding lower lip, Tattnall was feared in his younger days as a cutlass expert. His directive from Mallory was to make the Confederate ironclad "as destructive and formidable to the enemy as possible." Mallory added, "Do not hesitate or wait for orders, but strike when, how, and where your judgment may dictate."[44]

The *Virginia* left dry dock on April 4, 1862. Tattnall was instructed by Mallory to attack the Union transports in Hampton Roads which, in turn, the *Virginia*'s commander hoped would provoke the *Monitor* into battle, but bad weather and mechanical problems delayed the Virginia's departure for several days. As the *Virginia* waited to return to action, George McClellan launched his 121,500-man army up the Peninsula. The Army of the Potomac, however, was stopped in its tracks on April 5, 1862, by Major General John Bankhead Magruder's Warwick–Yorktown Line. Magruder's ability to deceive the Union commander into believing the Confederates outnumbered the Federal Army, coupled with the *Virginia*'s ability to guard the Confederate Army's James River flank, prompted McClellan to besiege the Confederate fortifications, and Yorktown became the focus of McClellan's siege engineering. Robert E. Lee, then military advisor to President Jefferson Davis, wanted the *Virginia* to strike at the Federal transports in the York River, but Mallory preferred that the *Virginia* defend Norfolk and confront the *Monitor.*

Tattnall knew that his ironclad's engines were unreliable, and he did not believe the *Virginia* could pass the Union forts without serious damage. He wrote Mallory:

> I have been aware from the first that my command is dangerous to my reputation, from the expectations of the public, founded on the success of Commodore Buchanan, and I have looked to a different field from his to satisfy them. I shall never find in Hampton Roads the opportunity my gallant friend found. [45]

Nevertheless, Tattnall was willing to take on the *Monitor,* declaring, "I will take her! I will take her if hell's on the other side of her."[46]

Tattnall understood that the Union plan was to lure his ironclad into deep water where once "in close conflict with the *Monitor,*"[47] the *Virginia* would be rammed by various Union gunboats. It was common knowledge that multimillionaire shipowner Cornelius Vanderbilt had donated his yacht just to be used to ram the *Virginia.* The Confederates had also concocted their own plan to destroy or capture the *Monitor.* Information gleaned from an issue of *Scientific American*, which contained a detailed report on the Union ironclad, indicated that the *Monitor* could be boarded and captured by disabling the crew. Midshipman R. C. Foute wrote:

> We have four small gunboats ready to take the party, some of each division in each vessel. One division was provided with grappling irons and lines, another with wedges and matters, another with tarpaulins, and the fourth with chloroform, hand grenades, etc. The idea was for all four vessels to pounce upon the *Monitor* at one time, wedge the turret, deluge the turret by breaking bottles of chloroform on the turret top, cover the pilot house with tarpaulin and wait for the crew to surrender.

Foute added that the "plan was very simple, and seemingly entirely practical, provided we should not be blown out of the water before it could be executed.

On April 11, at 6:00 A.M., Tattnall's squadron moved down the Elizabeth River to Sewell's Point. Tattnall made a brief patriotic speech to the *Virginia*'s crew and concluded, "Now you go to your battle stations and I'll go to mine."⁴⁹ Josiah Tattnall then perched himself in an armchair on the top deck. The *Virginia* entered Hampton Roads at 7:10 A.M., and the Federal transports scattered to the protection of Fort Monroe "like a flock of wild fowl in the act of flight."⁵⁰ The *Monitor*, now reinforced by the iron-hulled *Naugatuck* (Stevens Battery) and armed with one 100-pounder Parrott rifle, stayed in the channel between Fort Monroe and the Rip Raps. The Union ironclad had strict orders not to engage the *Virginia* unless the Confederate ironclad moved out of Hampton Roads into the open waters of the Chesapeake Bay. Tattnall refused to take his ironclad out of Hampton Roads, and the *Monitor* would not accept the *Virginia*'s challenge. The *Virginia* steamed around in Hampton Roads from 9:00 A.M. to 4:00 P.M. While the Confederate ironclad held the attention of the entire Federal fleet, the CSS *Jamestown* captured two brigs and an Accomac schooner off Newport News Point and towed them to Norfolk. The *Virginia*, flying the captured transport's flags upside down under her own colors as an act of disdain, fired several shells at the *Naugatuck* and returned to Gosport Navy Yard. Tattnall was praised for his prudent, yet gallant, actions on April 11.

However, time was running out for the Confederate Navy in Hampton Roads. On the evening of May 3, 1862, General Joseph Eggleston Johnson ordered the evacuation of the Warwick–Yorktown Line. Faced with defending both Norfolk and Richmond, Johnson chose to defend the Confederate capital. His retreat up the Peninsula uncovered Norfolk, forcing the Confederates to make plans to abandon the port city and naval base. When he learned of the Confederate Army's retreat, Mallory immediately telegraphed Tattnall, advising him that the Confederacy looked to the *Virginia* alone to prevent the enemy from ascending the James River.

The *Virginia* was now the lone sentinel guarding Norfolk, and she maintained a daily station off Sewell's Point. William Keeler of the *Monitor* remembered watching the "Big Thing" on May 7 as she

> ... again made her appearance and another just after dinner while she was in status quo under Craney Island, apparently chewing the bitter end of reflection and ruminating sorrowfully upon the future. She remained there smoking, reflecting, and ruminating till nearly sunset, when she slowly crawled off nearly concealed in a huge murky cloud of her own emission, black and repulsive as the perjured hearts of her traitorous crew. The water hisses and boils with indignation as like some huge shiny reptile she slowly emerges from her loathsome liar with the morning light, vainly seeking with glairing (sic) eyes some mode of escape through the meshes of the net which she feels in daily closing her in. Behind her she already hears the hounds of the hunter and before are the ever watchful guards whom it is certain death to pass. We remain in the same position we have occupied since the fight—a sort of advance guard for the fleet.[51]

The *Virginia*'s days of being "cock of the walk," as John Eggleston noted, were numbered. The Federals were tightening their noose around Norfolk

As the Confederates tried to remove valuable war material from Norfolk, President Abraham Lincoln decided to go to Fort Monroe to prompt more resolute action. Lincoln's focus was on Norfolk and CSS *Virginia*. A conference was held with Flag Officer Louis Goldsborough and Major General John Ellis Wool to discuss how the U.S. Navy could further support McClellan's march against Richmond. The President ordered a squadron, including the new ironclad *Galena* and the gunboats *Port Royal* and *Aroostoock*, into the James River on May 8, while the *Monitor* and *Naugatuck*, supported by several wooden warships including the USS *Susquehanna* and USS *San Jacinto*, moved past the Rip Raps and began their cannonade of Sewell's Point battery. When Tattnall heard the shelling, he immediately steamed his ironclad to contest the Union advance. While it appeared a second contest between the two ironclads might occur, Flag Officer Goldsborough ordered the Federal squadron to withdraw to its anchorage beyond Fort Monroe. Tattnall continued to steam around Hampton Roads for the next two hours, hoping that he might induce the *Monitor* to attack. Finally Tattnall, disgusted with the Union lack of aggression, ordered Catesby Jones to "fire a gun to windward."[52]

When Lincoln recognized that Norfolk could not be captured by a naval attack, he organized the landing of Union troops at Ocean View on the evening of May 9. Major General John Ellis Wool and Brigadier General Joseph King Fenno Mansfield marched their troops toward Norfolk and occupied the port city the next afternoon. The Confederate Army had already evacuated Norfolk. Major General Benjamin Huger, commander of the Department of Norfolk, was seized with panic when the *Galena* entered the James River. Huger believed that his 10,000-man command would be cut off from its retreat via Suffolk by the U.S. Navy. He left with such haste that he neglected to inform Tattnall of his retreat.

On the morning of May 10, the *Virginia* was at her mooring off Sewell's Point when Tattnall noticed that the Confederate flag was no longer flying from the Confederate fortifications. The Sewell's Point battery appeared abandoned, so Tattnall immediately dispatched his flag lieutenant, John Pembroke Jones, to Craney Island to find out what had happened. Jones soon learned that the Confederate Army was gone, the navy yard was in flames, and the Union army was en route to Norfolk. Tattnall was furious. He had attended a conference with Benjamin Huger on May 9, during which they decided that the *Virginia* should be given ample notice of any withdrawal, enabling the Confederate ironclad to move up the James River to serve as a floating battery defending Richmond.

Tattnall realized that an effort must be made to get the *Virginia* up the James River toward Richmond. The other possibilities—he could take his ironclad out and attack the Union fleet, perhaps destroying several enemy vessels before sinking in a blaze of glory, or he could try to take the *Virginia* out to sea en route to another Southern port—were not advisable. The pilots advised that his choice of course could only be achieved if the huge ironclad could reduce her draft from 23 feet to 18 feet in order to cross Harrison's Bar. The crew immediately went to work throwing coal, ballast, and everything else overboard except the ironclad's guns and ammunition. The *Virginia* had been lightened, but around 1:00 P.M. on May 11, the pilots informed Catesby Jones that the *Virginia* still could not cross the bar; the wind was coming from the west rather than the east, blowing the water away from the bar and making it even more shallow. There was little Tattnall could do. In addition, the lightning had made the *Virginia*, according to Ashton Ramsay, "no longer an ironclad," and therefore unable to engage the Federal fleet.[53]

Now, the *Virginia* would have to be destroyed to prevent her capture. She ironclad was run aground off Craney Island, and the crew slowly debarked using the ironclad's two cutters. After three hours the crew was safely ashore and combustibles had been spread throughout the ship. Catesby Jones and John Taylor Wood lit the fire and then rowed for shore, "by the light of our burning ship." "Still unconquered, we hauled down our drooping colors, their laurels all fresh and green," lamented Ashton Ramsay, "and with mingled pride and grief gave her to the flames."[54] It was, as Richard Curtis reflected, "a sad finish for such a bright beginning."[55] The crew then marched twenty miles to Suffolk, where Tattnall sadly telegraphed Mallory, "The *Virginia* no longer exists."

When Mallory learned of the *Virginia*'s destruction, he exclaimed, "May God protect us and cure us of weakness and folly."[56] John Mercer Brooke blamed the *Virginia*'s destruction on "poor leadership and lack of harmony within the Government."[57] The Federals were overjoyed, as S.R. Franklin remembered:

> It was a beautiful sight to us in more senses than one. She had been a thorn in our side for a long time, and we were glad to have her well out of the way. I remained on deck for the rest of the night watching her burning. Gradually the casemate grew hotter and hotter, until finally it became red hot, so that we could distinctly mark its outlines, and remained in this condition for fully half an hour, when, with a tremendous explosion, the *Merrimac* went into the air and was seen no more.[58]

The CSS *Virginia* was, without question, the most successful Confederate ironclad. The *Virginia* won the race, albeit for just one day, to win naval supremacy in Hampton Roads, thereby becoming the first ironclad to sink another warship in modern history. The *Virginia*'s brief career ended somewhat ingloriously, yet the Confederate ironclad achieved everlasting fame for her role as one of "the founders," as Franklin Buchanan wrote, "of iron-clad warfare at sea." Indeed, the *Virginia* and her antagonist, the *Monitor*, ushered in a new age of naval design when they fought in Hampton Roads.

Although the brilliant Swedish-American John Ericsson received most of the credit for the *Monitor* as the ship design of the future, it was the *Virginia*'s ramming of the *Cumberland* and the total destruction of the *Congress* that proved beyond a doubt the power of iron over wood.

The career of the CSS *Virginia* is an amazing story. This makeshift ironclad destroyed two major Union warships, fought another ironclad to a draw, and secured strategic control over Hampton Roads for two months, which helped tip the balance in favor of the Confederacy during the Peninsula Campaign. The *Virginia* achieved more in its brief lifespan than any other Confederate ironclad. Indeed, the *Virginia*'s service followed Franklin Buchanan's March 8 "Sink before Surrender" exhortation. Despite her destruction on May 11, 1862, the *Virginia* left in her wake a stunning example of improvisation, innovation, heroism, and leadership.

CHAPTER 5

Believe Only Half of What You Read About the Battle of Hampton Roads
Mabry Tyson

PERHAPS THE MOST FAMOUS NAVAL BATTLE IN UNITED STATES history, the Battle of Hampton Roads, pitted the Confederate ironclad CSS *Virginia* (ex-USS *Merrimack*) against the blockading fleet of the United States Navy, including the *Cumberland*, *Congress*, *Minnesota*, and the ironclad *Monitor*. As a turning point in naval technology, and as a dramatic battle in the Civil War, this battle has been popularized throughout the years and continues to be taught as one of the central battles of the conflict.

While the cannon were fired only on March 8 and 9, 1862, both sides continued to fight to claim victory for decades. Immediately after the battle, stories flew around the country on newly installed telegraphs. Northern and Southern newspapers and politicians each claimed victory for their side. But, as with any breaking news story, reporters and eyewitnesses had only partial information. While it would have been prudent to follow Ben Franklin's maxim, "Believe none of what you hear and half of what you see," instead rumors spread rapidly about the situations on the opposing vessels. Those wild rumors fueled the fame of the battle. It would be years before the participants could shed more light on the events. The emotional importance of this battle and the greater conflict fired the divergent views of the outcome.

Writing about this battle some twelve years later, former Assistant Secretary of the U.S. Navy Gustavus Vasa Fox stated: "Exaggeration may be a necessary device of war, but not of history."[1] During wartime, each belligerent has an inherent interest in interpreting the results in his own favor. Historians, however, have a duty to review the evidence and discount partisan reports when reviewing the battle. Even today it is common to find articles or books that repeat the myths of 1862. Any modern author that reiterates the exaggerations and inaccuracies is guilty of negligent intellectual dishonesty.

Facts Agreed Upon by Both Sides

Both the *Virginia* and the *Monitor* were experiments in progress in early March, 1862. The South had been converting the USS *Merrimack* into an ironclad for many months, delayed by other demands of the war. In response, the North built several vessels to counter the potential threat of the Southern ironclad. The *Monitor* was rushed to completion but, as with any new design, she had unanticipated flaws that delayed her appearance. Initially, steering difficulties delayed her a few days. As she headed for the fateful battle, she almost foundered during a storm in the open sea.

Although there is no written record indicating the South was aware of the status of the *Monitor*, the Confederates must have known she was nearing completion. For whatever reason, after months of delay, the Confederate Navy seemingly rushed the *Virginia* into battle. While this vessel was mostly invulnerable above water, its gunports were gaping holes in its armor. Shutters for the gunports had just arrived and were hurriedly placed on the bow and stern ports;[2] a few more days' delay would have allowed the installation of the shutters on all the gunports. The decision had been made to engage the Federal fleet at the earliest possible moment, but the same storm that nearly sank the *Monitor* delayed their plans until Saturday morning, March 8, 1862. Even then, reports indicate construction workers were still on the ship as it sailed. Lest word leak out, the crew was told this was a trial run, but the officers of the James River Fleet had been alerted that this was indeed a trial by fire. The true plans were concealed from even the crew of the *Virginia* until they were well on their way.

During this first day of the Battle of Hampton Roads, the *Virginia* sailed into the midst of the Federal fleet. Initially bypassing the *Congress*, she rammed the *Cumberland* just up the James River from Newport News. The two ships were locked together as the *Cumberland* began sinking, but eventually the *Virginia* broke away, losing her ram in the process. The captain of the *Congress*, wishing to avoid the same fate, ran his ship aground off Newport News. The guns of the *Virginia* raked the *Congress* until she was forced to surrender. As the other Confederate ships accepted the surrender under the white flag of the *Congress*, and attempted to remove the officers and wounded from her, Union forces on shore fired on the ships. The *Virginia*, unable to complete the capture of the vessel, fired hot shot to ignite the *Congress*, which exploded hours later. Return fire from the shore reportedly so infuriated *Virginia*'s Flag-Officer Franklin Buchanan that he personally returned fire with a musket. As a result, he received a minié-ball through his leg that required his removal to the navy hospital early the next morning.

Command of the *Virginia* passed to the Executive Officer, Lieutenant Catesby ap Roger Jones. On Sunday, he commanded the *Virginia* as she returned to Hampton Roads to continue the attack on the *Minnesota*, which had grounded the previous afternoon. The *Monitor*, under command of Lieutenant John Worden, had arrived overnight and interjected herself into the fight. The battle continued for several hours with neither vessel being seriously injured until a rifle shell from the *Virginia* damaged the pilothouse of the *Monitor*, injuring Worden. The *Monitor* then withdrew to shoal water, out of range of the *Virginia*. Worden passed command to Executive Officer Lieutenant S. Dana Greene. Precisely how much time passed remains open to question, but we know that in the early afternoon, the *Virginia* headed back toward Sewall's Point and Portsmouth. The *Monitor* then returned to the *Minnesota*.

Disputed Interpretations

The Confederates had an overwhelming victory on March 8, leaving the Union Navy scrambling to remove its ships from the threat of the seemingly invulnerable *Virginia*. The panic spread even to Abraham Lincoln's Cabinet. According to the press of the day, the results of March 9 also seemed clear-cut to each side, but each side saw those results differently.

The Confederate press claimed victory on March 9 based on the fact that the *Monitor* withdrew from the battle and stayed away as long as the *Virginia* waited. From the southern shores of Hampton Roads, the damage to the *Monitor* was invisible. She appeared to have withdrawn without damage, which only strengthened the idea that victory belonged to the *Virginia*. The Union papers' victory claims were based on assumptions that the *Monitor* literally chased a sinking *Virginia* out of Hampton Roads. After the war, the Union claims dominated the popular press, school texts, and history books.

It is easy to understand why both sides competed in the post-war battle for memory and vindication. The importance of victory at Hampton Roads far outstretched the outcome of one battle. England was waiting in the wings. If the Confederacy looked to have a good chance to secure independence, perhaps based on technological superiority, it was believed that England might yet come to the aid of the South. The Union could not let this happen.

The officers and men of the *Virginia* felt frustrated and dishonored by the inaccurate accounts of the battle that claimed the *Virginia* had retreated in defeat. Particularly galling was the claim for prize money, initially submitted in 1869, for the *Monitor*'s officers and crew, requesting a prize for the eventual destruction of the *Virginia*.

Likewise, the *Monitor*'s officers and crew were bothered by questions about the battle. In 1868, Captain Worden wrote to the secretary of the navy with an account of the battle in response to Lieutenant Greene's being "annoyed by ungenerous allusions to the fact that no official record existed at the Department, in relation to [Worden's] opinion of his conduct on that occasion."[3] Reportedly the questions continued to haunt Greene. Late in 1884, the same year that the prize claim was definitively rejected, and immediately after submitting an article on the battle for publication in the *Century Illustrated Magazine*, he took his own life.

Reaching for the Truth

Quite naturally, the traumatic Civil War occupied the attention of both sides long after the fighting stopped. Lectures, articles, and books recounted the stories of the veterans to eager audiences. Both sides wished to honor their heroes, glorious victories, and valiant efforts. Grievances were not soon forgotten.

Most of the officers and a number of the men who crewed the two ironclad ships told or wrote their stories of the battle. Catesby Jones, this author's great-grandfather, wrote one such account in 1874, based on his 1862 official report and letters from the other officers both during and after the war. As he died three years later, this was his definitive report.

Jones's wife, Gertrude Tartt Jones, outlived him by fifty years. She had lost her husband and wanted to right his honor by correcting what she believed were misconceptions perpetrated by the wartime

Union reports that claimed the *Virginia* retreated in defeat. Family stories recount that she spent every afternoon writing letters trying to get the story corrected.

In April 1890, for example, she wrote to the former Confederate Chief of the Signal Corps and Secret Service Bureau, Colonel William Norris, about creating a new pamphlet containing articles on the battle. Norris, who called Catesby Jones one of the finest men he had ever met, was a witness to the battle and had written an article about it eleven years earlier. Extracts from Gertrude Jones's letters show her concerns and indicate what she hoped to create:

> I know no words that can convey to you the interest I take in the narrative by Capt. Jones, and also yours, and the injustice I feel in the Northern people—not being magnanimous enough to give the credit of that victory to the Confederate's Virginia.... Can you not put your wits to work, and get them to tell the truth again? If this be true that the Monitor was so disabled, I think it great injustice to attach so much blame to the young officer as Ericson[sic] does, calling him "A miserable officer who ran off," I don't like injustice to even an enemy, the truth and nothing more is all we want.
>
> ...I would like to have in a little book for my children, and to vindicate the fair fame of the officers and men, but more particularly my husband, the commander of the Virginia in that remarkable battle, his narrative and ours both endorsed by others in short remarks....[4]

Mrs. Jones wanted to include statements or articles from Union naval officers that she felt had reported the event accurately, and she wanted to "get them to tell the truth again." Even today, the stories based on the initial rumors and misinformation continue to be presented as fact. Instead of a "little book," today's means of presenting the facts of the battle is a web site. In the spirit of Mrs. Catesby ap Roger Jones, and as her great-grandson, I continue to encourage the review of the facts about the Battle of Hampton Roads at the CSS *Virginia* Home Page (cssvirginia.org). This web site specializes in providing historical material from all the participants, eyewitnesses, and other individuals with special knowledge about the battle. With the testimony of both sides, readers can realize which are true and which are not.

Other officers of the *Virginia* also expressed their concerns. Third Assistant Engineer E. A. Jack wrote in his *Memoirs* for his wife about what he termed

> ... the untruthful reports that we were beaten and were in a sinking condition ... In our school books, from which the children of this generation are getting their knowledge of our country's history, this untruth is stated, in spite of assertions that there is no truth in it from distinguished foreign naval officers, federal officers who witnessed the fight, and Confederates who participated in it.[5]

Third Assistant Engineer E. V. White added in 1891:

> An incident on this point will illustrate the prevalence of an incorrect record of the case. Some two years ago, when in New York, I visited the Cyclorama illustrating the fight, then on exhibition, when, during the course of his lecture on the subject to the spectators, the manager made statements that were not facts, and, interrupting him, I called his attention to the same. He motioned me to hold my peace, and, after finishing his talk, he came to me and said he was well aware of the errors he was circulating, but that in order to make his show popular, he was forced to state what he did.[6]

The battle between the two ironclads was by then so famous that entrepreneurs built buildings just to tell the story. Besides the Cyclorama in New York, Merrimack and Monitor buildings were built in Jamestown, Virginia (for the 1907 Tercentennial Exposition), Chicago, Philadelphia, Seattle, and Denver as late as 1910.

Sources of the Popular Misconceptions

The newspapers and magazines of the day were the primary source of (mis)information to the public. Both the Confederate and Union ironclads had been highly anticipated, even dreaded, for months. When the *Virginia* decimated the Union fleet in Hampton Roads on March 8, the shock waves were felt immediately throughout the North, while the South rejoiced. Then, just one day later, the *Monitor* arrived and survived the battle with the seemingly unstoppable *Virginia*. Both sides claimed victory. Desperately in need of good news to counteract the previous day's disaster, the Northern newspaper articles reported as fact such rumors as that the *Virginia* was sinking and had retreated or that the *Monitor* had put shot through the *Virginia*, apparently not caring whether there was any way for the Union forces or witnesses to know if such stories were true or not.

The newspapers made immediate heroes of the men on the *Monitor*, the ship itself, and the designer Ericsson. Once committed to this story, there would have been no easy way to recant and explain that their statements were perhaps exaggerated. As will be seen later, Ericsson vehemently urged Fox not to publish information from the *Virginia* as it would upset "the satisfaction of the country" and would "amaze people" who had been told a different story "by several patriotic writers."

Because of the importance of the battle, witnesses remained eager to tell how they saw the event. It is hard to say whether some of them consciously distorted the truth or simply adapted the rumors they had heard to explain what they could not really have observed. Certainly the linguistic style of the day lent itself toward embellishments.

A number of newspapers carried similarly inaccurate descriptions, apparently from the same unnamed witness. The primary source seems to have been Chaplain A. B. Fuller, whose popular accounts are given in an 1863 book:

> The *Merrimac* tried to run the *Monitor* down, and thus sink her; she only got fiercer shots by the opportunity she thus gave her little antagonist. And so it went till the proud *Merrimac*, disabled, was glad to retire, and, making signals of distress, was towed away by her sorrowing consorts.[7]

In reality, Fuller would have found it hard to see such "signals of distress" from a distance of about four miles, even had he known what the Confederate signals were. The gunboats that accompanied the *Virginia* did not tow her. Moreover, he certainly could not claim to know the emotions of the officers or crew of the *Virginia*. Yet, his accounts were carried by the newspapers and contributed to the general belief that the *Virginia* withdrew.

Books that told the military history of the war repeated their own versions of the facts. In *Farragut and our Naval Commanders* (1867), J. T. Headley wrote:

> But it was soon evident that the *Merrimac* was getting the worst of it. Worden had found his way into her vitals, and would soon send her to the bottom, and so she wheeled out of the conflict and under the convoy of two tugs, limped away to her moorings. The *Monitor* followed her a short way, but Worden having received orders to act strictly on the defensive, and not leave the fleet, he soon ceased to follow his thoroughly humbled antagonist.[8]

At best, Headley must have been relying on those initial, incorrect reports. By repeating them as facts in his book, he gave them added credence, and reinforced this false information. But even Headley should have known that Worden was not in command at that point.

One of the recurring statements in Northern reports is that the *Virginia* retreated in a sinking condition. Charles Morris wrote:

> Then it came to an end. The *Merrimac* turned and ran away. She had a need to,—those on shore saw that she was sagging down at the stern. The battle was over. The turreted iron-clad had driven her great antagonist from the field, and won the battle. And thus ended one of the strangest and most notable naval combats in history.[9]

The *Virginia* had suffered some damage to the bow in the collision with the *Cumberland* and the subsequent ramming of the *Monitor* without the benefit of the ram. Jones was concerned about a leak, but any such leak was not significant. Chief Engineer Ramsay reported to him that the "skin of the vessel is plainly visible in the crank-pits."[10] E. A. Jack reported that the bilge pumps were not required to do extraordinary duty nor was there any alarm in that section of the ship.[11]

Jones had two seemingly contradictory worries. He was concerned about the ship taking on water and thereby increasing its draft, making it more likely to run aground. He also was concerned that the enemy might fire at the hull of the vessel, where there was minimal protection. When the *Virginia* left Portsmouth on March 8, the shield extended only five inches under the water. A well-placed shot would have punctured the minimally protected hull. As the ship used shell, gunpowder, and coal, the ship raised in the water because of the decreased weight. She also had lost her prow and an anchor. If the *Virginia* had her steam up for twenty-four hours, her coal consumption might have been one percent of her tonnage, which might have raised the ship 1.5 to 3 inches.[12] If the distribution of the weight was toward the stern, the bow would have been higher relative to the stern. This might explain Jones's concern that the vulnerable hull (towards the bow) was close to being exposed because the ship was lighter, and yet, to a Union observer, the ship might appear to be sinking at the stern. Jones does report, "The lower end of the forward end of the shield was awash."[13] This slant from bow to stern is only a hypothesis, not confirmed, but it might explain some discrepancies.

The South also has its embellished reports of the battle. Norris's 1879 article is so obviously zealous that the details cannot be trusted. Jones described an 1874 version of the article as "spirited." From Norris's 1879 article:

> The flying foe is moving two feet to our one but, rapidly firing, we chase her until we have no longer an inch of water under our keel—we have been brought up, all standing by the shoal.
>
> From the commencement of her flight, the *Monitor* had made no reply to our fire, and now her nimble heels have secured her a place of safety, miles distant, on Hampton Shoals. Although the great distance made it a waste of precious ammunition... we fired five more shells at her. As well as we could distinguish, three of them struck, but the last two, though fired from our pivot gun, could not reach, *and to none of them did we get any reply*.[14]

Positions of the Ships

The major point of disagreement is whether the *Monitor* withdrew from the battle due to her injuries and whether she stayed out until she could return safely when her opponent no longer threatened her. To understand this, it will help to understand where the ships were on that fateful day. Unfortunately, most accounts give differing descriptions of where the ships were.

A view of Hampton Roads itself (see survey chart) may help us understand the activities on March 9. The four shades of water indicate depths as of 1852 (the most recent information before the war): The lightest shade along the coast is water that is too shallow (less than 10 feet at mean low tide) for the *Monitor*; the next lightest represents water that the *Monitor* could navigate except at low tide (10–12 feet at mean low tide, 12.5–14.5-feet at mean high tide); the darkest (12–22 feet at mean low tide) represents the area the *Monitor* could navigate easily but is too shallow for the *Virginia*. The central area describes where the *Virginia might* travel—however, the soundings on the chart are not sufficient to indicate where the *Virginia could* safely travel throughout the area. It appears that the pilots of the *Virginia* generally were conservative, but still the *Virginia* grounded during the battle.

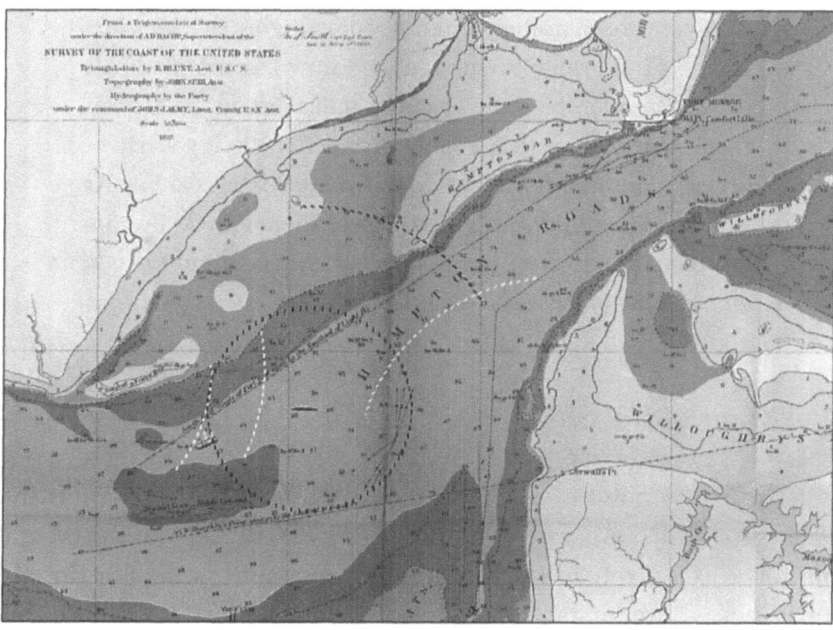

The map must be considered illustrative, not definitive. As with any chart, there may be areas that were not marked that were shallower due to local features on the bottom. Also, the contours of the bottom might change after any storm and surely changed in ten years from the time of the soundings until the battle. However, the larger features are clearly visible. On the map you can see the shallow Middle Ground, the North Channel, and the South Channel. The *Virginia*'s pilots obviously felt the North Channel was too dangerously shallow. On the first day, the *Virginia* snaked up the narrow channel of the Elizabeth River, past Sewall's Point, then steamed southwest through the South Channel and northwest to attack the *Cumberland* west of Newport News Point.

The map shows the author's best estimate of the position of the grounded *Minnesota*, based on reports and maps of the day.[15] She traveled a "straight line" from Fort Monroe to Newport News before grounding. Reports vary on how far she was from Newport News. The two white arcs centered on Newport News demark 1.5 and 2 miles distance. The position shown for her puts her just at or beyond the limits of effective range of the *Virginia* when the *Virginia* had been close to Newport News after destroying the *Congress*. The stern of the *Minnesota* was toward Fort Monroe.

The *Virginia*, of course, was steaming around on March 9. Jones reports that the pilots would not take her within one mile of the *Minnesota*. The red circle has a one-mile radius around the *Virginia*. Reports put the *Virginia* generally east of the *Minnesota*. When the *Virginia* ran aground, her bow was toward the *Minnesota*.

The reports vary as to where the *Monitor* withdrew after Worden was injured. Generally, she is described as being in shoal water and to have headed to Fort Monroe or Hampton Creek. One of her crew indicates they withdrew three miles away. William Tindall, a witness as a Union soldier who wrote perhaps the best-researched study on the battle,[16] recalls that the *Monitor* went more than halfway to Fort Monroe. The outermost red arc indicates two miles distance.

If the *Monitor* went inside Hampton Bar, generally north or north-northeast of the *Virginia*, she would have been in shoal water and well out of the range of the *Virginia*'s guns. More likely, the *Monitor* headed two to three miles directly toward Fort Monroe, where the shoal water was not far from deeper water. At three miles, she would have been within range of the protection of the guns of Fort Monroe. Jones, not knowing the *Monitor* had been possibly seriously damaged, had little reason to pursue the seemingly invulnerable *Monitor* with his ship that he knew was vulnerable.

A Review of Union Authorities

With the popular press reporting the great victory of the *Monitor* chasing the *Virginia* away, did the navy also feel this was true?

Assistant Secretary of the Navy Fox arrived at Hampton Roads on that Sunday morning, March 9. He was on the *Minnesota* when the *Monitor* returned to her after the battle and he went aboard to assess the situation. He obviously spoke to Worden (before he was taken that afternoon to Baltimore) and Greene. Fox later wrote that he was "the nearest [person] to the *Virginia* outside the *Monitor*."[17]

By early the next morning, Fox ordered Liuetenant Thomas O. Selfridge, a more experienced officer from the *Cumberland*, to take command of the *Monitor*. This move is probably more a reflection of the importance of the *Monitor* in light of the concern over the *Virginia* than it is a reflection upon the conduct of Greene. However, Fox, perhaps intentionally, passed over Greene when he wrote: "Lieutenant J. L. Worden, who commanded the Monitor, handled her with great skill, assisted by Chief Engineer Stimers."[18] Certainly Fox was in no position to remove Greene, given that no other officer was in the least familiar with this unique vessel. Still, as revealed in his letter to his parents, Greene was obviously sensitive that he had been replaced.

Late in the battle, when the two ships were touching, some men on the *Virginia* prepared to board the *Monitor*, but she dropped off astern.[19] Perhaps Worden had seen the boarders, as on March 10, President Lincoln wrote to Secretary of the Navy Gideon Welles: "I have just seen Lieut. Worden, who says the '*Monitor*' could be boarded and captured very easily—first by boarding, by wedging the turret, so that it would not turn, and then by pouring water in her & drowning her machinery. He is decidedly of opinion she should not go sky-larking up to Norfolk."[20]

It is unclear when Worden realized this and whether this had anything to do with the order to withdraw after Worden's injury. The result was an order that the *Monitor* was not to engage the *Virginia*. That order proved frustrating to officers and sailors on both sides. Just ten days after the battle, Fox testified before the U.S. Senate. His testimony is rarely mentioned in even modern descriptions of the battle:

> *Question:* Why did not she [the *Monitor*] follow the *Merrimac*?
> *Answer:* She was disabled herself, and it was not known to what extent.... The more vulnerable part of the vessel being apparently very much injured, they hauled off to see what the damage was....[21]

Certainly Captain Van Brunt of the beleaguered USS *Minnesota* felt the *Monitor* had withdrawn as he described in his official report:

> [T]he rebels concentrated their whole battery upon the tower and pilot-house of the *Monitor*, and soon after the latter stood down for Fortress Monroe, and we thought it probable she had exhausted her supply of ammunition, or sustained some injury. Soon after the *Merrimac*, and the other two steamers headed for my ship.... I ordered every preparation to be made to destroy the ship, after all hope was gone to save her.[22]

Greene described the battle a number of times over the years, but each description changes the events. In his official report, dated March 12, 1862, Greene did not mention withdrawing at all to attend to Worden or to assess damage to the vessel. Furthermore, he claimed that the ships continued the action for forty-five minutes after Worden was injured!

> At 8:45 A.M. we opened fire upon the *Merrimack* and continued the action until 11:30 A.M., when Captain Worden was injured in the eyes by the explosion of a shell from the *Merrimack*, upon the outside of the eyehole in the pilot house, exactly opposite his eye. Captain Worden then sent for me and told me to take charge of the vessel. We continued the action until 12:15 P.M., when the *Merrimack* retreated to Sewell's Point and we went to the *Minnesota* and remained by her until she was afloat.[23]

Yet on the same day, Greene wrote to Ericsson:

> Our noble and gallant captain was wounded near the close of the fight, and I was called on to take command of the vessel.... I put five shot of 170 pounds straight through this infernal machine, and wounded her captain. Lieutenant T. O. Selfridge is at present in command, and as soon as the *Merrimac* makes her appearance we are going to lay this battery alongside of her and stay there until one or the other sinks.[24]

Since the gunners in the turret could not tell the effect of their shots, Worden (in the pilothouse) would pass word back about the effects. Considering the fact that no shot entered the *Virginia*, it is not clear how Greene (who was firing the guns in the turret) thought he had put shot through it. Greene took credit for wounding Buchanan (wounded by a minié-ball and not on board) when he could not possibly have known who was wounded, when, or how.

Even more surprisingly, he spoke of attacking the *Virginia*. Just two days before he wrote this, orders had been passed to the *Monitor* not to engage the *Virginia*. Surely, as executive officer, he must have been aware of the order! Two days later, on March 14, Greene was more candid in a letter to his parents describing the problems he found at the pilothouse:

> On examining the pilot-house, I found the iron hatch on top, on the forward side, was completely cracked through. We still continued firing, the tower being under the direction of Steiners. We were between two fires—the *Minnesota* on one side, and the *Merrimac* on the other. The latter was retreating to Sewall's Point, and the *Minnesota* had struck us twice on the tower. I knew if another shot should strike our pilot-house in the same place, our steering apparatus would be disabled, and we should be disabled, and we should be at the mercy of the batteries on Sewall's Point. We had *strict* orders to act on the defensive, and protect the *Minnesota*.[25]

His concern for the safety of the *Monitor* seems to be a proper reason to have withdrawn. The *Virginia* was targeting the pilothouse and surely would have continued to fire. Chief Engineer Alban Stimers, Ericsson's assistant, was most familiar with the workings of the ship and would have advised him. Although Ericsson later claimed that the damage was unimportant at the time, the commanding officer felt that the ship was in danger. Even though he had orders to protect the *Minnesota*, he could not protect her if the *Monitor* was at the bottom of Hampton Roads.

If the *Monitor* withdrew because either Worden or Greene felt she would be captured or destroyed, it is clear that the navy and Lincoln would not want this to be known. The press (and the history books) proclaimed Union victory. The gloom that swept the nation just the day before was reversed. Any official report by Worden would have been embarrassing.

Lucius E. Chittenden, register of the Treasury under President Lincoln, first published an often-quoted account in 1891. Later it was published in a book that listed Worden and Greene as authors, and is often incorrectly considered authoritative. Chittenden recounted a gathering with Lincoln on the deck of the *Monitor* in Washington some weeks after the battle. A portion of the story quotes Greene but may be inaccurate since it was not published until nearly thirty years after the event and Greene could not review it. These descriptions that wander so far from the truth may not accurately reflect what Greene said. However, given the stories in the press, and the disadvantage to the navy had he told what he had written his parents, it is hard to imagine what he could have said that was the truth without revealing a withdrawal by the *Monitor*. This story was consistent with his official report regarding continuing the action after the injury. Greene (reportedly) described what happened after Worden was injured:

> I kept the *Monitor* either moving around the circle or around the enemy, and endeavored to place our shots as near amidships as possible, where Captain Worden believed we had already broken through her armor.... Once we ran out of the circle for a moment to adjust a piece of machinery, and I learn some of our friends feared that we were drawing out of the fight. The *Merrimac* took the opportunity to head for Norfolk. As soon as our machinery was adjusted we followed her, and got near enough to fire a parting shot.[26]

Information about the battle leaked out piecemeal until the 1880s. Greene's letter to his parents was first published in 1865 but may not have been widely known until the mid-1880s when it was published again.

When Worden wrote his account of the battle in 1868, he claimed that after his injury, he felt the pilothouse was seriously disabled and gave the order to sheer off—but before sending for Greene. He said that Greene (who five days later wrote that the damage made the *Monitor* vulnerable to a single shot) found the damage was less serious than he thought and that the vessel's head had turned in the direction of the enemy but "before we could get at close quarters with her [the *Virginia*] she retired." He reports that it was a "short time" after he was taken to his quarters until he was told the *Virginia* had retired.[27]

Beginning in 1869, bills were introduced to give prize or relief money to the crew of the *Monitor* for their fight with the *Virginia*. These died in the Committee of Naval Affairs until 1882, when a bill was returned favorably from the Committees of Naval Affairs of both the House and Senate.

Former Confederates were incensed by the thought that the vessel that had fled from them was entitled to prize money. They argued that the presence of the *Monitor* had no bearing on the later decision by the Confederates to destroy the vessel. The bill's near passage inspired yet another flurry of articles that drew renewed attention to the battle.

The bill was again submitted in the next Congress and was again sent to the Committee on Naval Affairs. This time, the House's Committee on Naval Affairs recognized a number of blatantly false statements that had been given in support of the bill such as "The *Merrimack* finally retired from the battle-ground in a disabled and crippled condition, retreated to Norfolk and immediately went into dry dock to prevent her from sinking. The evidence of these facts is most reliable and authentic, and it is not understood that up to this point there is any denial or controversy as to their existence."[28] The committee reported numerous official documents, both Union and

Confederate, that countered the claims made in support of the bill. It also found that all prior claims for relief or prize money were awarded only where the vessel was sunk or captured. In May 1884, the committee recommended that the bill be denied. This ended the matter.

With the renewed attention on the Battle of Hampton Roads, the *Century Illustrated Magazine* requested several articles on the subject by key surviving participants in the battle. Greene wrote his final description of the battle for this series:

> In the confusion of the moment resulting from so serious an injury to the commanding officer, the *Monitor* had been moving without direction. Exactly how much time elapsed from the moment that Worden was wounded until I had reached the pilot-house and completed the examination of the injury at that point, and determined what course to pursue in the damaged condition of the vessel, it is impossible to state; but it could hardly have exceeded twenty minutes at the utmost. During this time the *Merrimac*, which was leaking badly, had started in the direction of the Elizabeth River; and, on taking my station in the pilot-house and turning the vessel's head in the direction of the *Merrimac*, I saw that she was already in retreat. A few shots were fired at the retiring vessel, and she continued on to Norfolk.[29]

If this version is taken as truth, Greene implies that any withdrawal was unintentional. By "moving without direction" he must mean that no one was actively in command of the *Monitor*. Rather than continuing the action for forty-five minutes after Worden was injured, he now claims it was only twenty minutes until they turned back. He gives no reason why he decided to return. Was it because he felt their orders required his return—despite the fact that he felt the vessel could be disabled by a single shot? Was it because his crew petitioned him to rescind the order (Seaman Hans Anderson wrote that Greene ordered the *Monitor* to withdraw and that the crew tried to have the order rescinded)? Was it because the *Virginia* was already leaving?

Lieutenant William Jeffers assumed command of the *Monitor* on March 13. Once the *Virginia* was no longer a threat to the *Monitor*, Jeffers reported a number of problems in the *Monitor* on May 22. In his report he alluded to the fact that the navy took advantage of the exaggerated reports on the *Monitor*:

> The opportune arrival of this vessel at Hampton Roads, and her success in staying the career of the *Merrimack*, principally by the moral effect of her commander's gallant interposition between that vessel and the *Minnesota*, caused an exaggerated confidence to be entertained by the public in the powers of the *Monitor*, which it was not good policy to check.[30]

In 1874, Fox had been invited to prepare his own account of the battle. To prepare a complete report, he needed information that was only known by the Southern side. He initiated a series of letters with Jones who, in turn, asked for input from his officers. Fox also collected information from a number of Union officers. In this letter, he mentions that the *Monitor* retired first, based on statements from both sides. He must have known this from his own observations as well.

> I observed your officers corroborate your statement that the *Monitor* first retired. Parker's account, written after consultation with Worden, admits this. One of your shells bent one of the wrought iron logs of the pilothouse, disabled Worden, and threw off the loose plate of iron which covered the square top of the P. house. Worden then

ordered her to withdraw, when the injury being found to be slight and the command given to the 1st Lt.³¹

Before publication, Fox submitted Jones's information to Ericsson. Ericsson's reaction was intense, feeling this "rebel statement" would "be more damaging than probably any incident of my life." Two statements in his letter reveal, by today's standards, a shocking attitude of perpetuating self-serving myths. In contrasting his opinion to Ericsson's, Fox wrote, "Exaggeration may be a necessary device of war, but not of history,"³² and "The truth of history can hurt nobody and should not be concealed. So far as my administration is concerned I should wish no credit at the expense of truth from whatsoever source it emanates."³³

Importantly, Ericsson placed the blame for the withdrawal of the *Monitor* squarely on the shoulders of Greene. In doing so, he implicitly acknowledged that the *Monitor* did discontinue the fight. His assistant, Chief Engineer Stimers, probably passed all he knew back to Ericsson. Fox initially sent Jones only his response to Ericsson's letter. But when he could not convince Ericsson to change his mind, he forwarded the letter to Jones to explain why, after months of collaboration, he was going to renege on his commitment to publish Jones's input. He urged Jones to publish his story in the *Southern Historical Society Papers*. In fact, Jones had already submitted his article.

> I am at a loss to understand why you have opened a fresh discussion about the *Monitor* and the *Merrimac* fight, so happily disposed of by several patriotic writers to the satisfaction of the country—I may say to the satisfaction of the whole world.
>
> No one knows better than yourself the shortcomings of that fight, ended at the moment the crew had become well trained, and the machinery got in good working

order. Why? Because you had a miserable executive officer who, in place of jumping into the pilot house when Worden was blinded, ran away with his impregnable vessel. The displacements of the plate of the pilot house, which I had designed principally to keep out spray in bad weather, was really an advantage, by allowing fresh air to enter the cramped iron walled cabin—certainly that displacement offered no excuse for discontinuing the fight—the revolving turret and the good steering qualities of the *Monitor* rendering it unnecessary to fire over the pilot house.

Regarding the rebel statement before me, I can only say that if published it will forever tarnish the lustre of your naval administration, and amaze our people, who have been told that the Merrimac was a terrible ship, which but for the *Monitor* would have destroyed the Union fleet and burnt the Atlantic cities—in fact, that the *Monitor* had saved the country.

Need I say that Jones' statement will be published in the professional journals of all civilized countries, and call forth sneers and condemnation from a legion of Monitor opponents. Poor Count Platen and Alderspanes, the criticism and blame that will now be heaped upon them by the present kings party, will be insupportable.

How the changes will be wrung on the statement of the *Merrimac*'s commanding officer, that the Cumberland could have sunk his vessel (admitted to be "unseaworthy," the hull being covered with only one inch plating), yet the Monitor was unable to inflict any damage, not a man on board the *Merrimac* wounded or killed. But the unarmed Cumberland destroyed two guns, wounding and killing several of the *Merrimac*'s crew.

Again the *Monitor*, when challenged to come out,

"hugged the shore under the guns of the fort." Counter statements, even if believed, would never be published. But I have said enough.

Should the rebel statement be published, its effects will be more damaging than probably any incident of my life.

Please find your several documents enclosed.

Yours truly,
J. ERICSSON

P.S.—The original, written under strong emotion, being nearly unintelligible, forward the copy.

Yours,
J. ERICSSON
CAPT. G. V. FOX, Boston[34]

The Truth and Nothing More Is All We Want

Eyewitness accounts are often believed accurate. Yet several factors belie their reliability. The "fog of war" is probably responsible for different reports differing in many ways. Confusion is a natural byproduct of intense action. Wishful thinking will also cloud participants' thoughts. Each person wants his side to win and often will interpret what he sees in that light. Each side may also engage in propaganda, making claims that are not justified. Some may think, as did Napolean Bonaparte, that "History is a lie agreed upon." Students of history must gather as much evidence as possible and evaluate according to a number of criteria:

- Was the person that provided the evidence in a position to know it?
- Has he been consistent? Is the evidence consistent with

other evidence? Is it consistent with what might be expected to have happened?

- Has the person been truthful in the past? Has he embellished his stories?
- Is the evidence self-serving?
- Is there some way to find a common interpretation amongst divergent views?

The brave men of the *Virginia* and *Monitor* (as well as men of the *Cumberland* and *Congress*) were clearly heroes. They fought a fierce battle in experimental vessels under intense physical conditions. However, as eventually acknowledged by both sides, one side retired first that day. The men of the *Virginia* should be recognized as the victors of the Battle of Hampton Roads, March 8 and 9, 1862.

Former *Virginia* engineer E. A. Jack, who kept in contact with several veterans, including the *Monitor*'s Acting Master, Samuel Howard, understood the potential for conflicts between history and memory. In 1891, Howard wrote about the problem of inaccurate accounts of the battle—an appropriate way to conclude this chapter.

> I have never seen a true statement of the engagement by any one so far, all want their side to have the best of the matter, and so it will be to the end of time. People may talk about the affair a hundred years hence, and all the talk and all the writing that may be done will not alter one iota, it will remain where it was twenty-nine years ago, *and so must it be*.[35]

CHAPTER 6

Victory without Glory? The Battle of Hampton Roads in Art

Harold Holzer

IN 1862, JUST A FEW WEEKS BEFORE THE BATTLE OF HAMPTON Roads, Union Admiral Samuel F. Du Pont, commander of the Atlantic blockading squadron, wrote an unusual letter from on board his flagship, the USS *Wabash*, far out at sea, to describe a young man who had recently enlisted for two years' service. The volunteer was "a son of Russell Smith, the artist," Du Pont wrote, clearly impressed that his new sailor "sketches and takes ships beautifully—he has a collection of all our steamers that will be very curious one day."[1]

Du Pont was certainly right about the young shipboard artist. Xanthus Russell Smith proved to be both talented and prolific. Ultimately, with works gracing all the great institutional collections that house Civil War art, he in fact became one of the best-patronized, and best-known marine artists of the mid-nineteenth century. If his work has grown unfamiliar since, there is a reason—one that helps to remind modern Americans how little known most Civil War naval art really is, and why.

Smith served on board ship between 1862 and 1864. We do not know a thing about how, when, or even if he expeditiously sent his most newsworthy drawings and sketches on to publishers, agents, or galleries. Most likely, he did not. Land-based battlefield artists like Winslow Homer, by comparison, by using the United States mails, or hopping on board trains and traveling to publishing centers like Philadelphia or New York themselves, could quickly transport their first-hand action sketches to picture weeklies like *Harper's Weekly* and *Frank Leslie's Illustrated Newspaper,* or to printmakers like Currier & Ives, which in turn promptly engraved or lithographed them and widely distributed them while the scenes they portrayed were still fresh.[2]

Not so with the marine artists. They were, after all, stuck on board ship, out of communication with their constituencies and potential patrons on land. They amassed sketchbooks, but in most cases, it took time before land-based Americans got to see the results of their experiences. Xanthus R. Smith's superb works, including several showing Admiral Du Pont's picturesque flagship, seldom made it to wide public view in a timely manner. Marine artists simply had no opportunity to display their works, or see to their adaptation into popular prints, while the war raged. Smith's greatest works were painted after the war ended.

Actually, Smith was one of the few artists who served at sea at all. As Admiral David Dixon Porter pointed out:

> Naval ships did not travel with ... sketchers. There was no room for these on board ship, and if perchance some stray ... should get on board, the discomfort of a man of war, the exacting discipline, and the freer life in camp sent him back to shore, where in most cases he only remembered his association with the Navy as a trip without any satisfaction, and with no desire to do justice to the work of the naval service.

Even the ambitious Smith admitted: "[I] was able to keep busy with my sketchbook and pencils" only when time permitted.[3]

But in the end, such specialists faced an even greater challenge than isolation in their efforts to portray Civil War naval battles: they were confronted with the suddenly changing technology of naval warfare, and the subsequent decline of the picturesque on the high seas. Amidst this profound revolution, the traditions of marine art changed abruptly and artists were compelled to all but celebrate machines.

Confronting this challenge, Civil War naval artists reserved their greatest creative outburst—and their most influential show of Union morale building—for the high-tech battle that ironically ended the era of romance in both naval warfare and its art: the Battle of Hampton Roads. The most un-picturesque encounter of all provided the greatest inspiration to artists, who instantly recognized its importance. In part through their pictorial evocations, many of them produced despite the obstacles that usually inhibited publication of naval prints, the duel between the *Monitor* and the *Virginia* became the greatest naval event of the Civil War. Students of iconography and popular culture should remember that the duel not only revolutionized the nature of naval warfare itself, but naval art, too.

Nathaniel Hawthorne, who wrote insightfully about the war in a memorable 1862 essay for the *Atlantic Monthly*, fully grasped the importance of this fabled engagement. The *Monitor*, he sneered, "the strangest-looking craft I ever saw... could not be called a vessel at all; it was a machine." The ship "looked very queer," the author concluded, wondering: "How can an admiral condescend to go to sea in an iron pot?"

Predicted Hawthorne sourly:

> All the pomp and splendor of naval warfare are gone by. Henceforth there must come up a race of engineermen and smoke-blackened cannoneers, who will hammer away at their enemies under the direction of a single pair of eyes; and even heroism—so deadly a grip is Science laying on our noble possibilities—will become a quality of very minor

importance, when its possessor cannot break through the iron crust of his own armament and give the world a glimpse of it.[4]

Hawthorne was not totally correct: Admiral David Glasgow Farragut would later prove at Mobile Bay that personal heroism was still possible even in the machine age. Farragut's personal bravery in the face of enemy fire—fire aimed at him from a Confederate iron ship, as it transpired—from on board his graceful wooden flagship USS *Hartford*, inspired one of the greatest of all Civil War paintings, and made the aging admiral a hero.[5] But it was an exception to the trend that was so powerfully launched at Hampton Roads, and consecrated by painters and printmakers. The *Monitor*'s fight against the *Virginia* did not advance the romantic aesthetic in art; it created an altogether new aesthetic in its place, one that celebrated the modern machine, not handsome ships or brave sailors.

In artistic terms, the *Monitor* was a homely "cheese-box," as Hawthorne had observed, and it symbolized northern industrialism, not gallantry. The *Virginia*, clumsily refitted atop the hulk of an old wooden ship, looked as fearfully monstrous as it first proved to the Union fleet, before the *Monitor* steamed to the rescue the following day. That the two vessels nonetheless changed naval war forever in March 1862 was powerfully suggested in a painting rendered by an artist we know only as "HH," the initials he wrote on his canvas depicting the *Virginia* ramming the helpless wooden ship USS *Cumberland* at Hampton Roads on March 8. English artist Charles Sidney Raleigh was inspired to paint a similar scene. And portraying the identical moment, yet another painter, W. B. Matthews, chose a title that neatly summed up the artistic transfiguration: *Last of the Wooden Navy*. His work would be engraved and widely distributed to the print-buying public.[6]

Similarly, the Scottish-born artist Alexander Charles Stuart focused on the destruction of another of the doomed wooden warships of the Federal fleet, the USS *Congress* (Fig. 1), in yet another scene that reflected the Confederate ironclad's dominance at Hampton Roads the day before the arrival of the *Monitor*. But like the others, Stuart's nostalgic view of the dramatic transformation of the wooden age at sea was painted more than a decade after the events at Hampton Roads—in 1875.

Printmakers, far more quickly than artists, perceived the news value of the Hampton Roads engagement, and even lacking, for the most part, reliable firsthand eyewitness sketches or descriptions of the duel, rushed fanciful pictures onto their presses to satisfy understandable public hunger for such visualizations. But since Northern print publishers sold their works almost exclusively to pro-Union audiences, the New York lithographer Currier & Ives's first, newsworthy print of the *Virginia*'s rampage against the Union fleet, focusing on the sinking of the *Cumberland* (Fig. 2), probably attracted few appreciative customers, even though it celebrated the personal bravery of the doomed ship's commander for ordering a final broadside against the Confederate ironclad as his ship went down. Northern audiences were likely not in the mood to display images of a day so devastating that no comparable destruction against the United States Navy would occur again until Pearl Harbor, nearly eighty years later.

Fortunately, for both the artists and the Union, the *Monitor* steamed to the rescue the next day, and the war's first all-technology battle began. Printmakers followed suit, and emphasized the one-on-one encounter as well. The Mariners' Museum owns one of the great representative collections of these works on canvas and paper.

In most of these pictures, invariably produced in the Union, the symbolism was remarkably consistent: holy white smoke was usually shown billowing from the *Monitor;* evil-looking black smoke spewed from the *Virginia*. Perhaps the smoke really did look like this on March 9, 1862: if so, it provided fortuitous high-tech symbolism for pro-Union artists and their patriotic audiences.

Typically, Currier & Ives reached the masses before the competition, with a print entitled *The Great Fight Between the "Merrimac" & "Monitor"* (Fig. 3), the first of several lithographs it produced to commemorate the ironclad duel, and like its print of the sinking of the *Cumberland*, based on a sketch allegedly made on the scene by a Norfolk eyewitness named F. Newman. But perhaps there was too much *Merrimack* and not enough *Monitor* in this, likely the firm's initial interpretation, in which the hulking Confederate ironclad, shown in the foreground, dominated the scene and all but obliterated the little *Monitor* with its bulk and spewing smoke. So the publishers quickly added to its list a revised interpretation of the event, subtitled *Terrific Combat Between Monitor 2 Guns and Merrimac 10 guns* (Fig. 4). This lithograph (and several similar states of the print) are believed to be the work of Flora Bond (Fanny) Palmer, one of Currier & Ives's best artists, and though she is seldom so acknowledged, probably also the most accomplished female marine artist of the nineteenth century. Her effort rejected the simplistic white-smoke-black-smoke imagery, and suggested instead, through both image and words, that this had been a David and Goliath contest. As the caption declared: "The little 'Monitor' whipped the 'Merrimac' and the whole 'School' of rebel steamers." In truth, the *Virginia* was not "whipped" at all but merely driven off; and at the height of their duel, the Union fleet outnumbered the "school" of Confederate steamers by 219 to 15. But a patriotic myth was born in such early graphics—all of them from the Union side.[7]

There was no artistic response from the South. By 1862, Confederate printmaking was already teetering on extinction. Chronic shortages of paper, ink, and artists in the region had crippled picture production, dooming its publishing industry. The few southern engravers—the elderly and the infirm—who remained civilians in the midst of Confederate mass-conscription were usually assigned to government work: producing images for official stamps and currency. Thus, the production of popular prints that could be displayed in loyal Southern homes soon vanished altogether, especially after two of the three print publishing centers of the South, Baltimore and New Orleans, either stayed loyal to the North or fell into Union hands, after which pro-Confederate publishing was discouraged, and sometimes censored.[8]

The same pathetic decline could hardly be said for the Confederate Navy: the Confederacy began the war with no navy of its own, no shipyards, and few professional sailors. Despite these handicaps, it seriously challenged the Union for dominance of the rivers and seas, and even preceded it in ironclad technology. But despite the *Virginia's* deadly early assaults at Hampton Roads, not a single Confederate artist was ever known to have recorded her triumphs.

Its one-on-one duel with the *Monitor* the next day proved newsworthy enough to arouse and inspire printmakers not only in the Union (Figs. 5, 6, 7), but also in Europe. America's own foreign-speaking population was served by a Chicago-made lithograph with a caption in German (Fig. 8), based on a painting by William Torgerson, a little-known nineteenth-century artist whose only other contribution to the Civil genre appears to be a painting of sleek-looking blockade-runners nestled in the safety of a Bermuda harbor.[9] Prints were not conceived only as wall decorations for the family parlors; others were engraved in smaller format as plates for history books (Figs. 9, 10), one of them the work of an under-appreciated Connecticut engraver of portraits, bank notes, and animals, Oliver Pelton.[10] And the ironclad battle would remain a staple for lithographers who went on to publish retrospective series of Civil War images a generation after the guns had ceased. Both Kurz & Allison of Chicago and Louis Prang of Boston issued best-selling chromos (see Fig. 21) of the encounter for their memorable, rival series of naval and land battle scenes issued in the 1880s.[11]

In the end, no naval battle of the Civil War ever inspired as much artistic commemoration. The only event of the entire Civil War to rival it was the Battle of Gettysburg, the fabled land encounter that enjoyed the advantage of attracting many more reporters and photographers to the scene of the action.

Fascination with ironclad technology may be responsible for inspiring much of this work. Interior scenes of the *Monitor's* Berth Deck (Fig. 11), for example, appeared in *Harper's Weekly*, helping picture buyers become familiar with the heroic sailors who had lived inside the vessel virtually like canned goods. Similarly, the interior of its revolutionary gun turret inspired a separate-sheet print by Endicott & Co. of New York (Fig. 12).[12] Their print was one of many that celebrated the *Monitor's* turret as a technological marvel, all but ignoring reports by those who manned her in battle that it was "difficult if not impossible to control," and had a "perplexing" effect on sailors who found it difficult to "keep the bearings...shut up in a revolving drum."[13]

Not surprisingly, even the ironclad's launching pad, the Continental [Shipbuilding] Works in Greenpoint, Brooklyn, proved fascinating enough in and of itself to inspire its own elaborate Endicott lithograph (Fig. 13), a busy and skillfully rendered birds-eye view of the site as viewed from the Manhattan side of the East River. It is a scene not only of creation, but also of celebration—a triumph of Union technological and industrial superiority—populated by pleasure crafts and their enthusiastically patriotic crews and passengers raising their hats in jubilation as another iron vessel slips into the river.

Iron ships and their heroes would appear in a wide variety of artistic media. Rival commanders John Worden and Catesby Jones, who were rarely depicted in paper images that tended to emphasize technology over humanity, would be portrayed by an unknown but talented artist on a scrimshaw whale's tooth (Fig. 14), and both of their ironclads appeared on several ornate souvenir silver spoons (Fig. 15)—even the renowned Tiffany & Co. produced one such sterling silver example. Also serving the souvenir market were highly decorative enamel spoons (Fig. 16), and even a boxed set of playing cards, one deck featuring the *Monitor* (Fig. 17), and the other the

Virginia (Fig. 18). The *Monitor* was also celebrated on illustrated sheet music covers,[14] and even in a giant cyclorama, now lost except for one surviving panel and a print loosely based on the vanished giant picture.

Eventually, the fine arts followed suit. Painters like Xanthus R. Smith produced formal canvases of the naval battles at Hampton Roads, in Smith's case a *Monitor-Merrimack* painting commissioned to decorate the Philadelphia Union League club, which had been founded in 1864 to celebrate Abraham Lincoln, emancipation, Republican political successes, and the restoration of federal authority. There could be little doubt, even before Smith was invited to contribute his painting, that the *Monitor* had contributed to each.[15] Alexander Charles Stuart created a M*onitor-Virginia* companion canvas (Fig. 19) to his view of the *Virginia* attacking the USS *Congress* (see Fig. 1). Little-known nineteenth-century painter Thomas C. Skinner produced a vivid and richly colored scene of his own (Fig. 20). And William Torgerson, who had also crafted that handsome canvas of sleek blockade-runners at port in Bermuda, contributed a *Monitor-Merrimack* scene that was promptly adapted for a lithograph (see Fig. 8).

Not for years did artist Julian Oliver Davidson, who provided the vivid watercolor that served as the model for Prang's postwar Hampton Roads chromolithograph (Fig. 21), concede pictorially, in a dark, seldom-published drawing showing Union monitors foundering in a gale, that early ironclads were in truth flimsy-looking and far from seaworthy. To Hawthorne, who proudly observed that the shell-scars left on the seemingly impregnable *Monitor* by the *Virginia*'s guns looked reassuringly like "imperceptible dents," the Union ironclad not only looked safe: "the thing looked altogether too safe." Heavy seas off Cape Hatteras proved the author wrong.[15]

Davidson's drawing[17] provides a haunting visual reminder of how the original *Monitor* had capsized in a storm, a catastrophe that, not surprisingly, inspired few pictorial commemorations. The death of the original *Monitor* off Cape Hatteras, only nine months after the Battle of Hampton Roads (Fig. 22), proved an artistic anticlimax, as did the destruction of the "monster" *Merrimack* at the hands of her own crew, to avoid capture by the Union. As an eyewitness observed from a nearby vessel as the *Monitor* went down, "the victor of the first iron-clad conflict, the savior of our naval forces, plunged with a dying struggle at her treacherous foe"—the untamable sea—"and was seen no more."[18] Except, that is, in prints, for ironclads—the new technology of the new navies—lived on in public memory, thanks in large part to the artists.

New York printmakers Endicott & Co., for thirty years the most prolific publisher of marine prints in the business, eventually issued prints of thirty-eight different Union monitor-class ironclads (See Fig. 23), for sale at $1.50 apiece; and eight United States ironclads depicted in storms for $2.00 each, marketing them to the families of their active crews, and, later, to their veteran officers and sailors. They became and remained favorites for the survivors and their relatives.[19]

Their popularity signaled a revolution not only in how wars were fought at sea, but in how walls were decorated at home—no small measure, in mid-nineteenth-century America, of patriotism and memory. In Endicott's influential 1862 print, *The First Naval Conflict Between Iron Clad Vessels* (Fig. 24), just as Hawthorne had predicted, the "race of engineermen" emerged the new heroes. None of the decorative portraits surrounding the main scene of the battle portrayed the captain of the *Monitor*, John Worden, who had the bad luck to be disabled during the fighting. (Worden would in fact be honored with few print tributes while he lived, while inventor John Ericsson inspired at least one engraved portrait in life as well as a major print tribute after his death—see Figs. 25, 26). Instead, crowning the image were pictures of the "caloric engine" that powered the Union ironclad, and inventor Ericsson, who became far more famous than the man who commanded his vessel at

Fig. 1. Alexander Charles Stuart (Scottish-American, 1831–1898), *CSS Virginia Attacking USS Congress*. Oil on canvas, ca. 1875, 18 1/8 x 30 1/8 inches. (All illustrations from the Mariners' Museum collections; accession no. 1950.0562)

Fig. 2. [Nathaniel] Currier & [James Merritt] Ives, after F. Newman, *The Sinking of the "Cumberland["] by the Iron Clad "Merrimac", Off Newport News Va. March 8th 1862 / The Cumberland went down with all her Flags flying destroyed, but not conquered. Her gallant Commander Lieut. Morris, calling to his crew, "Give them a Broadside, boys, as she goes."* New York, 1862. Hand-colored lithograph, 1862, 13 1/4 x 9 1/2 inches. (Accession No. 1933.0460)

Fig. 3. Currier & Ives, after F. Newman, *The Great Fight Between the "Merrimac" & "Monitor," March 9th 1862. / The First Battle Between Iron-Clad Ships of War.* New York, 1862. Hand-colored lithograph, 9 1/2 x 12 1/2 inches. (Accession No. PE35)

Fig. 4. Currier & Ives, after Fanny Palmer, *The First Fight between Iron Clad Ships of War. / Terrific Combat between the "Monitor" 2 Guns and "Merrimac" 10 Guns / In Hampton Roads, March 9th 1862 . /In which the little "Monitor" whipped the "Merrimac" and the whole "School" of Rebel Steamers.* New York, 1862. Hand-colored lithograph, 7 5/8 x 12 5/8 inches. (Accession No. PE34)

Fig. 5. Henry Bill, *The First Battle Between "Iron" Ships of War / The "Monitor" 2 guns. / The "Merrimac" 10 guns . /The Merrimac was crippled and the rebel-fleet driven off*. Hartford, Connecticut, 1862. Lithograph, 14 3/8 x 20 1/4 inches. (Accession No. 2002.0030)

Fig. 6. [George W.] Hatch[, Jr.] & Co., *The Splendid Victory of the Ericsson Battery Monitor. / Disabling the Rebel Battery Merrimac, 10 guns and Steamers Jamestown & Yorktown, in Hampton Roads, March 9th, 1862*. New York, 1862. Lithograph, 12 7/8 x 19 3/4 inches. (Accession No. 1935.0622)

Fig. 7. Edward Sachse & Co., after Charles Worret, *The Naval Engagement between the Merrimac and the Monitor at Hampton Roads on the 9th of March, 1862 / Drawn on the Spot by Charles Worret, Sergt. 20 Rgt. N.Y.V.* Published by C. Bohn, Washington, D.C., 1962. Lithograph, 8 3/8 x 16 1/2 inches. (Accession No. 1933.0409)

Fig. 8. [Charles] Shober & Carqueville, after William Torgerson (active 19th century), *Striden Emellan / "Monitor" och "Merrimac" / Vid Hampton Roads d. 9 Mars 1862*, signed lower left in stone: *Wm. Torgerson*. Chicago, 1877, published as a premium for *Nya Verldens*. Lithograph, 18 x 27 1/2 inches. (Accession No. 1968.0350)

Fig. 9. Johnson & Fry after Alonzo Chappel, *Naval Conflict in Hampton Roads—Action Between the Monitor and Merrimac.* New York, 1863. Steel engraving, 5 1/2 x 8 inches. (Accession No. 1938.0292)

Fig. 10. Oliver Pelton (b. 1799), *First Naval Combat Between Iron Vessels.* Hartford, published by Hurlbut, Williams & Co., 1862. Steel engraving, 4 1/2 by 7 inches. (Accession No. 1938.0290)

Fig. 11. Printmaker unknown, *Berth Deck [of the USS Monitor]*. New York, 1862. Woodcut engraving, one of a series of interior views of the *Monitor*, published in *Harper's History of the Great Rebellion*, 1866. Size of entire page, 11 1/8 x 13 7/8 inches. (Accession No. 1993.0050)

Fig. 12. [William and Francis] Endicott & Co., after a woodcut illustration in *Harper's Weekly*, April 12, 1862, *Interior View of the Turrets of / The Monitor Fleet*. New York, ca. 1862. Lithograph, 6 3/4 x 10 1/2 inches. (Accession No. 1970.0476)

Fig. 13. Endicott & Co., *Continental Works, Green Point, Brooklyn. / T. F. Rowland, Proprietor. / Iron Ships, Iron Bridges, Boilers, Tanks and General Iron Work. Vessels of Every description furnished and ready for sea. Builder of U.S. Iron Clad batteries.* New York, ca. 1863. Lithograph, 18 3/8 by 33 3/4 inches. (Accession No. 1934.1043)

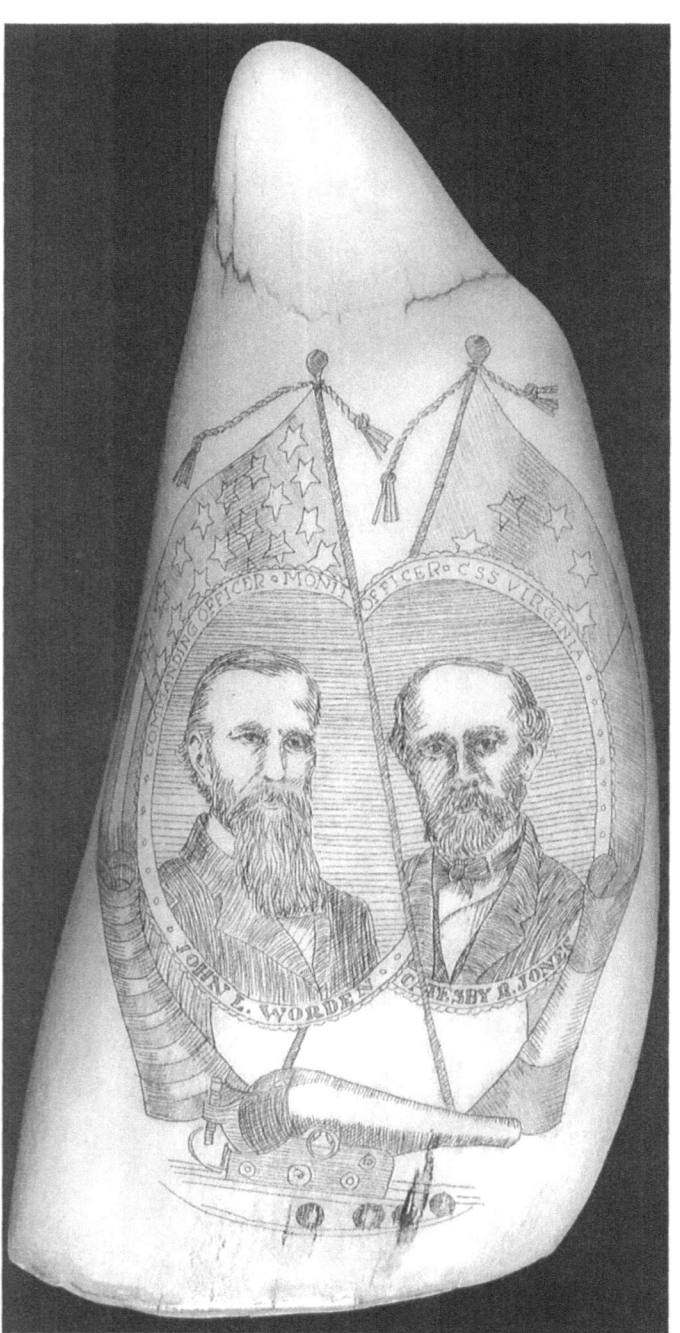

Fig. 14. Artist unknown, [Scrimshaw on sperm whale's tooth showing commanders John L. Worden and Catesby R. Jones on one side, with Union and Confederate flags behind portraits, Dahlgren gun in foreground; and on the other, the battle between the *Monitor* and *Virginia*, with wooden ship—perhaps the U.S.S. *Minnesota*—in background, surrounded by patriotic devices]. Inscriptions: "United We Stand / Divided We Fall" (on banner surmounting portraits); "March 9, 1862, at Hampton Roads / Naval Duel of CSS Virginia and the Monitor" (beneath battle scene). Height: six inches. (Accession no. 1971.0007)

Fig. 15. Paul-Gale Greenwood Co., *Merrimac and Monitor*, [souvenir spoon, featuring crossed rifles and swords, anchor and line, portraits of Captain John Smith and Pocahontas, an American eagle, an American battleship, a caravel under sail, and the dates 1607–1907. New York, ca. 1907. (Accession No. 1948.0005)

Fig. 16. Paul-Gale Greenwood Co., *Merrimac and Monitor / March 8* [sic] *1862* [souvenir spoon]. New York, n.d.. Ceramic over sterling silver, 6 inches high. [Accession No. 1948.0007)

Fig. 17. A[ndrew]. Dougherty, [Souvenir deck of cards with inscription: "To commemorate / The greatest event in naval history / The substitution of iron for wood." New York, ca. 1862–74. These cards represent the Union—*Monitor*—side. Each card 3 9/16 x 2 1/2 inches. (Accession No. 1947.0066)

Fig. 18. A. Dougherty, [C.S.S. *Virginia* playing cards, from the same boxed deck as illustrated in Fig. 17] (Accession No. 1947.0066)

Fig. 19. Alexander Charles Stuart, *USS Monitor and CSS Virginia*. Oil on canvas, ca. 1875, 17 3/4 x 30 inches. (Accession No. 1950.0559)

Fig. 20. Thomas C. Skinner (worked 19th century), *Battle Between Virginia and Monitor*, 1875. Oil on canvas, 32 x 42 inches. (Accession No. 1935.0013)

Fig. 21. L[ouis]. Prang & Co., after J[ulian]. O[liver]. Davidson (1853–1894), *Battle Between the "Monitor" and "Merrimac," March 8, 1862*, also known as *"The Monitor and Merrimac." The First Fight Between Ironclads*, signed lower right in stone: *J. O. Davidson*. Boston, 1886. Chromolithograph (also called an "aquarelle facsimile print"), 15 x 21 1/2 inches. (Accession no. 1945.0427)

Fig. 22. Artist unknown, *Wreck of the Ironclad Monitor*. New York, published by *Harper's Weekly*, January 24, 1863. Woodcut engraving, 7 x 9 inches. (Accession No. 1970.0304)

Fig. 23. Endicott & Co., *U. S. Monitor / Passaic / Built by the Continental Iron Works.* New York, ca. 1863. Lithograph, 12 3/8 x 24 inches. (Accession No. 1934.1194)

Fig. 24. Endicott & Co., after C[harles]. Parsons, *The First Naval Conflict Between Iron Clad Vessels. / In Hampton Roads, March 9th 1862 [with views of the Captain's cabin, tower, turret machinery, engine room, wheel house, and ward room, surmounted by an American eagle with flags, a portrait of Ericsson, and images of the berth deck and caloric engine, and a sectional view of the vessel].* Copyrighted by A. S. Lotridge, New York, 1862. Lithograph, 13 1/2 x 21 inches. (Accession No. 1933.0384)

Fig. 25. J[ohn]. C[hester]. Buttre, after a photograph by R. A. Lewis, *Lieut. John L. Worden* [with facsimile signature]. New York, ca. 1862. Steel engraving, 5 3/4 x 4 3/4 inches. (Accession No. 1969.0193)

Fig. 26. Manhattan Art Co., *Captain John Ericsson. The Famous Swedish Inventor and Engineer. Born in Wermland, Sweden, July 31st, 1803. Died in New York, March 8th, 1889.* New York, ca. 1889. Lithograph, 21 1/2 by 18 3/4 inches. (Accession No. 1947.0621)

Fig. 27. Calvert Litho. Co., *The First Encounter of Iron-Clads / Terrific Engagement Between the "Monitor" and "Merrimac" / Hampton Roads, Virginia, U. S. A., March 9th, 1862. / This fight settled the fate of the "Wooden Walls" of the world and taught all nations that the War-Ship of the future must be—like the McCormick Harvester—a Machine of Steel.* Detroit and Chicago, 1881. Lithograph, after the *Cyclorama of the Monitor and Merrimac* exhibited at Toledo, Ohio. Chromolithograph, 23 1/8 x 35 1/16 inches. (Accession No. 1933.0557)

Hampton Roads. On March 9, 1862, technology surpassed heroism as the inspiration for naval art.

Perhaps none of the so-called *Monitor-Merrimack* prints more coldly testified to this extraordinary iconographical metamorphosis than a chromo issued by the Calvert Lithography Company of Detroit and Chicago in 1881, reproducing a Battle of Hampton Roads cyclorama then on view in Toledo. *The First Encounter of Iron-Clads* (Fig. 27) is artistically superior in many respects—skillfully depicting raging battle, rampant destruction, and even the loss of life in background scenes of Union sailors leaping into the sea to escape one of the wooden warships destroyed by the *Virginia*. Of course, the scene also unforgivably compresses two separate days of action into a single image, but that is not its only remarkable distinction.

The picture is also notable for the inset pictures that appear in its upper right-hand, and lower left-hand corners, prints of McCormick Harvester steel products that the viewer is invited to infer are as tough and immune to damage as was the *Monitor*. McCormick, which copyrighted and no doubt commissioned the print, was neither shy nor subtle about making such outrageous claims in images ostensibly created to honor Civil War sacrifice. In a similarly panoramic chromo of the Battle of Shiloh, the firm had gone so far as to show a McCormick Reaper sitting in the middle of the carnage-filled battlefield, having survived artillery fire and rifle shots to testify nobly to the endurance of its hardy product.[20] Blatant and self-promotional as it was, the chromo appropriately marked the tipping point in Civil War art—when reverence for the machine at least equaled reverence for man.

Nathaniel Hawthorne was not the only literary figure who took note of this change. Herman Melville realized it, too. In one of the poems from his volume of *Battle-Pieces*, he took what he called "a utilitarian view of the *Monitor*'s Fight"—presaging with uncanny accuracy what a generation of artists would make of the duel. To make his point, he even took pains to rhyme "heroic" and "caloric." It was not the most felicitous of constructions, but it rather dramatically showed how technological heroism had replaced bravery of the personal kind—in art and war alike:

> Hail to victory without the gaud
>   Of glory; zeal that needs no fans
> Of banners; plain mechanic power
> Plied cogently in War now placed—
>   Where war belongs—
> Among the trades and artisans.
> Yet this was battle, and intense—
>   Beyond the strife of fleets heroic;
> Deadlier, closer, calm 'mid storm;
> No passion; all went on by crank,
>   Pivot, and screw,
> and calculations of caloric.
> Needless to dwell; the story's known.
>   The ringing of those plates on plates
> Still ringeth round the world—
> The clangor of that blacksmith's fray.
>   · The anvil-din
>   Resounds this message from the Fates.
> War shall yet be, and to the end;
>   But war-paint shows the streaks of weather;
> War shall yet be, but warriors
>   Are now but operatives; War's made
>   Less grand than Peace,
> And a singe runs through lace and feather.

Naval warfare, as Melville sensed, changed forever at Hampton Roads. "Hail to Victory without the gaud of glory," he proclaimed. But glory still existed; it simply called for "mechanic power," not "gaud" and "banners." Visually evoking these sentiments in its chromo, the McCormick company proclaimed in its caption: "This fight settled the fate of the 'wooden walls' of the world and taught all nations, that the warship of the future must be—like the McCormick Harvester—a Machine of Steel."

Art helped teach all nations the same cold, but accurate, lesson.

CHAPTER 7

"This Country Now Occupies the Vantage Ground": Union Monitors vs. the British Navy
Howard J. Fuller

ON AUGUST 5, 2003, THE NATIONAL OCEANIC AND ATMOspheric Administration (NOAA) and the U.S. Navy at last salvaged the turret of the original ironclad-battery USS *Monitor*, complete with dents[1] from the famous battle of Hampton Roads (March 9, 1862) against the CSS *Virginia,* or *Merrimack*. Along with the ship's anchor, engine, shaft and propeller, it seems that history is finally catching up, piece by piece, with America's most famous—and most misunderstood—class of warship.

It is important, then, to clarify exactly *why* the *Monitor* was so very important to the Union during the Civil War. Controversy always has surrounded the vessel, from whether or not she was a successful warship to her legendary status as the product of either American mythmaking or simple historical fact.[2] Yet her inventor, John Ericsson, made it very clear what a monitor was about when he named her:

"The Navy Department at Washington having, shortly before the launch, requested me to suggest an appropriate name for the impregnable turreted steam battery, I addressed a letter to the assistant secretary of the navy, saying: 'The impregnable and aggressive character of this structure will admonish the leaders of the Southern Rebellion that the batteries on the banks of their rivers will no longer present barriers to the entrance of the Union forces. The iron-clad intruder will thus prove a severe monitor to those leaders.'"

Usually when this letter is quoted the passage above is followed by the concluding statement: "On these and many similar grounds, I propose to name the new battery *Monitor*." "But," Ericsson continued,

> There are other leaders who will also be startled and admonished by the booming of the guns from the impregnable iron turret: Downing Street will hardly view with indifference this last "Yankee notion," this monitor. To the Lords of the Admiralty the new craft will be a monitor, suggesting doubts as to the propriety of completing those four steel ships at three and a half million apiece. On these and many similar grounds, I propose to name the new battery *Monitor*.[3]

If we are to better evaluate the monitor-class of warship it is essential for us to first explore the full historical context of this letter to Gustavus Fox (the assistant secretary), dated January 20, 1862.

Effect of the Trent Affair

Ericsson's allusion to Downing Street was aimed at the recent New Year's Day conclusion of the *Trent* Affair, when the two captured Southern emissaries to England and France, James Mason and John Slidell, were released from Federal incarceration, and a third American conflict with the British Empire—this time in the midst of a civil war—was barely avoided.[4] The end of the *Trent* Affair was the greatest diplomatic humiliation suffered by President Abraham Lincoln's administration, especially since it came at the end of a British cannon (although even the generally bellicose *New York Herald* accepted the rationale that disavowing the seizure of Mason and Slidell from the *Trent* vindicated America's traditional policy of "freedom of the seas," while depriving the South of its greatest hope—a war between England and the Northern states.)[5] Had Lincoln refused the ultimatum of Lord Palmerston's government to free the Confederate commissioners seized on the high seas, no amount of international law at the beginning of 1862 could have prevented the huge Royal Navy from counter-blockading the North and overwhelming its coastal defenses.[6] This was even more so since most navies were still measured by overall numbers of wooden steamships (themselves classed by overall numbers of guns), despite the fact that the broadside-ironclad HMS *Warrior* was finally ready for sea and the *Monitor* herself, at the time Ericsson named her, was only ten days from launching. Even as early in the Civil War as June, 1861, Palmerston was keen to utilize ironclads in a show of force against the Union, for "their going could produce no bad Impression here, and depend upon it as to Impression in the United States the Yankees will be violent and threatening in Proportion to our local weakness and civil and pacific in Proportion to our increasing local strength."[7]

Congress was more than bitter about the Union's weakness, exclaiming that England's "standard of right has been, is, and will be, the interests of England. There is nothing in the law of nature or of nations that will stand in the way of her imperious will."[8] British naval might seemed behind British political and legal right. At the same time, however, *Blackwood's* magazine recognized that "the Americans have been coerced into an act of justice, which they performed with the worst possible grace; and we are frankly assured that a time is coming, when they mean to take ample vengeance for present humiliations. It appears, then, that a war with the Federal States of America is only deferred. If not imminent, it is pretty sure to come sooner or later."[9]

Thus the original *Monitor*, according to Ericsson, was now openly intended to deter at least the wooden ships of the Royal Navy from further influencing U.S. policy. Indeed, when Cornelius Bushnell, Ericsson's earliest backer, first exhibited the *Monitor* plans to Secretary of the Navy Gideon Welles, in September 1861, he announced that an anxious President Lincoln "need not further worry about foreign interference; I [have] discovered the means of perfect protection."[10]

British Reaction to the Monitor

The reaction of Great Britain to news of the battle of Hampton Roads was extraordinary. Only a few illustrations reveal a remarkable transformation of attitude. In reply to Ericsson's published letter on the naming—and nature—of the *Monitor*, the London *Times* stated:

> We are much obliged to Mr. Ericsson for his hint. We take the warning as it was given, and acknowledge with all frankness that this last Yankee notion merits all the attention which he claims for it. . . . At Washington, says our Special Correspondent, the common remark is that the naval supremacy of Great Britain is disposed of. We don't think it will be disposed of quite so easily, and yet the conclusion has really better warrant than usual. . . . Six months ago the Secretary of the Admiralty described our active force afloat as 19 line-of-battle ships, *two iron-cased frigates*, 38 frigates and corvettes, and 90 sloops. Of all this force there are but two vessels that could be relied upon to meet such a ship as the *Monitor*.[11]

In Parliament it also was tellingly reflected that "the great question of iron-plated ships against wooden vessels had been brought to an issue, and, happily, without any action on our part." News of the American naval battle, with its impervious ironclads, struck even deeper against government plans already underway for exorbitant coastal fortifications. It was to save face for Palmerston's anti-French forts—and his own expensive sea-going ironclad program—that the Duke of Somerset, the First Lord of the Admiralty, famously ridiculed the *Monitor* as "something between a raft and a diving bell" in the House of Lords. The prime minister himself, never very confident in the partially-armored *Warrior*, which he privately expressed to Somerset to be "a fine yacht, but not an efficient Ship of War," now defended her in the Commons as "a very splendid ship"—almost solely on the basis that she was at least seagoing, unlike "floating batteries."[12] "Only think of our position," wrote Foreign Secretary Lord Russell to Palmerston, "if in case of the Yankees turning upon us they should by means of iron ships renew the triumphs they achieved in 1812–13 by means of superior size and weight of metal."[13] The U.S. Minister to Britain, Charles Francis Adams, meanwhile noted that "the effect is to diminish the confidence in the result of hostilities with us. In December we were told that we should be swept from the ocean in a moment, and all our ports taken. They do not talk so now."[14]

Ericsson's Definition of Naval Power

Shortly after the *Monitor* checked the *Virginia* at Hampton Roads, Ericsson wrote Secretary of State William Seward that "the state of the naval defences of the country being so intimately connected with its international relations, I deem it my duty to report to you that under orders from the Secretary of the Navy, keels for 6 vessels of the Monitor class of increased size and speed have already been laid." Their ultimate purpose was to destroy ocean-going broadside-ironclads, through a combination of greater maneuverability, lighter draft for coastal operations, greater protection in the form of low freeboard submersion, thicker, more concentrated armor, and deadlier firepower—now measured in caliber of gun, not numbers. These "recent developments in naval warfare," Ericsson declared, "tend to prove that this country now occupies the vantage ground."[15] With ship-to-ship superiority confirmed, it would be suicide for a maritime power such as England to risk either wooden steam ships-of-the-line or her magnificent, though comparatively lightly armored, broadside-gunned ironclads for at least the crucial duration of the Civil War—the most vulnerable period in the nation's *international* as well as domestic history.[16]

This was confirmed in September, 1862, following Lincoln's Emancipation Proclamation, when the British cabinet, fearing a grisly slave uprising in the South reminiscent of the ferocious Sepoy Mutiny in India (1857-8), debated a French proposal to co-intervene.[17] It was Secretary for War Sir George Lewis who put in a printed memo what practical factor, among others, influenced their decision not to try and stop the Civil War. Even if Britain and France had "the right to intervene", he wrote, large trans-Atlantic deployments (of "peace-keeping" troops) were "difficult and expensive," suggesting bitter memories of the recent war in the Crimea against Imperial Russia, while "the wooden ships of Europe would encounter the small iron-cased steamers of America, which, though not seagoing ships, would prove destructive in the ports and rivers."[18]

This was a conclusion, moreover, that the Admiralty also reached. Although he strongly objected to Union monitors as a model for the Royal Navy in general, the commander-in-chief of the North American and West Indian Station, Vice Admiral Sir Alexander Milne, recognized that their potency for harbor and coast defense had completely upset the balance of power in North America. Following news of the naval action at Hampton Roads, Milne, surveying at Bermuda the most powerful British fleet ever assembled, wrote privately to an Admiralty Board member that "if these ships of the line now here were cut up into small vessels, they would be of use to me, but except for Demonstrations clear of *Merrimac* and *Monitor*, they are no use...."[19] The Controller of the Royal Navy (the influential equivalent of Fox), Admiral Robert Spencer Robinson, also acknowledged Ericsson's "riddle" for British naval supremacy. With various Union ironclad descriptions before him, and from American newspapers and Royal Navy officers under Milne's command, Robinson reported that "there appears to be no novel or important principle elucidated by these constructions." Those that "seem to possess sea going qualities," particularly the experimental broadside-ironclad USS *New Ironsides*, "are in no way superior to the French *Gloire* or *Invincible* or the Ships of the *Royal Oak* class." The obvious bulk of the armored Federal warships were "mere Rafts carrying very few heavy guns propelled at moderate speed, and though perfectly well adapted for the Inland waters of that great Continent, and most formidable as Harbour Defences, are not in any sense sea going Ships of War,"

> This is not said with any view of disparaging the Skill and industry which has been displayed in their construction, still less with any intention of undervaluing the enormous defensive power which has thus been developed: a power which I believe renders the Americans practically unassailable in their own waters
>
> If again, Admiral Milne means that we have not yet an Iron plated Flotilla capable of going into the inland waters, rivers and Harbours of the United States, and when there, able to fight an Action on equal terms with the description of Vessels which will be found awaiting us, he is perfectly right and it will be only necessary to observe that such a proceeding on our part is simply impossible.[20]

The Threat of Foreign Interference Grows

Congress, meanwhile, was in a spending mood far beyond the needs of the Union Navy. Ten million dollars was appropriated for

"20 more ironclads," in addition to the $1.5 million already invested for the three initial prototypes, the *Galena, New Ironsides*, and *Monitor*. After Hampton Roads, this figure was raised to nearly $30 million—and another $10 million was devoted to Union coastal fortifications.[21] This was followed closely by a $10-million bill calling for an improved interior canal network that would link the Great Lakes with the Mississippi River—all in anticipation of hostilities with England.[22] Even the first transcontinental railroad was urged on the floor of the House by reason that it would help protect California from strategic isolation in an Anglo-American conflict.[23]

Nor were these considerations entirely groundless. British reinforcements to Canada, although themselves defensive by nature, were seen as threatening, while Napoleon III's extended imperial "visit" to Mexico, with large French military and naval forces, only heightened a sense that the United States was now surrounded by European enemies—the nightmare scenario that prompted the Monroe Doctrine in 1823—as much as it was divided from within by "Southern traitors." What started as the North's "personal" irritation with Queen Victoria's Proclamation of Neutrality at the start of the conflict (which automatically granted the Confederates belligerent rights), nearly turned to war over the *Trent*, and ever-present was the threat of British and French intervention in the conflict, whether to relieve themselves of the cotton shortage imposed by the Union blockade or for strictly humanitarian reasons.[24] Britain's largely ruling-class sympathy with the Southern aristocracy, in addition to its contempt for popular democracy, also was well known. As William Howard Russell of the London *Times* confided in his diary:

> There is after all great satisfaction among the representative property men & tories [sic] in England with the rupture in America & I confess for one that I agree in thinking this war if it be merely a lesson will be of use.... Had there been a possibility in human nature to make laws without

faction & interest & to employ popular institutions without intrigue & miserable self seeking the condition of parts of the U.S. does no doubt cause regret that it did not occur here, but the strength of the U.S. employed by passion interest self seeking became dangerous to other nations & therefore there is an utter want of sympathy with them in their time of trouble & England regards the North without fear favour or affection & in spite of liberty rather favours the South.[25]

When British subjects began constructing and manning fast blockade runners, commerce raiders, and even ironclad rams for the Confederacy—utilizing British naval bases in Halifax, Bermuda, and the West Indies—the American Civil War took on a different dimension, which historians tend to overlook, though the phrase "Anglo-Rebel" fills contemporary newspapers, political debates, and private letters.[26] Indeed, the greatest threat to the survival of the nation throughout the American Civil War arguably came from the Great Powers, not the South. It is significant that the first official naval history of the Civil War saw the Union Navy's primary victory as having "saved us from foreign intervention that could not have been otherwise avoided," (adding almost as an afterthought), "while at the same time its labors in putting down the rebellion have been far greater than has been generally supposed."[27] When we recall what foreign recognition and assistance meant for the original thirteen colonies struggling for independence, we can see how important this hope was for the Southern states. How long could the Confederacy hold out without blockade—running to and from England?[28] As the Chairman of the Senate Foreign Relations Committee, Charles Sumner, informed his English friend, Richard Cobden, "our people are becoming more and more excited, &c., there are many who insist upon war. A very important person said to me yesterday—'we are now at war with England, but the hostilities are all on her side.'"[29]

Union Responses to an "Anglo-Rebel" Threat

The result of this attention on the "Anglo-Rebel" threat was the development of ironclad-killing weapons, the monster 15- and later 20-inch Rodman and Dahlgren smoothbores, mounted in both the new fortifications and the monitors, respectively. Fox confirmed this strategy when he wrote to the Navy's Bureau of Ordnance that the U.S. had to "keep pace, and lead, if possible, in the production of smooth bore and rifled guns of such calibres and velocities as shall be irresistible *against anything possible to construct which will cross the ocean.*"[30] The Bureau subsequently proved Fox and Ericsson's belief that the 15-inch gun would be supreme at effective combat ranges. "Target 57," which included a large, 5-inch thick, rolled iron plate from John Brown & Co. of Sheffield, was punched clean through, in addition to "Target 51," a rolled plate 6 inches thick procured from a reputable French manufacturer.[31] According to J. P. Baxter, "when Fox sent [Ericsson] a plan of one of the Laird rams... [he] replied 'such a gingerbread affair must not come near our XV-inch bulldogs in their impregnable kennels.'"[32] It also is important to note that the "fever" over Confederate ironclad-rams rather added to this concern than vice versa.

Yet Ericsson, Fox, and the Union Navy's ambitions reached far beyond the American coastline. Even as Ericsson boasted to Seward of the geo-strategic value of the *Passaic*-class coastal monitors he also wrote to Fox that "the national contest for supremacy is now fairly inaugurated," for to break up any distant blockade of the Northern States, or engage broadside-ironclads on the open sea, Ericsson also proposed a "super" monitor-ram fully twice the size of the original. The vessel would continue to forgo the tactical weaknesses associated with sails and rigging in combat (in addition to the much larger crew of sailors needed to work them), in favor of a massive coal carrying capacity of 1,000 tons. Low freeboard of hull, also permissible without masts, would continue to allow the maximum concentration of armor along the waterline while forming an unusually steady gun platform for the heaviest possible guns—mounted behind 15 inches of turret armor. Gigantic engines in the larger hull were expected to make 16 knots.[33] "Sir William [Armstrong] may do his best," wrote Ericsson, "but we will make floating targets which he cannot demolish and guns that will sink any thing his country can put to sea."[34]

Added to this, Welles informed Congress in his annual report dated December 1, 1862, that "we must have a formidable Navy, not only of light draught vessels to guard our extensive and shallow coast, but one that with vessels always ready for service, and of sufficient size to give them speed, can seek and meet an enemy on the ocean."[35] The result of this appeal was the establishment of the League Island dockyard at Philadelphia to facilitate the construction of a full-scale, wide-ranging ironclad navy that had nothing to do with the prosecution of the war against the Rebellion and everything to do with a war against British naval and maritime supremacy. The following year Welles also revealed plans for a class of "super-*Alabamas*," "with which to sweep the ocean, and chase and hunt down the vessels of an enemy."[36]

By 1864, it was this combination of plans and proof in the shape of warships already built and under construction that led Admiralty-appointed naval observer Captain James G. Goodenough, R.N., to report to the worried British minister to the United States, Lord Lyons, that "this country is preparing for war against a maritime power by aiming at destroying its commerce and protecting its [own] ports with vessels of a peculiar construction, and by breaking a blockade of any its ports with [the] aid of swift, manageable, invulnerable vessels."[37] Nor was this development necessarily inconsistent with the Union's foreign policy. Lincoln himself declared towards the end of the Civil War that "England will live to regret her inimical attitude toward us." The resolution of the *Trent* Affair was "a pretty bitter pill to swallow," Lincoln said, "but I contented myself with believing that England's triumph in the matter would be short-lived, and that after ending our war successfully we would be so powerful that we could call her to account for all the embarrassments she had inflicted upon us."[38]

Conclusion

Understanding the monitors means understanding that the Civil War was not exclusively one of North vs. South, but an international contest between the two great English-speaking peoples of the mid-Victorian era. The "iron shield" of the American republic—struggling for its survival against slave-holding factions from within and from British support via commerce raiders and blockade runners from without—was Fox and Ericsson's idiosyncratic force of monitors, which the Royal Navy simply could not challenge. On December 23, 1861, at the height of the *Trent* crisis, Ericsson wrote to Welles that, "our gun boats or floating batteries, since they lack speed, size and many other potent elements of the large European iron clad war ships will be worthless unless absolutely impregnable and capable of carrying the heaviest ordnance." The original *Monitor*, still under construction, possessed "the properties called for, requiring only increased substance of turret plate and to be armed with 15-inch guns to bid defiance to any war ship afloat."[39] Following the ironclad stalemate at Hampton Roads, Ericsson further assured the secretary that the new, enhanced monitors were "exactly what we most need" on the basis "that there are no vessels yet produced in Europe that could sustain an encounter with the fleet of turret vessels now building under your orders."[40]

Previously, Welles had replied to the Senate Naval Committee's request for particulars on the Navy's ironclad lineup that "the Department does not propose to confine itself exclusively to any particular plan yet offered but proposes to avail itself of the experience which will be gained in the construction of those now going forward, one of which will soon be tested in actual conflict." This referred to the expected duel with the converted *Merrimack* and of the three original Union ironclads contracted, only the *Monitor* would possibly be ready in time. He also noted, however, that "the ends proposed for the gunboat class is to reduce all the fortified sea ports of the enemy and open their harbors to the Union army."[41] This was a significant caveat not mentioned by Ericsson, who based his conception of a superior ironclad more on a concentrated, thicker armor scheme and larger though fewer guns; specifically, an ironclad-killing ironclad, or "machine."

Because of this discrepancy, the *Passaic*-class monitors proved to be of limited value in bombarding Confederate land works, as demonstrated during the great naval assault on Charleston's defenses of April 7, 1863, where a rapid suppressing fire counted more than individual weight of shell.[42] Their defensive powers, on the other hand, were extraordinary. At less than 800 yards USS *Passaic* (844 tons, with a crew of only seventy) was struck thirty-five times in under forty minutes, though firing only thirteen times in return. A month before, she had been struck thirty-four times in an attack against Fort McAllister. "One of my officers who was below," reported her commanding officer, Captain Percival Drayton, "tells me that at one time in a few seconds he counted fifteen shot which passed over his head just above the deck, and at times the whistling was so rapid he could not keep count at all."[43]

In fact, by the end of 1863 Welles was responding to a complaint from another monitor captain that

> Neither the XI inch smooth bore nor the eight-inch rifle can penetrate the armor of the rebel iron clads, and in a contest with them, only the 15 inch gun can be effective, according to the experience derived from the contest between the *Atlanta* and the *Weehawken*. In a contest with sand batteries, broadside vessels are required, so that it is

immaterial whether the guns are 15, 11 or 8 inch. Against the exposed masonry of forts we have the testimony of our own officers and the rebels that the 15 inch gun is the most effective. [44]

Then again, when the Confederate States Navy ventured to oppose these monitors, the results were disastrous. The casemate-ram CSS *Atlanta* was forced to surrender after five shots from the monitor *Weehawken* (June 17, 1863); the mighty *Tennessee* was pounded into submission at Mobile Bay (August 5, 1864), first by the 11-inch guns of the river monitor *Chickasaw*, and then the 15-inch guns of the *Manhattan*; while the *Virginia II* was heavily damaged by the double-turreted *Onondaga* at Trent's Reach (January 24, 1865).[45] At the same time, public and professional opinion in Great Britain was turning against the broadside-ironclad principle.[46] The London *Mechanics' Magazine*, jubilantly quoted by *Scientific American*, wrote that "the fleet of experimental iron-clads, of which the *Warrior* is the type, must, if they are to be in a condition to cope with the armor-plated ships of foreign powers, be reconstructed.... The remedy is a bitter pill for the Government to swallow; but there is no avoiding it."[47] Even the London *Times* admitted that, for all intents and purposes, "a perfect Ironclad is an imperfect seaboat"—a momentous though unconscious distinction between what may be termed tactical and strategic naval supremacy.[48] Which was more important, and upon which was the other based?

What we see, therefore, in the recent salvaging of the original *Monitor* is not just a forgotten warship; indeed, the *Monitor*'s place in American and naval history has been assured since 1862. What we see is the primary weapon in a *forgotten war*—an entire dimension of the American Civil War—that was never fought. Probably as a consequence of their much more decisive though less obvious *deterrent* success, John Ericsson's monitors have been understood only in relation to Confederate defenses, rather than as a "national defense system" of the most sophisticated war machines of their day, conceived and manufactured on an unprecedented, industrialized scale against the offensive capability of the world's greatest naval power. In that respect, perhaps, they were the timely fulfillment of Thomas Jefferson's dream of strategic isolation secured by a host of comparatively inexpensive gunboats—not a "Blue Water" navy.[49]

CHAPTER 8

Who Won the Battle of Hampton Roads? A Historians' Debate
John V. Quarstein and Joseph Gutierrez

1. Describe the Strengths and Successes of "Your" Ship's Design

QUARSTEIN: The CSS *Virginia* was an experimental vessel; an amazing adaptation of available materials and a tribute to the C.S. Navy's ability to improvise. The achievement of building an ironclad within the weak, industrial infrastructure of the Confederacy is a mark of success. As a result of the tremendous effort and resources applied to the *Merrimack-Virginia* conversion project, the CSS *Virginia* became one of the most successful warship designs of the Civil War. The ships submerged ends gave this adaptation greater stability. The *Virginia*'s sloped, armored casemate enhanced the ironclad's shot-proof qualities by causing shot to glance off. Furthermore, providing the two layers of 2-inch ironclad plate with 24 inches of layered wooden backing gave the casemate greater strength and flexibility to withstand shot. The

---

This debate was moderated by Anna Holloway of The Mariners' Museum.

Virginia also had a variety of weapons from which to choose, making the Confederate ironclad one of the most powerful warships to ply the waves during the war. The ironclad was designed to fight wooden warships and was armed with ten heavy guns. Four of these cannons were rifled. The 7- and 6.4-inch Brooke guns were capable of firing solid-shot, explosive shell and armor-piercing shot known as Brooke bolts. The Brooke guns were by far the most superior rifled naval cannon of the Civil War. The velocity, accuracy and hitting power of the Brooke guns gave the *Virginia* a major advantage. The two 7-inch Brookes were pivot-mounted with three gun ports each at the bow and stern giving these rifles a good field of fire. The *Virginia*'s armament included six 9-inch Dahlgren smoothbores and two of these Dahlgrens were specially modified to fire hot-shot. These cannons, coupled with the 1,500-pound cast-iron ram, made the *Virginia* a warship that could ram or blow-up its adversary. The *Virginia* also had some other advantages including good fire-control, effective rate of fire, and an imposing broadside. The ironclad's size gave it a large crew to use when boarding enemy vessels or when acting to repel boarders. To summarize, the *Virginia*'s cannon, ram, and sloped-casemate gave it an advantage.

GUTIERREZ: The first point I want to make is the *Virginia* did not prevail against the *Monitor*. The *Virginia*'s strengths did not overcome the weaknesses of the *Monitor*. Sir Francis Drake thoroughly understood the sailing ships of his day and the sailing ships of the mid-nineteenth century would have not been so alien to him. However, the *Monitor* was something new and represented such a break with the past, that neither Drake nor any other figure from the past would have easily understood the "cheese-box on a raft." The *Virginia* was essentially a sailing vessel that had been armored and represented the past. The *Monitor* however, represented the future, where guns would be housed in rotating armored turrets, armor belts would surround warships at the waterline, and the commanding officer's battle station would be in a command center. As he designed the vessel, John Ericsson was creating new devices, which in the rush to complete the ship were immediately incorporated into the design. Such inventions as forced-air ventilation may not have worked as well as hoped, but they did work and are in use today. The *Monitor*, while not a comfortable vessel, was an effective man-of-war. Its objective on March 9, 1862, was to stop the *Virginia*. The *Virginia*'s shot and shell failed to penetrate the *Monitor*'s armored turret where the vessel's two powerful 1-inch Dahlgren guns were located. The *Monitor* was clearly the faster and more maneuverable vessel and throughout the engagement; it was able to dance around the *Virginia*. The rotating turret allowed the guns to be aimed and fired regardless of the direction the bow was pointing. The turret sounded the death knell of the traditional broadside. While the *Monitor*'s low freeboard, designed to prevent the ship's hull from being an easy target, would pose challenges, on March 9th the *Monitor* performed brilliantly. The enemy stated the *Monitor* was successful. When the *Virginia* failed to penetrate the armor, she tried to ram. When she failed to ram, she tried to board the *Monitor*. None of the tactics the *Virginia* tried could stop the *Monitor*. As a result Ericsson's vessel was hailed throughout the North.

2. *What Are Your Ship's Fighting Capabilities?*

QUARSTEIN: The *Virginia* introduced several new weapons technologies as well as reintroducing the art of ramming. The ram is a critical tool. The steam-powered *Virginia* was able to save gunpowder by ramming wooden vessels. "Like a bayonet charge of infantry," the ram became, virtually overnight, an emotional tactical tool that instilled fear in the enemy. A whole class of vessels was reintroduced during the war. Whether made of iron or wood, each of the "rams" hoped to re-create the *Virginia*'s quick destruction of the *Cumberland*. At the 1866 battle of Lissa, the Austrian fleet relied on rams not guns to destroy the Italian fleet. The *Virginia* has Brooke rifles, which gave the Confederate ironclad effective firepower. The two hot-shot 9-inch Dahlgren's also added to the *Virginia*'s ability to destroy any wooden ship she might encounter. If the *Virginia*'s armaments and ram made her a death knell to wooden warships, the Brooke bolt gave the Confederates an advantage against most other ironclads. Unfortunately, these projectiles were not available on March 9, 1862; but, they would be used in subsequent engagements with Union ironclads to great effect.

The *Virginia* also had good shot-proof qualities thanks to the design of its casemate, which is based on the Barnard principle. Developed by John G. Barnard, who later became chief engineer of the Army of the Potomac, the concept featured a casemate with a 36-degree slope that prompted shot to ricochet or bounce off the sides of the *Virginia*. The casemate also provided the Confederates with good firepower and field of fire from its broadside and pivot gun positions. Grated hatchways and the conical pilothouse gave the *Virginia*'s officers good vision, which enhanced the ironclad's fire control. Not only did the *Virginia* have a variety of superior tools of war—the ram, rifled guns, hot shot guns and shellguns—but she also had the defensive capabilities that meant her crew were well protected in battle.

GUTIERREZ: The *Monitor* carried two 11-inch Dahlgren guns inside the turret. During the battle nineteen men were originally stationed in the turret, which was 20 feet in diameter. The turret rotated the guns to bring them to bear on the *Virginia*; the *Monitor* did not have to turn broadside as the *Virginia* did to bring its weapons to bear. While there were significant challenges related to starting and stopping the turret, it did work. Ericsson believed the problems associated with the turret rotation on March 9th, were due to the failure on the crew to properly maintain the system. Be that as it may, the turret represented a major breakthrough, and its effectiveness is clearly demonstrated during the engagement with the *Virginia*. With the turret the crew is protected—for example, the turret can turn away from the enemy when loading the guns. Another important fact to remember is the *Monitor* was a shallow draft vessel. Thus she could fight on rivers, in harbors, and places where the *Virginia* could not go due to her deep draft. The *Monitor* fought in Hampton Roads, at Drewery's Bluff, and at Malvern Hill. These examples clearly demonstrate the *Monitor*'s versatility; she fought the enemy's most successful warship, attacked a fort, and participated in joint operations by providing fire support to McClellan's troops. The *Monitor* represented the future, the *Virginia* the past.

3. *What Were Your Ship's Most Significant Command Decisions?*

QUARSTEIN: Before I detail the command decisions, I want to remind you of the fighting capabilities of the *Monitor* at Drewry's Bluff. It could not even fire at the Confederate fortifications because the *Monitor* could not elevate its guns. Added to this, the *Monitor* exhibited the lack of any effective fire control while engaging the *Virginia* on March 9. The Union ironclad failed to cause any damage to the *Virginia* during the battle.

As for command decisions, there is no doubt that Franklin Buchanan provided the Confederacy with dynamic and effective leadership on March 8, 1862. His dramatic speech to his crew when the *Virginia* first entered Hampton Roads gave an impetus to achieve victory against what appeared to be overwhelming odds. Buchanan transformed a shakedown cruise into an aggressive strike against an unsuspecting Union fleet. This surprise tactic enhanced his opportunities to destroy Union wooden warships before the arrival of Union ironclads. The flag officer's determination helped the *Virginia* destroy every Union ship in its path on March 8, 1862. The dynamism of Buchanan's strike against the Federal fleet in Hampton Roads sent shockwaves throughout the Union command that reached all the way to Washington, D.C. New York City appeared threatened by the unstoppable "Rebel Monster." Almost every Federal suffered from a dreaded disease in the summer of 1862 thanks to Buchanan's decision to ram the *Cumberland*—" ram fever" or "*Merrimack*-on-the-brain"

Once Buchanan is critically wounded, Catesby ap Roger Jones assumes command and continues to exhibit fine leadership qualities on March 9. Even though he realizes that he has the wrong ammunition available to fight against the *Monitor*, Jones strives to strike at the one vessel he knows his ship can destroy—the *Minnesota*. Events will not allow Jones to destroy the Union frigate; however, he does fight the *Monitor* to a draw on March 9. Jones's return to Gosport Navy Yard, once the *Monitor* is apparently damaged by a shell striking the pilothouse, is prompted by several factors, including the receding tide, leaks in the *Virginia*, need for more effective ammunition and other repair and resupply issues. Jones is fully determined to return to fight the *Monitor* when conditions favor a Confederate victory.

Josiah Tattnall would eventually replace Buchanan as the *Virginia*'s commander. On several occasions Tattnall will try to beckon the *Monitor* into battle; yet, the *Monitor* refuses. Tattnall's ironclad has a new ram and Brooke bolts all designed to give the *Virginia* an advantage in any contest with the *Monitor*. Josiah Tattnall most influential decision is when he decides to scuttle the *Virginia*. Even though he would have rather taken his ship to another port or, at least, to attack the Union fleet and "die game," Tattnall destroys the *Virginia* and sends the crew to Drewry's Bluff where they play a critical role in blocking the Union fleet's advance against Richmond via the James River.

GUTIERREZ: The first of the *Monitor*'s fateful command decisions was the decision to stay at Hampton Roads. Captain John Marston, who was acting as commander of the North Atlantic Blockading Squadron forces in Hampton Roads, had been ordered by the secretary of the navy to send the *Monitor*, upon her arrival, to Washington, D.C. It's not usually a good career move to ignore the orders of the secretary of navy if you're a serving officer. However, Marston recognized that best use of the *Monitor* would be to counter the immediate threat the *Virginia* posed to the wooden ships in Hampton Roads. Thus he ordered the *Monitor* to protect the *Minnesota*. John L. Worden, the *Monitor*'s commanding officer made the second critical command decision when he determined to place the *Monitor* between the *Virginia* and the *Minnesota*. The worst day in United States naval history, until the sneak attack by the Japanese on Pearl Harbor, was March 8, 1862, and the Union Navy had reason to fear the *Virginia* when she approached the *Minnesota*. The *Monitor* was about one-half the size of the *Virginia* and was untested. Captain Henry Van Brunt of the *Minnesota* wasn't going to sit idly by while a small, untested ship tried to protect his vessel. Thus the *Monitor* was a target for both ships and was effectively caught in crossfire for a period of time. The *Virginia* quickly turned its full attention to the *Monitor*. While the *Monitor* did have fire control problems, the *Virginia* was unable to take advantage of the *Monitor*'s challenges. The attempt to board the *Monitor* by the *Virginia* was recognized and Worden had canister loaded in the guns. He was able to anticipate the movements of the rather sluggish *Virginia* and dodged her attempts to board and ram.

4. Which Ship Boasted the Most Successful Combat Record?

QUARSTEIN: Well, of course it's got to be the glorious and noble CSS *Virginia*. It is the *Virginia* that inflicts on the U.S. Navy its greatest defeat until Pearl Harbor. The *Virginia* destroys two major Union warships on March 8. In addition, this Confederate ironclad inflicts 247 casualties, damages the USS *Minnesota* and USS *St. Lawrence*. The *Virginia* disables the gunboats *Dragon* and *Zouave* as well as destroying two transports and a schooner. Without question, these statistics give the *Virginia* a greater kill ratio than any monitor in the Union fleet. When the *Virginia* returns to Hampton Roads on April 11, 1862, the *Monitor* refuses to engage, which allows one of the *Virginia*'s consorts, CSS *Jamestown*, to capture two brigs and a schooner off Hampton Creek. Furthermore, the *Virginia*'s mere existence blocks the Union fleet's access to the James River for over two months, which negatively impacts upon Major General George McClellan's Peninsula Campaign. Once the *Virginia* is sadly given to the flames by her own crew, so that she is sunk rather than surrendered, her crew is taken intact to Drewry's Bluff. There, manning Confederate naval guns, they repel the Federal fleet inflicting serious damage to the USS *Galena* and, of course, forcing the *Monitor* back down the James River. This retreat prompted John Taylor Wood to call out to the *Monitor*, "Tell Jeffers that's the wrong way to Richmond." I put it to you that it is the CSS *Virginia* that has the most glorious and effective combat record, not only of any Confederate ironclad, but of any other ironclad that served in Hampton Roads.

GUTIERREZ. Keep in mind the objective of the *Virginia* was to sink the *Minnesota*. The *Virginia* failed to accomplish her objective on March 9th. The *Monitor* came within a few miles of Richmond; how close to Washington, D.C. did the *Virginia* get? Not only did the *Monitor* prevent the *Virginia* from accomplishing her objective, within a short time she threatened the capital of the Confederacy. She provided fire support for McClellan's troops at Malvern Hill during an attack by Lee's forces. By all accounts, the *Monitor* was extremely successful.

5. Why Do You Insist That Your Ship Wins the Battle of Hampton Roads?

GUTIERREZ: First the *Monitor*'s objective was to protect the *Minnesota* while the *Virginia*'s goal was to sink the *Minnesota*. The *Virginia* was unable to accomplish its objective while the *Monitor* was not only able to save the *Minnesota* but was also able to prevent the Confederacy from destroying the Union fleet at Hampton Roads. I concur that, following Worden's injury, it took some time for Executive Officer Samuel Dana Greene to move from his post in the turret and gain control of the *Monitor*. No less an authority than John Taylor Wood, an officer on board the *Virginia*, recognized the *Monitor*'s victory when he stated, "Although there is no doubt that the *Monitor* first retired, for Captain Va Brunt, commanding the *Minnesota*, so states in his official report, the battle was a draw, so far as the two vessels engaged were concerned. But in its general result the advantage was with the *Monitor*." Even the enemy recognized the *Monitor*'s victory. We can do no less.

QUARSTEIN: The bottom line is that the *Virginia* did achieve its goal in destroying several Union vessels and secured control of Hampton Roads at the very moment that the Union army planned to use the harbor as a base for operations against Richmond. Yes, the *Virginia* did not destroy any more wooden ships on March 9th, but it was the "mistress of Hampton Roads." The mere existence of the undefeated CSS *Virginia* closed Hampton Roads and the James River to the Union's use at the very moment McClellan's Peninsula Campaign intended to use these transportation resources. The *Virginia*'s ability to defend Norfolk and guard the Confederate James River flank against any Union advance delayed McClellan's march against Richmond for over a month, which contributed to his eventual defeat. So, the overall goal of the Confederates in Spring 1862 was to save Richmond from capture. The *Virginia* and her crew played a significant role in achieving this goal.

6. Which Ship Do You Think Had the Greatest Influence upon the Peninsula Campaign?

QUARSTEIN: Well, I have already alluded to the *Virginia*'s influence upon the Peninsula Campaign. The *Virginia* closed the James River and access to the river was a critical component of McClellan's campaign. His concept was to use the James and York rivers to carry his troops and to guard his flanks. McClellan believed he could rapidly move to Richmond using these rivers before the Confederates could consolidate their military resources to defend their capital and largest industrial center. The *Virginia* disrupted this entire concept. It closed the James River and controlled Hampton Roads. It forced McClellan to concentrate on the York River, which was closed by Confederate batteries. In fact, the Union naval command was so afraid of the *Virginia* that the U.S. Navy refused to attempt to run past the Confederate Gloucester Point and Yorktown batteries. The CSS *Virginia* caused a dreaded sickness amongst the Union commanders—ram fever. The *Virginia,* without doubt, altered, changed, and disrupted the Union high command's goals for victory in Spring 1862 by its very existence. It paralyzed the movement of the Union fleet, it paralyzed the movement of the Union army and, in doing so, contributed greatly to the Union campaign's failure.

GUTIERREZ: Confederate secretary of navy Stephen R. Mallory had a vision of the *Virginia* attacking Northern cities. That would have had a major impact on the campaign. However, that did not happen. The *Monitor* was held in reserve to prevent the *Virginia* from attacking the Union transports in the York River. While it is true that McClellan was denied the use of the James River, it was but for a short while. By May 8 a Union squadron was in the James, and on May 15 Union naval forces fought an engagement with desperate Confederates at the gates of Richmond. The *Virginia* was available to Confederate forces for only a brief period.

7. *Which Ship Had the Greatest Technological Impact?*

GUTIERREZ: Is there a question here? Don't we know the answer? Monitors will serve in the United States Navy until 1937. While Ericsson's design had a number of challenges, it did represent the future. To this day, modern warships use rotating turrets, which provided protection to the crew and weapons. The Confederates at Drewry's Bluff were amazed that the *Monitor* could be moved without the crew being exposed to enemy fire. The fact that the *Virginia*'s anchor and rudder chains were exposed impacted upon the crew's ability to maneuver the ship. In modern warfare we demand that crews are reasonably protected, that fire control is effective, and that human needs are at least minimally accommodated. From turrets to forced-air ventilation, the *Monitor* represented the future. Ericsson's vision of a warship represented the future. While monitor class vessels were still in use in the twentieth century, *Virginia*-style vessels disappeared with the Confederacy.

QUARSTEIN: We may see many technological advances in the USS *Monitor*, but there are some technological advances that the *Monitor* did not have. I never heard anyone say that the *Monitor* was seaworthy. I want to take you to December 31, 1862, and that clarifies the failure of the monitor class as an ocean-going vessel. I must also point out that every time a monitor-class vessel encounters a Confederate fixed fortification, it is repulsed. While this class of warship was designed by Ericsson as an offensive weapon, monitors are unable to capture or reduce Confederate fortifications at Drewry's Bluff or Charleston. So the monitor design featured some marvelous innovations, but these innovations were not fully developed. The *Monitor* had serious weaknesses that threatened the very well-being of the crew as well as the ability to achieve Union tactical and strategic goals.

8. Which Ship Had the Greatest Impact on the Civil War?

QUARSTEIN: There could be no other: CSS *Virginia*. I say the *Virginia* merely because of its design. There was no other ironclad during the Civil War that won such a victory as the CSS *Virginia* did on March 8, 1862. No monitor can compare to this achievement. I think, moreover, that the Confederates developed a casemated ironclad well suited to their industrial infrastructure. I might add that no Confederate port was captured by sea when there was a Confederate ironclad based on the *Virginia* design protecting it. These ironclads helped to keep these vital ports open, which give the Confederacy a lifeline that helped to keep it afloat. Richmond would fall only when the last port fell, and the last port fell as a result of a land operation—not due to the actions of a Union monitor.

GUTIERREZ: It is interesting to note that the definition of success becomes a question of whether monitors destroyed Confederate forts. The question should be: "Which ship had the greatest influence on the Civil War?" *Monitor*-class vessels appeared and patrolled off every major Confederate port. The Union had the industrial might to produce a large number of monitors and armorclad vessels. Charleston was attacked, Mobile Bay was attacked, Wilmington, was shelled. Union monitors operated on most of the Confederacy's major rivers, often in support of Union troops. Most of the Confederacy's ironclads were destroyed before they were completed, and those that were actually completed usually had very poor engines. The Union's iron vessels helped split the Confederacy, enforced the blockage, captured Southern ports, and provided fire support for Union troops. Confederate ironclads never threatened or blockaded Union cities nor were they able to prevent their ports to falling to Union forces.

9. *Which Ship Leaves the Greater Legacy?*

GUTIERREZ: We have talked about this from several different perspectives. The *Virginia* was a sailing ship made into an ironclad. The *Monitor* was an iron warship, an entirely new design. The *Monitor*'s turret protected her gun crew and key machinery was located below the waterline and was protected not only by iron armor but also by the water itself. No longer would a captain have to turn broadside to the enemy to bring his most powerful weapons to bear. There were those that worried during the battle that the *Monitor* would win by destroying the *Virginia*'s propeller, which, while protected on the *Monitor*, was unprotected on the

Virginia. The *Monitor* represents a major change in ship design, a significant step in the evolution of the warship. The *Virginia* does not. Shortly after the battle, the London *Times* noted: "Whereas we had available for immediate purposes 149 first-class warships, we now have only two, these being the *Warrior* and her sister *Ironside* (*Black Princess*). There is not now a ship in the English navy, apart from these two, that it would not be madness to trust to an engagement with the *Monitor*." Europe recognized the *Monitor* for what she was: the future.

QUARSTEIN: I will merely tell you that in the Commonwealth of Virginia many recognize the CSS *Virginia* as an important symbol of our state's contribution to the Southern war effort. After all, the ironclad was made in Virginia, by Virginia workmen using Virginian iron and wood, and she was crewed by many Virginians who fought in the vessel in Virginian waters making a heroic record that still is honored today. The *Virginia* is a symbol of the lost cause; but, she is also a symbol of a major transition in naval warfare. It is also the ship that inflicted upon the U.S. Navy its greatest defeat until Pearl Harbor. The *Virginia*'s legacy is that she was an equal partner in the ironclad revolution that forever changed naval warfare.

CHAPTER 9

Discovery and Recovery—
The Modern History of the USS
Monitor: A Personal Memoir
Jeff Johnston

MANY PEOPLE ARE NOT AWARE THAT THERE ARE TWO HISTOries of the *Monitor*—not only that of her epic encounter at the Battle of Hampton Roads, but also the *second* dramatic battle she fought: the age-old battle of man against the sea. Unfortunately for the *Monitor*, she lost. As the *Monitor*'s paymaster said: "What the fire of the enemy hits failed to do, the elements have accomplished." That was no small statement.

The *Monitor*, in tow of the steamship USS *Rhode Island*, left Hampton Roads on December 30, 1862, and headed for points south. Those points south eventually would have been her final port of call, and the ironclad would have taken part in the attacks on Charleston; but, as we all know, she did not make it. She ran into severe weather off the coast of Cape Hatteras and, despite heroic efforts by its crew and the crew of the USS *Rhode Island*, they could do nothing to keep her afloat.

Sixteen people lost their lives on the night the vessel sank, among them three sailors from the *Rhode Island*. The United States Navy awarded five Congressional Medals of Honor that night to the crew of the *Rhode Island*, three of them posthumously. Men in small boats had pulled out against 20-foot seas and done everything possible to get to the *Monitor* and rescue her crew.

But just after 1 A.M., the *Monitor* was lost forever, at least so everyone thought. When the *Monitor* went down, probably the best thing that ever happened for us today is that she sank in 240 feet of water. Had she been in water that was more salvageable, the ship would have been quickly raised and scrapped; she would have gone the way of every successive class of monitor vessel, and she would not have existed today at all. Instead, with the exception of a few writings, the *Monitor* was lost to memory. Then, in 1953, a retired postmaster decided that he wanted to find and raise the *Monitor*, have it brought back and made into an exhibit. That year, he petitioned the secretary of the navy to properly abandon the vessel, and that is no easy feat for the United States Navy. He was granted a meeting with the secretary, who, agreeing that the vessel held no significance except for historic interest or to make her right for salvage and recovery agreed—probably for the only time in its history— to abandon a military vessel.

Fortunately, they did not find the *Monitor* back then. The retired postmaster from Massachusetts did offer a $1,000 reward for anyone who could provide the location to help him recover the wreck of the USS *Monitor*. He began receiving tips, and some historical accounts even talk about picnickers in the 1880s sitting underneath the Cape Hatteras Lighthouse watching the *Monitor*'s turret at low tide. One gentleman insisted that he saw the *Monitor* 1,500 yards off the coast of the lighthouse. We know now that they were probably talking about a wreck named the *Oriental* and what they were seeing at low tide was the ship's boiler.

The discovery of the real *Monitor* was no accident. People had a pretty good idea of where to look, thanks to the surviving logbook of the USS *Rhode Island*. Still, the night the *Monitor* sank was a dark New Year's Eve in a coastal gale. Dead reckoning by the sailors onboard the *Rhode Island* put them at thirteen nautical miles south-southeast of the Cape Hatteras Lighthouse. The wreck was eventually discovered at sixteen miles south-southeast; that is not bad dead-reckoning for the middle of the night and in the most inclement conditions.

The recent, successful search for the *Monitor* came about because of a multitude of organizations. It began with a man named Doc Edgerton of MIT. Edgerton had a great interest in underwater technologies and underwater imagery, and he was looking to go out to sea and test a new piece of equipment in the area of the Graveyard of the Atlantic. The Graveyard of the Atlantic is aptly named. In fact, it is estimated that between the Virginia and South Carolina borders there are two- to three-thousand shipwrecks off the coast and up on the beach. Nineteenth-century sailors called it the Cape Horn of the Atlantic. It is a hard place to work, and a hard place to sail around. Fortunately we do not have too many of these encounters nowadays, but the reason that the *Monitor* was so far offshore is that she was trying to get around the part of Cape Hatteras called Diamond Shoals. The *Monitor* could easily sail over Diamond Shoals but the vessel that was towing her could not.

Thus, modern explorers had a pretty good idea by the *Rhode Island*'s log of the area where they wanted to look. With researchers and archeologists from the State of North Carolina's Division of Archives and History and Duke University, this multi-faceted team pulled together and went out and conducted a series of surveys off the coast of North Carolina.

The search narrowed it down originally to three sites and, subsequently, down to two. The project archeologist, Gordon Watts, who helped discover the wreck, can tell you some great stories about it; one of the most interesting is that when they first discovered the ship, it took them almost a year and a half to verify that they actually had the *Monitor* because no one expected her to be upside down. Everybody expected the imagery that came back would show her sitting upright on the bottom, turret in place. As the legend goes, Gordon's wife walked up to the table one day when they were all sitting looking at all these photographs that were laid out and said, "Of course it's the damn *Monitor*, it's upside down." She turned the pictures around and everybody said, Oh yeah, it is the *Monitor*!

That created a whole new series of problems, including the fact that at that time period, the *Monitor* was in international waters. Because she was no longer a U.S. Navy warship, she was ripe for salvage and salvage does not necessarily mean historical recovery. Everybody began looking around for a way to protect this ship because they wanted to announce to the public that it had been found. We had found one of the most historically significant ships in the history of the United States and we could not tell everybody where it was because we couldn't guarantee we could protect it. They went back to the federal government and the only thing that was on the books that could potentially protect the *Monitor* was the new Reserves and Sanctuaries Marine Estuarial Act. That is a very long title for protecting pretty fish and coral reefs and other things that archeologists refer to as bioclutter.

At that time the *Monitor* site was designated as a cultural resource sanctuary. It was designed particularly to protect an American shipwreck. This is something that had nothing to do with the Sanctuaries Act. There was a lot of flack caught over it. And then, unfortunately for the *Monitor*, nothing was done except for some early survey work. Archeology, after all, is not necessarily about recovery; it is about study, preservation, learning, trying to interpret history, our heritage, and our culture. NOAA's stance on the site, because it did appear to be fairly stable, was literally, no pun intended, to monitor the site.

The next big milestone occurred on the 125th anniversary of the battle between the *Monitor* and the *Virginia*, The Mariners' Museum was selected as the principal repository for the growing *Monitor* collection. NOAA is not in the museum business but we have found a great partner here. In fact, you can walk around this museum and see that we definitely made the right choice to come here.

After all this study and survey, for the most part, the wreck was determined to be relatively stable, but by the late '80s and early '90s we started looking at the *Monitor* in a whole different light. It iwas, after all, an iron ship in salt water. It did not take a brain surgeon, a conservator, or an archeologist to figure out that it was destined to fall apart. There is a rate of deterioration with wrought-iron and cast-iron metals. It works out to be about a tenth of a millimeter a year. Based on that, parts of the *Monitor* no longer existed.

In 1991, an incident took place that changed everything. The Coast Guard caught a private fishing vessel out of Cape Hatteras illegally anchored on the site. In such circumstances, Coast Guard regulations forbid a vessel from cutting its anchor unless officials can physically escort the vessel back to shore. They were about to do just that when they received a distress call three miles farther out. When the Coast Guard left the scene, the fishing boat raised its anchor and when it did, it cracked open the back of the wreck like an egg. It was hooked into the propeller shaft or the skeg—we are not certain exactly which—but the end result was that an area that was relatively stable in the stern and stabilized with the covering marine growth— the concretion that grows on it—was suddenly and dramatically destabilized. That is when we started crying wolf, saying, "The *Monitor*'s falling apart, the *Monitor*'s falling apart." We had corrosion experts come out and look the site and they told us that the *Monitor*, as a shipwreck, was going to be unrecognizable in ten years. We could not sit by and let that happen.

Fortunately, John Broadwater, our director, was at last given a mandate from Congress to revise our management plan and come up with a plan for what we wanted to do with the *Monitor*. The problem was, they did not give us any money. This is where our partners came out of the woodwork to help us. We came up with a management plan that took two years to draft. We sent it out for peer and public review. It covered the gauntlet of options from literally doing nothing and letting nature take its course, allowing the wreck to naturally deteriorate and fall apart (fortunately everybody agreed that was just a tremendous waste), down to reburying the site completely until new technologies might, in fifty or sixty years, allow us to return and perhaps raise the entire vessel.

It proved impossible to raise the entire vessel. The *Monitor* is an ironclad, made of iron and wood, and these materials require different treatment. So even if we did recover the entire hull, it would have come apart and realistically it would never have been put back together to a point where any of us could recognize it. Raising the entire vessel was just not feasible. Our next preferred option was to try to stabilize portions of the hull and recover some of its key components. The main component was obviously the turret, which is the one piece of the *Monitor* everyone wanted to see. Because of the collapse that took place in 1991, we went out in 1998 on a shoestring budget and worked with a local dive organization, the United States Navy Mobile Diving and Salvage Unit 2 out of Little Creek.

Archeology and salvage: two bad words to start mixing together. This is what the professional community told us: You cannot do this with United States Navy divers because these guys know nothing about archeology. But we gave them archeological supervision, and proved the opposite. They just needed to be told what to do and how to do it, and that is where NOAA came in. We worked with a man who at that time was our prime advocate, Lieutenant Christopher Murray, who is now a captain in the United States Navy. He rented out a contract vessel that was sitting over in Little Creek. For the first time in history, we had non-government divers working with navy divers and we went out and we raised the John Ericsson original.

The propeller also gave us the opportunity to test what we were going to run into in treating some of the large items from the wreck. The conservation process might seem daunting when one sees it first-hand—all a visitor sees is a big old, murky tank of water. But for iron objects, it is basically very simple: reverse electrolysis. Basically one uses a series of electrodes or anodes and, eventually, because sea salts and chlorides have penetrated ferrous metals all the way to the core, you must get these out. Today, the prop looks beautiful. We allowed the marine growth that was covering it to tell us when it was ready to come off; we did not peel it off. Iron submerged in salt water goes through a molecular change until the surface becomes almost graphite, and it sticks to marine growth better than it does to the metal itself. So, if one allows that surface to solidify in its own time, that marine concretion starts peeling off when it is ready. In the case of the propeller, we got down to the original mold and pattern marks on the blade.

The *Monitor* is also a story of humans. The human aspect jumped out at us one day six months further into conservation. We were cleaning the propeller and found the initials WK chiseled into one the blades. We told everyone we didn't do it. Then we learned that when the *Monitor* went to the Washington Navy Yard in October 1862 for an overhaul, they scraped her bottom, and evidently one of the yard workers felt bold enough to leave his mark on history.

After we got the prop up, a comprehensive plan was finalized in 1998, and everything was given approval. Congress told us we had done a great job, go to it. They still did not give us any money. So, again, we went back to our partners and everybody jumped forward and agreed that the next logical step in order to get the turret up was to first get the steam engine out. The steam engine itself is an incredibly complex piece of machinery. We were looking at going out and recovering something that was 26 feet wide overall and 18–20 feet long with a bunch of appendages hanging off a cast iron cylinder. It is a combination of materials: brass, glass, bronze, leather, cork, steel, cast iron, and wrought iron. All these metals react differently in a marine environment. The one thing we did not want to have to do was disassemble the steam engine under water. We wanted to make sure that if we brought it up, we brought it up intact and that it would make it to the museum intact.

The engineering firm with which we worked at the time came up with a concept to raise this high-rise lying upside down at the bottom of the ocean. We knew we had not seen half of the engine because it had been buried. So we knew we were going to have to excavate it and gently lift it up out of the wreck until we were sure it was free, and then bring it to the surface. To be able to rig the engine and gently lift it up out of the wreck had a tremendous amount of appeal to us because otherwise we would have had to rig it and snatch it up off the bottom just to keep the dynamic motion from the sea from slamming it into the bottom.

We threw a multitude of tools at the *Monitor*. One thing we have learned over the years is that we have an incredibly long list of what does not work at 240-feet off Cape Hatteras. The list of what does work is much smaller. Realistically, it came down to men on the bottom of the ocean with hammers and chisels, popping rivets until we freed the engine from the site. Then, twenty-eight days after we started, we lifted it up, brought it back, and put it on a transport barge. We did not lose a piece or a part off the engine.

After we recovered the engine, we knew that the next big step was to get the *Monitor*'s gun turret up. As a design for a warship, it was very innovative. As a construction process, it was pretty unremarkable. John Ericsson never bothered to patent the revolving gun turret because he said there was never a time in his life that he did not know the concept of a revolving gun turret. He was simply the first person ever to put it into play. The turret is made of eight layers of 1-inch-thick iron plate, bolted together around a small skeletal structure. (One of my jobs in the recovery process was to learn how the ship was put together so we could best figure out how to take it apart.)

Because the gun turret, too, was upside down, we had to deal with the 11-inch Dahlgren guns as well. But the first big issue was the roof. The turret roof made a great roof, but a miserable floor. Unfortunately, that is what we confronted, because it had come to rest upside down. It was a compression fit. Ericsson originally wanted to hermetically seal the turret, as he referred to it, with a solid plate roof. The Navy Department insisted that there was a very human need for sailors to see daylight. So Ericsson agreed to put a perforation in the roof. We thought we knew what a perforated roof would look like based on later-class monitors. We know now that we were wrong. We could have just gone down and hooked rigging onto the turret and lifted the cylinder to the top, but that is all we would have had; we would have had the cylinder, but lost the contents. The first night we were doing the excavations, we hit both cannons, which made me happy, but realistically, I had no doubt they were there, because the guns could never have come free of the truss system of diagonal braces.

We faced the additional possibility of encountering human remains. It was unheard of to think we were going to lift this to the surface and just take a chance that the roof was going to hold and drop, so we kept going round the table. Even when the steam engine was out, we faced an armored belt sitting on top of it; armor 5 feet high, and 36 inches thick. To get the armor belt off to get access to the turret, we were going to have to remove an approximately 45-foot-long section of armor belt and 29-foot x 40-foot section of the deck. The decking was not that big a problem because the deck was starting to crumble before our very eyes. Deck plates were dropping off and falling off and falling down around the turret. We knew we had to get this off quickly, because if the wreck collapsed down around the turret, in all likelihood it would destroy the turret completely.

As I noted, we had a long list of what works off Hatteras, a longer list of what does not, and what does not work well at 240 feet are hydraulics. Hydraulic tools are what we were primarily relying on to cut it, and they were not working. We had tools that would cut wood, we had tools that would cut iron. We did not have a combination tool that would cut wood and iron to everybody's satisfaction. Navy divers were going to have to go in and disassemble sections of the armor belt by hand. From the archeological historical viewpoint, we thought this was great—we were going to see how this thing was put together.

We knew the plates had to have a stagger pattern on them but we did not know exactly what it was, and we were going to learn all this in the process. The problem we faced is that while pieces of the deck around the turret were crumbling away to nothing, the armor belt had given us no indication that it was even starting to sag or drop anywhere along the turret. That meant that it was in incredibly good condition. Ship worms had made their way in to the armor belt and bottom plate, but as you got down into it where the armor was the thickest, the wood was perfect. We encountered 140-year old oak that was as shiny and as good as the day the ship was made—just waterlogged. That was pretty impressive, but it made the job of cutting it tremendously difficult. We had to go in and use an underwater oxygen acetylene torch and burn the spike-heads to a point that they would collapse so we could jack the plates away.

The one tool found that did work flawlessly was a 20,000 PSI water gun. The Navy calls it a hydro-blaster. It's like the 7-foot-long robo-gun that one uses to wash a car, except this would take the paint right off. It did a beautiful job of cutting the wood. Once we could go in and cut gaps in the wood, navy divers could come back down with rods and cut the spikes until we actually started separating the large sections of the armor belt. Ultimately, we picked up an entire 45-foot section, swung it 50 feet out from the wreck and sat it back down, and it was in beautiful condition.

There was a lot of angst on-site because we knew that as soon as we lifted the deck and the armor belt off the top, we were going to lose visibility. One thing about Hatteras, it always kicks our butts when we are working out there: the bottom currents slow down the work and make it impossible to see. We got to a point when we had no bottom currents for a week; the Gulf Stream went away, and all the particulate matter we put in suspension in the water column stayed there. We lost site of the turret and the armor belt, and stopped working.

When we were able to lift the deck and the armor belt, we also dropped a tremendous amount of debris back down into the site. That debris was primarily coal because, as I mentioned, when the *Monitor* sank stern first, the outboard sides of her hull on the aft-end section were coal bunkers. When the *Monitor* left Hampton Roads, she was fully provisioned, with 40 tons per bunker. We knew we were going to revert to the old navy tradition of coal heaving. There was no other way.

So, how did we get this thing up off the bottom? We did not have the money for a gigantic turret recovery structure, besides which it was not really feasible. There were several early concepts. The navy liked some and we did not. We liked others and the navy did not. Then, one day, our engineers arrived all grinning and unveiled a plan we all knew would work. It was called the spider and the claw and it addressed all the concerns we had about being able to safely get the turret off the bottom. The theory was to lower the spider down, jet into position over the turret, pick it up, set it over, put it on a platform, and then cinch everything back together snatch it up off the bottom. It sounds easy, but realistically it was anything but. Yet it worked.

Once the excavation had gone far enough inside, the turret was rigged and picked up. The crane boomed it around and, with the two stabbing guides, it hooked it and set it back on the bottom. Picture perfect. Nothing to it. Everything works this flawlessly off Cape Hatteras. The reality of it is, when we set the spider in the water, it hit a piece of deck plate on the bottom and it scraped the side of the turret; it took us almost two extra weeks to get it into position. Murphy doesn't live there, but he spends a lot of time off Hatteras. After we had cleared all the debris, and we got everything in place, divers went around with pinch bars and poked and prodded the bottom, checking to see if we somehow we missed a deck plate. At first, there was a whole bunch of unhappy faces. The claw scraped the side of the turret, but it did no damage. It actually did us a favor because it allowed the divers to slowly jet each leg into position. We hooked it to a couple of points forward in the wreck and, with a "comealong" as we excavated it, pulled the whole thing forward and it settled right down on top of the turret. All we had to do was jack the legs back into position. But we began running out of money because it took so long to get the claw structure into position. Then, three days before we were scheduled to leave, a tropical depression formed north of us, one formed south, and yet another gathered steam on top of us. Then the currents came back, and we could not even get a diver in the water. I watched a surface diver crawl across the bottom and jump off the stage; the current took him like a kite. When he finally hit bottom, he had to crawl across on his hands and knees, using his dive knife just to get back so that we did not have to pull him up by his helmet.

Somehow, on an August day, we lifted the turret, brought it to the surface. I have worked many ocean recoveries, but this is, without doubt, one of the more flawless ever. The turret came up in beautiful condition, better than any of us could have ever hoped. The recovery structure proved its merits: nothing moved.

We still had a couple of days left on site, but we were unable to back into the water and get to work because the currents persisted and we were unable to leave the turret sitting on deck. We had to get it back to The Mariners' Museum. As great as my job is, this is where my job got better, because we did not have to empty the turret completely, all the way down to the contents. We were able to do the majority of the excavation here at the museum in a controlled environment.

Inside the turret is a great place to go to work. You look around, see the port cannon, the side of the carriage, the grunion and the barrel running out. Amazingly, the gun ports are still blocked. Of course, there was a lot of mud, a lot of dead and dying marine life which had to be removed. As nice a place as it was to come to work, it smelled awful. The more we worked, the more the excavation proceeded, the more details we found. We had a list of what we were hoping to find inside. But a gun turret is a weapon of war, not something in which sailors kept personal effects. Yet we did have accounts of sailors trying to leave the ship before it sank, and officers telling them they could not take their sea bags, to throw them back. So, were they on top of the turret, or inside on the berth deck? What we found were some of the historic features that we all talk about in the *Monitor:* the diagonal braces, and the breach of the starboard gun. Ericsson, being the genius that he was, also designed the turret to take dents. The whole purpose of the armor was for cannon balls to hit and bounce off, and we found the dents.

We also found remains: two incredibly articulated sailors. This is where our partners jumped in. The skeleton remains were removed, we sent them out to the military's Central Identification Laboratory in Hawaii and they began working putting names to the faces so we do not have to re-inter them in a national cemetery as unknown sailors off the USS *Monitor*. In abandoning ship that fateful night, one survivor must have realized that he was wearing a big old sailor's wool overcoat, and he was not going to go swimming in it, so he tossed it off. As the excavation ran on, we found all the buttons for that U.S. Navy overcoat.

The state of preservation inside the turret was amazing. We believe the turret silted up and buried within months after the vessel sank. This is where we found the lion's share of the good material: a fine shot ladle, for example, and an 11-inch rope-handled rammer head once used to shove cannonballs into the Dahlgren guns. It was not a glamorous job. Those people who remained outside in cold weather sifted through freezing buckets of mud that we were bringing out from the wreck. Others thought they kept smelling kerosene. Actually, they were smelling pine tar because there was a tremendous amount of rope everywhere in the turret and all we found were just pieces and parts and fragments.

Just underneath one box we found a beautifully preserved officer's boot. Because we had already found two skeletal remains, the first thing we thought was: did we have a third guy? The other two still had their boots on. We were pretty glad to see there were no bones inside this one. Later, we found the sole for it nearby. Behind the roof rails, all the way down, we excavated to the gun slides, revealing a unique feature of the *Monitor* itself: the diagonal braces in which the original cannons rested. When they first lifted and tested the turret at the Continental Ironworks, it was reported a failure because it would not lift up off the deck. This is when the term "Ericsson's Folly" came into use. We knew historically, via text, that the way Ericsson fixed the problem was to cut those diagonal braces and add turnbuckles. Merely by jacking the turret up its central shaft, they could actually tighten up the turret with these turnbuckles and it helped raise it up off the deck. But there is no surviving plan describing this design innovation, and no one alive had ever seen them. Then there are the gun carriages themselves—the only ones of their kind ever built. They were Ericsson's design specifically for the *Monitor*, rescued almost intact as well.

History did tell us that at the Washington Navy Yard after Hampton Roads, the *Monitor*'s guns were engraved to commemorate the battle between the *Monitor* and the *Virginia*. History says one cannon read "*Monitor*-Merrimac-Ericsson," and the other, "*Monitor*-Merrimac-[John]Worden." When we found the guns, we did not know what to expect but there it was: on the starboard gun, *Er* and *on*—the remains of the name *Ericsson*. And then, digging down to the roof rails, we found silverware—the last thing we ever expected to encounter in the wreck. Its condition was phenomenal.

Francis Butts was a sailor onboard the *Monitor* and is directly responsible for the question most often asked about the *Monitor*. Butts claims to have been the lone sailor inside the *Monitor*'s turret—he claims to have been a lot of places that he probably was not. But he also made the claim that he took the *Monitor*'s scared, wet, agitated, howling, black cat and for its own safety placed it into the muzzle of one of the guns and then put the tamping back in. I do not believe the story—for several reasons. For instance, Butts claimed to be the only person in the turret that fateful night—but that is the only way in or out of the vessel. Has anyone ever tried to take a wet, agitated cat and stuff it into an 11-inch opening?

Still, the more we dug, the more we researched, and the more human the story seemed to all of us involved with the project. There was the spoon engraved "Jacob Nichols, Norman K. Atwater, George Fred Ericsson, Samuel Augee Lewis." These were four officers who were all lost onboard the USS *Monitor* when she sank on December 31, 1862. It is a story of people, not just a story of battle and combat, and that how we came to view the story of the *Monitor* when we took her out of her underwater grave and brought her artifacts, large and small, to The Mariners' Museum.

PORTFOLIO

Highlights from The Monitor Center Collection

The revolving gun turret of the U.S.S. *Monitor*—designer John Ericsson's history-altering technological innovation—ended up resting face down, beneath the weight of the ship's hull, when the ironclad sank off Cape Hatteras on December 31, 1862. But it was successfully brought to the surface by the National Oceanic and Atmospheric Administration and the U.S. Navy on August 6, 2002, and transferred to The Mariners' Museum a few days later. The turret, currently undergoing conservation to remove more than 140 years of encrustation, will be the centerpiece of the new U.S.S. *Monitor* Center at The Mariners' Museum. It is seen here being hoisted from the ocean floor; resting in its newly designed conservation tank; and from above, lying in the tank upside down. (MNMS.2002.001.185A)

"I have the honor to report that the engines and propeller of the Ericsson Battery have been operated by steam this day and that their performance was highly satisfactory." So telegraphed the Union Navy's Chief Engineer and Superintendent, Alban C. Stimers, on December 31, 1861—ironically, one year to the day before the *Monitor* sank. This is the original, vibrating side-lever engine, recovered by Navy divers in July 2001, and now resting upside down in a solution of sodium hydroxide to arrest the corrosion process while conservators work on the engine. The 400-horsepower engine consists of hundreds of separate pieces made from different materials. Before John Ericsson developed this compact design in the 1840s, steam engine pistons took up far more space, and were vulnerable to enemy fire since they rose above the waterline. (MNMS.2001.003.230)

Usually portrayed blasting away at the C.S.S. *Virginia* in all the period paintings and prints of the Battle of Hampton Roads, these XI-inch Dahlgren guns of the U.S.S. *Monitor*, each more than ten feet long, were made at the West Point Foundry in Cold Spring, New York, in 1859. The cast-iron guns were still in place, inside the ironclad's turret, when it was recovered from the *Monitor* National Marine Sanctuary. On September 9, 2004, crews from Northrup Grumman Newport News, NOAA, and The Mariners' Museum gingerly removed the guns and placed them in separate conservation tanks for restoration. The two guns were engraved in large letters at the Washington Navy Yard seven months after the Battle of Hampton Roads: *Monitor and Merrimac / Worden* and *Monitor & Merrimac / Ericsson*, re-christened for the commander and inventor of the ironclad, respectively. (MNMS.2002.001.469

Another extraordinary relic of the Union's first ironclad warship is its 1,300-pound anchor, before and after restoration, and now on display at The Mariners' Museum. (MNMS.1987.002.03A)

The original brass engine register of the *Monitor*, 10-3/8 x 4-3/4 inches in size, was mounted to the engine with four fasteners. A visible dent was probably caused by impact during the fatal shipwreck of December 31, 1862. The engraved inscription reads: *Monitor / Engine Register / 1862.* (MNMS.2001.003.210)

This unbroken brass, copper, and glass engine room thermometer still features such plainly visible inscriptions as: "Blood Heat," "Fever Heat," "Water Boils," and "Zero." Thermometers such as this one would have measured the intense temperatures inside the *Monitor* during the summer of 1862. (NMS.2001.003.133)

The original cast-iron *Monitor* propeller, before and after initial restoration, is nine-feet in diameter. The *Monitor* moved at achingly slow speed, yet it was considerably faster than the lumbering *Virginia*. (MNMS.1998.001.03A)

The ironclad's brass reversing wheel, more than two feet in diameter, is riddled with dents, cuts, gouges, and pits—though restoration experts and historians have yet to offer conclusions about how the damage occurred. (MNMS.2001.003.024)

A surviving, restored metal-and-glass lantern from the *Monitor*, manufactured by W. M. Porter in New York, was recovered from the sea bottom in 1977, lying in the sand near the ironclad's turret. Shown before and after restoration, it originally hung inside the vessel on a leather strap. The damage found to the glass is consistent with thermal shock that would have occurred when the hot lens of a lighted lantern plunged into cold water. Researchers discovered fragments of manufacturer Porter's name on what was left of the maker's label, and later found Porter himself—identified as a "lantern maker"—listed in the New York City directories for 1859–1861. (MNMS.1987.002.02)

These lantern sconces were recovered from the officers' wardroom and the engine room in 2001. Subsequent conservation of these and other gimbals revealed their beauty, testifying to inventor Ericsson's desire to create elegantly appointed interiors for the *Monitor*, including such crucial amenities as artificial light for the underwater sections of the vessel. But handsome as they were, the devices still did not illuminate the interiors to the satisfaction of the crew. "I have…seen no room as handsomely fitted up as ours," admitted Assistant Paymaster William Keeler. "The only objection is they are too dark. I have all my writing to [sic] by candle light & lamps are always burning in the ward room." (MNMS.2001.003.206)

A copper alloy bomb fuse, inscribed *ORD D* with a stamped anchor, and dated 1861, was recovered by NOAA some thirteen feet forward of the midships bulkhead. (MNMS.2002.001.157)

This dark-green glass wine bottle was probably in the officers' quarters when the *Monitor* sank, and somehow survived intact. (MNMS.1990.001.036)

A plain ironstone pitcher, made sometime after 1845 by Furnival & Co. in England, was also discovered intact in the wreck.
(MNMS.2000.002.08)

One of the most intensely personal of all the relics found in the ironclad's underwater grave is this ca. 1862 hair comb, patented by Goodyears in 1851, and stamped *U. S. Navy*. The comb is made of gutta percha (black hard rubber), and like the combs of today, has wider teeth on one side, narrower on the other. (MNMS.2002.001.203)

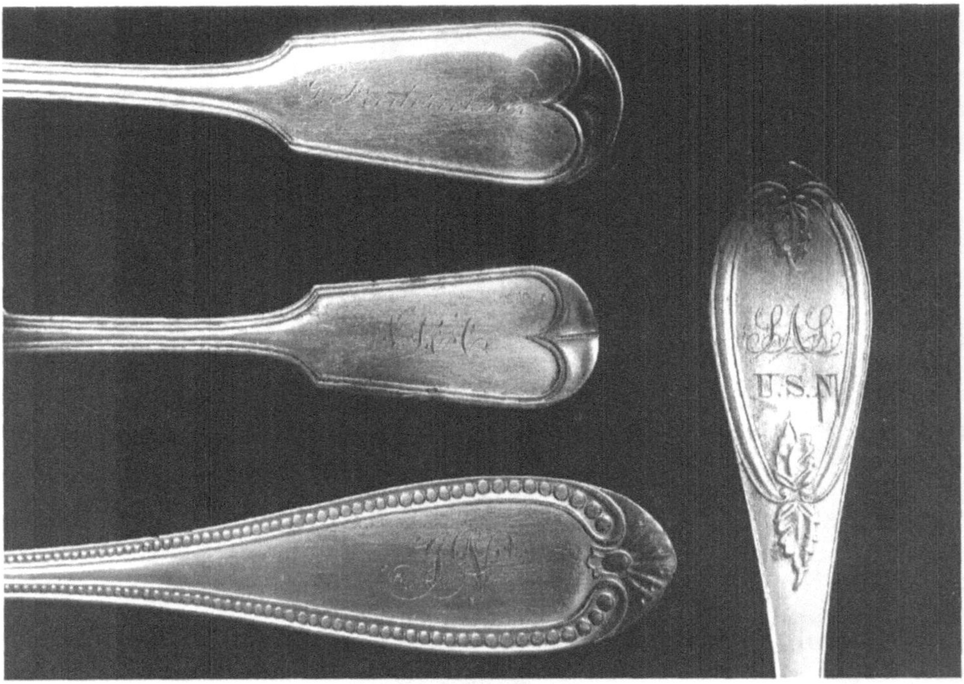

A number of metal spoons and forks have been unearthed in and around the *Monitor* wreck site off Cape Hatteras, some silver-plated, some extravagantly patterned, and others boasting the monogrammed naval insignia *USN*. Such artifacts vividly recall day-to-day life on board the ironclad. (MNMS.2002.001.438; 2002.001.204)

The *Monitor* was well outfitted with tools for emergency repairs, including these copper soldering irons, each boasting two puncture holes for hafting. (MNMS.2002.1-82-83-84)

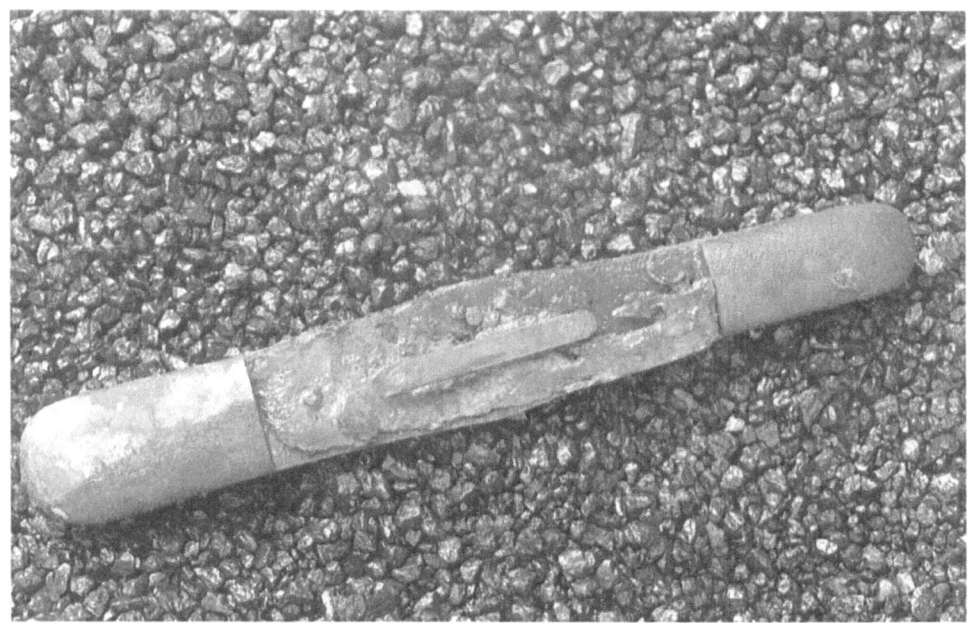

What is left of a four-inch-long metal pocketknife, badly rusted, suggests that it once featured an iron case with as many as two blades. The relic still boasts the remains of wooden-panel inlays. It undoubtedly belonged to one of the *Monitor's* crew. (MNMS.2002.001/193)

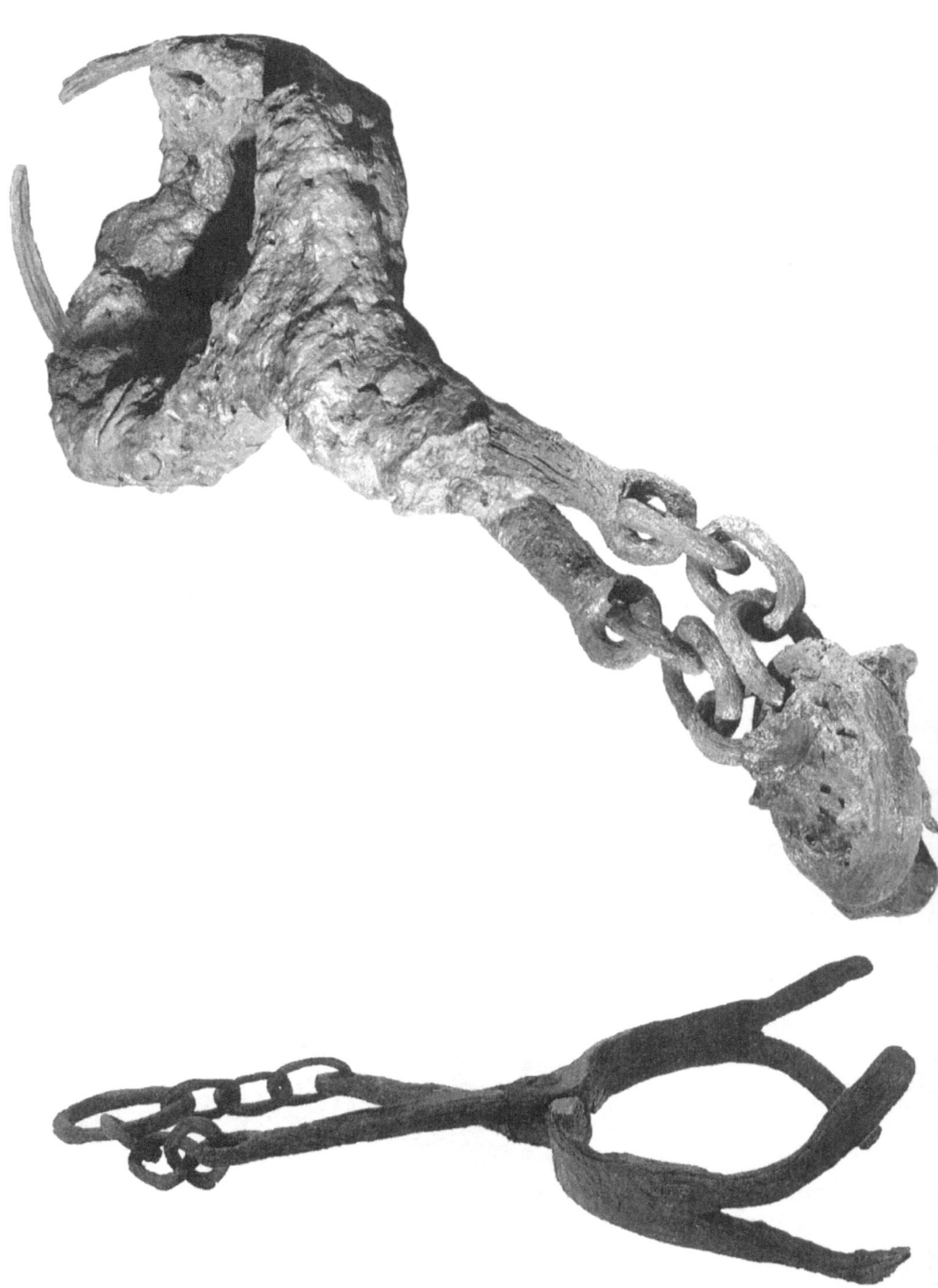

This wrought iron shot hook was used to raise and lower eleven-inch shot, weighing nearly 170 pounds each, into the *Monitor's* turret. The tongs worked with a scissor-like motion. (MNMS.2002.001.453)

Lieutenant John Lorimer Worden, commander of the U.S.S. *Monitor*, never achieved the fame of the ironclad's inventor, John Ericsson—perhaps because an injury during the Battle of Hampton Roads took him out of action in the midst of the historic fray. But Worden was famous enough to inspire this wartime engraving by New York printmaker John Chester Buttre, after a photograph by B. A. Lewis. This copy was presented to Worden by one J. M. Hudnut some twenty-three years after the battle: on April 30, 1885. Worden preserved it in his personal album. (The Library at The Mariner's Museum, PP 2559)

These eight *carte-de-visite* photographs of the *Monitor* crew were preserved in the album assembled by Lieutenant Worden. The veterans portrayed here, clockwise from upper left, are: Paymaster William Keeler; Executive Officer Samuel Dana Greene; Third Assistant Engineer Mark Sunstrom; Second Assistant Engineer Albert B. Campbell; Assistant Engineer John Watters III; Acting Lieutenant William Flye; Captain's Clerk Daniel Toffey; and Acting Master Louis Napoleon Stodder. (The Library at The Mariners' Museum, PP 2534, 2530, 2563, 2536, 2556, 2527, 2551, and 2535).

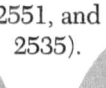

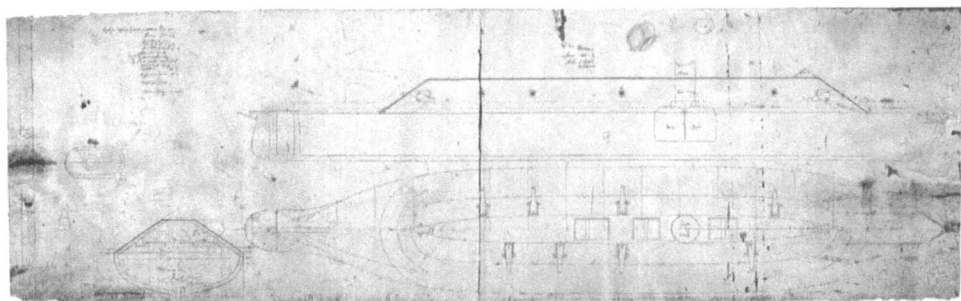

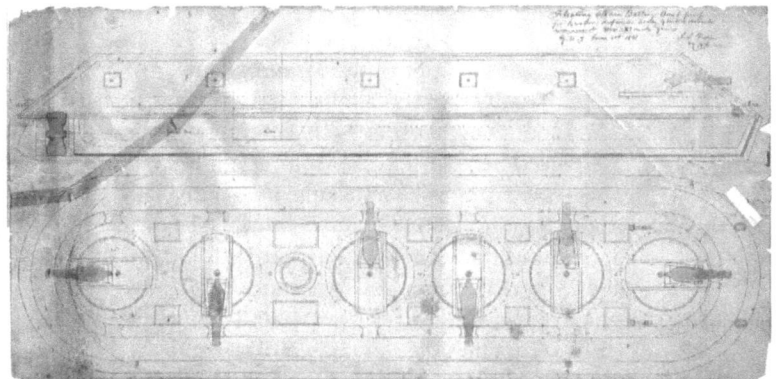

Among The Mariners' Museum's most significant recent acquisitions are these three historic, original design drawings for the *Monitor's* Hampton Roads adversary, the C.S.S. *Virginia*. The drawings, by Confederate Naval Constructor John Luke Porter, were tailored to the suggestions of Lieutenant John Mercer Brooke, who proposed an ironclad design with a casemate housing a battery of rifled guns. Porter adapted the concept to the recovered hull of the *Merrimack*, and later supervised the transformation of the old wooden frigate into an ironclad, creating all the project's plans. Shown on the following pages are Porter's Elevation and Plan View of a Floating Steam Battery, his Plan View for gun placement, and a hand-drawn cross-section. (The Library at the Mariners' Museum, CN 1650, 1651, 1655)

AFTERWORD

About The Mariners' Museum: The Collections

LOCATED IN A 550-ACRE PARK IN NEWPORT NEWS, VIRGINIA, The Mariners' Museum was founded in 1930 by Archer M. Huntington, son of the railroad magnate Collis P. Huntington. Archer Huntington was also a donor to libraries and other cultural institutions around the country. Unlike other maritime museums in the United States that specialize in U.S. naval and marine history, Mr. Huntington made the mission of the Museum to highlight "the culture of the sea"; all the world was to be represented, and today The Mariners' Museum continues to fulfill that mission.

The Mariners' Museum, one of the largest and most comprehensive maritime history museums in the world, houses a treasure trove of more than 35,000 items inspired by human experiences with the sea. For over seventy years, the Mariners' has illustrated the spirit of seafaring adventure, assembling a renowned and strikingly diverse collection of maritime artifacts including 90 figureheads; almost 1,500 ship models; more than 700 navigational instruments; archives holding more than 600,000 historical photographic prints and negatives; and more than 11,000 paintings, prints, drawings, engravings, and watercolors, including splendid examples of the Bard brothers James and John, Robert Salmon, Antonio Jacobsen, James Buttersworth, Fitz Hugh Lane, and Montague Dawson, among other masters. The Museum is also home to the third-largest maritime library in the world, with a collection of books, maps, charts, manuscripts, photographs, and other items that chronicle six centuries of maritime history. And now, the remains of one of the most famous ships in history, the USS *Monitor*, will find a permanent home in the USS *Monitor* Center, which will open in 2007.

The Mariners' Museum is currently in the middle of a $30 million capital campaign to raise funds for the construction of the Center, which will serve as the definitive national authority and repository for materials, research, and programming related to the history of the *Monitor* and the larger, and lesser known, story of the naval history of the Civil War. The USS *Monitor* Center is being developed in partnership with the National Oceanic and Atmospheric Administration.

The Museum's permanent galleries display incredible treasures. Among them Captain John Smith's map of the Chesapeake Bay, poet Robert Browning's gondola, the oldest known of its type in existence, and the polar bear figurehead from the vessel of Admiral Richard Byrd on his Antarctic expedition in the 1930s. All reflect the human use of the sea for transportation, commerce, food, battle, and pleasure.

The spectacular first-order lighthouse lens from the Cape Charles lighthouse welcomes visitors to The Mariners' fascinating *Chesapeake Bay Gallery*. Thematic exhibit areas interpret the Bay's early history, watermen, shipbuilding and military complexes, navigation, commerce, and recreation. Historical photographs, a working steam engine, fiber optic maps, videos, and hands-on activities complement the hundreds of maritime artifacts on display.

The Mariners' *Age of Exploration Gallery* chronicles the developments in shipbuilding, ocean navigation, and cartography that made the voyages of the sixteenth through eighteenth centuries possible. Ship models, rare books, illustrations, maps, navigational instruments, and other artifacts help bring the gallery to life. A hands-on "Discovery Library" allows visitors to examine reproductions of early navigational instruments and books.

The hallmark of The Mariners' Museum's collection is *The Miniature Ships of August F. Crabtree*, one of its most popular exhibits. From a primitive raft to a Venetian galleass decorated with 359 carved figures, these exquisitely detailed miniature ships depict the evolution of boatbuilding in an unparalleled display of craftsmanship by artist and carver August F. Crabtree.

Other galleries include the *Great Hall of Steam*, which offers a visual display of maritime steam engine history, and *Defending the Seas*, which tells the story of the U.S. Navy's important role in our nation's past, present, and future.

The International Small Craft Center, which opened on May 17, 2003, houses more than seventy-five vessels from thirty-six countries, including a gondola from Italy, canoes from Africa, sampans from China and Burma, and original mahogany Chris-Craft vessels.

The Library at The Mariners' Museum houses more than 78,000 volumes, 600,000 historic photographs, and one million archival items—including the boatbuilding archives of Chris-Craft Industries through the early 1980s.

The Museum Shop offers a unique collection of maritime books, prints, jewelry, and gifts. Visitors can also explore the 550-acre Mariners' Museum Park, which features the Noland Trail, a five-mile walking trail with scenic sites overlooking Lake Maury.

Notes

Preface
HAROLD HOLZER

1. William O. Stoddard, *Inside the White House in War Times* (New York: Charles L. Webster, 1890), 39.
2. Nathaniel Hawthorne, "Chiefly About War-Matters. By a Peaceable Man," *Atlantic Monthly* 10 (July 1862): 57–58.

2. Building the Ironclads
CRAIG L. SYMONDS

1. The largest naval guns of World War II were on the Japanese superbattleships *Yamato* and *Musashi,* each of which carried nine 18.1-inch guns in three turrets. The largest American naval guns of World War II were the 16-inch guns on the *Iowa*-class battleships.
2. Lincoln's proclamation of a blockade (April 19 and 27, 1861) is in Roy S. Basler, ed., *The Collected Works of Abraham Lincoln* (New Brunswick, N.J.: Rutgers University Press, 1953), 4:338–39, 346–47.
3. Craig L. Symonds, *The U.S. Naval Institute Historical Atlas of the U.S. Navy* (Annapolis, Md.: Naval Institute Press, 1994), 80–85.
4. Mallory to his wife, August 31, 1862, Stephen Mallory Papers, P.K. Yonge Library, University of Florida; Mallory to Congress, May 8, 1861, *Official Records of the Union and Confederate Navies in the War of the Rebellion* (Washington: U.S. Government Printing Office, 1894–1922), series 2, 1:742 (hereafter *ORN*).

5. John M. Brooke, "The Plan and Construction of the Merrimac," in *Battles and Leaders of the Civil War* (New York: Century, 1887–89), 1:715–16 (hereafter *B&L*); Jon L. Porter, untitled essay, *B&L*, 1:716–7; J. Thomas Scharf, *The Confederate States Navy* (New York: Rogers & Sherwood, 1887), 1:145–7; Craig L. Symonds and Harold Holzer, "Who Designed the CSS *Virginia*?" *Military History Quarterly* (autumn 2003): 6–14.

6. Indeed, the deep draft of the *Virginia* (22 feet) greatly inhibited its movements in the Battle of Hampton Roads.

7. Investigation of the Navy Department, February 26, 1863, *ORN*, series II, 1:783–4; Scharf, *Confederate States Navy*, 1:147.

8. John Quarstein, *CSS Virginia: Mistress of Hampton Roads* (Appomattox: H. E. Howard, 2000), 36–39.

9. Mallory to Conrad, May 8, 1861, *ORN*, series II, 1:742: Quarstein, *CSS Virginia*, 36; Charleston Mercury (October 30, 1861).

10. John Niven, *Gideon Welles* (New York: Oxford University Press, 1973), 365–66.

11. Bushnell to Welles, March 9, 1877, *B&L*, 1:748.

12. Ibid.

13. Ibid.

14. Smith to Worden, January 11, 1862, *ORN*, series I, 6:515; Welles, "The Building of the Monitor," *B&L*, 1:731n; Worden to Smith, January 13, 1861, *ORN*, series I, 1: 516.

15. Keeler to his wife, February 28, 1862, in Robert W. Daly, ed., *Aboard the USS Monitor: 1862* (Annapolis, Md.: Naval Institute Press, 1964), 18.

16. Ibid.

17. Subsequent testing proved that the 11-inch guns in the *Monitor* could have handled a charge as large as 30 pounds. With such a charge it is almost certain that the *Monitor*'s guns could have blasted holes in the *Virginia*'s iron casemate.

18. Keeler to his wife, February 28, 1862, in Daly, *Aboard the USS Monitor*, 18; George Geer to his wife, March 2, 1862, in William Marvel, ed., *The Monitor Chronicles* (New York: Simon & Schuster, 2000), 20.

19. Keeler to his wife, serial letter dated March 6, 1862, in Daly, *Aboard the USS Monitor*, 27.

20. William C. Davis, *Duel Between the First Ironclads* (Baton Rouge: Louisiana State University Press, 1975), 49.

21. Geer to his wife, March 2, 1862, in Marvel, *The Monitor Chronicles*, 21.

22. John Ericsson, "The Building of the Monitor," *B&L*, 1:741; Keeler to his wife, serial letter dated March 6, 1862, in Daly, *Aboard the USS Monitor*, 27–28.

23. Samuel Greene, "In the Monitor Turret," B&L, 1:721; Keeler to his wife, serial letter dated March 6, 1862, in Daly, *Aboard the USS Monitor*, 28–30.

24. Louis N. Stodder (as told to Albert Stephens Crockett), "Aboard the USS Monitor," *Civil War Times Illustrated* 1 (January 1863): 32; Greene, "In the Monitor Turret," B&L, 1:721; Keeler to his wife, serial letter dated March 6, 1862, in Daly, *Aboard the USS Monitor*, 30–31.

3. Iron Horse, Iron Coffin: Life Aboard the USS Monitor
DAVID MINDELL

1. Keeler's letters were published in Robert Daly, ed., *Life Aboard the U.S.S. Monitor, 1862: The Letters of Acting Paymaster William Fredrick Keeler, U.S. Navy, to His Wife, Anna* (Annapolis, Md.: U.S. Naval Institute, 1964).

2. Geer's letters are in The Mariners' Museum collection.

3. Nathaniel Hawthorne, "Chiefly About War-Matters. By a Peaceable Man," *Atlantic Monthly* 10 (July 1862): 43–61.

4. Greene to his parents, March 14, 1862, U. S. Naval Academy Library, Annapolis, Md., published in David A. Mindell, *War, Technology, and Experience aboard the USS Monitor* (Baltimore: Johns Hopkins University Press, 2000), 66.

5. Ibid., 66; from the Ericsson Papers in the New-York Historical Society.

6. Hawthorne, "Chiefly About War-Matters," 58.

7. John Worden, "The Monitor's First Trip," *Youth's Companion*, August 15, 1895.

8. Hawthorne, "Chiefly About War-Matters," 57.

9. Samuel Dana Greene, "In the Monitor Turret," in Robert Underwood Johnson and Clarence Clough Buell, eds., *Battles and Leaders of the Civil War*, 4 vols. (New York: The Century Company, 1887), 1:725.

10. Goldsborough to Welles, May 12, 1862, in Welles, *Report of the Secretary in Relation to Armored Vessels* (Washington, D.C.: U.S. Government Printing Office, 1864), 21–24, and Mindell, *War, Technology, and Experience*, 94–95.

11. From the Ericsson Papers at the Library of Congress.

12. Drayton to Welles, December 26, 1862, in Welles, *Report of the Secretary*, 31–32.

13. "A World on the Other Side," *Army and Navy Journal*, August 29, 1863; see also Donald Nevius Bigelow, *William Conant Church, and the Army & Navy Journal* (New York: 1952), 97, 153–54.

14. Mindell, *War, Technology, and Experience*, 114–16.

4. Sink Before Surrender: The Story of the CSS Virginia
JOHN V. QUARSTEIN

1. John W. H. Porter, *A Record of Events in Norfolk County, Virginia, from April 19, 1861, to May 10, 1861, with a History of the Soldiers and Sailors of Norfolk County, Norfolk City, and Portsmouth Who Served in the Confederate Army or Navy* (Portsmouth, Va.: W. A. Fiske, 1892), 8.

2. William Norris, "The Story of the Confederate States' Ship "*Virginia*" (Once *Merrimac*): Her Victory Over the *Monitor*; Born March 7th, Died May 10th, 1862" (Baltimore: John B. Piet, 1879): reprint in *Southern Historical Society Papers* (September 1916): 234.

3. *New York Times*, April 22, 1856.

4. Oliver W. Griffiths, "The New War Steamers," *The United States Nautical Magazine*, April 1855, 302–303.

5. Porter, *Norfolk County*, 12.

6. Ibid., 12–13.

7. U.S. Department of the Navy, *Official Records of the Union and Confederate Navies in the War of the Rebellion*, 30 vols. (Washington: U.S. Government Printing Office, 1894–1922), series 1, vol. 4, pp. 277–78 (hereafter cited as *ORN*).

8. John S. Long, "The Gosport Affair," *Journal of Southern History* 23 (May 1957): 155–72.

9. Porter, *Norfolk County*, 13.

10. *Richmond Daily Enquirer*, April 22, 1861.

11. *ORN*, 2, 2:78.

12. Ibid., 67–69.

13. *ORN*, 2, 1: 784.

14. John Mercer Brooke, "The *Virginia* or *Merrimac*: Her Real Projector," *Southern Historical Society Papers* 14 (January 1891): 32–33; Porter, *Norfolk County*, 331–332; *ORN*, 2, 1:784.

15. U.S. Department of the Navy, Subject File of the Confederate States Navy, 1861–1865, file HA, Miscellaneous, box 160, "Narrative of H. Aston Ramsay, Chief Engineer, Confederate States Steamer *Merrimack*, during her Engagements in Hampton Roads, 1862." Microfilm Series, M1091, Roll 13, RG 45, NA (hereafter cited as Ramsay Narrative).

16. *ORN*, 1, 7:758–759.

17. Porter, *Norfolk County*, 338.

18. George M. Brooke Jr., "John Mercer Brooke," 2 vols. (PhD dissertation, University of North Carolina, 1955), 2:763.

19. *ORN*, 1, 6:766.

20. William D. Henderson, *41st Virginia Infantry* (Lynchburg: H. E. Howard, Inc. 1986), 13.

21. John R. Eggleston, "Captain Eggleston's Narrative of the Battle of the Merrimac," *Southern Historical Society Papers* 40 (1916): 168.

22. *ORN*, 1, 6:776–777.

23. U.S. War Department, *The War of the Rebellion: A compilation of the Official Records of the Union and Confederate Armies*, 128 vols. (Washington: U.S. Government Printing Office, 1880–1902), series 1 (hereafter referred to as *OR*), 9:44.

24. Eggleston, 170.

25. Dinwidde Brazier Phillips, "The Career of the Iron-Clad *Virginia*, (formerly the *Merrimac*), Confederate States Navy, March–May 1862," Collections of the Virginia Historical Society (Richmond, Va.: Virginia Historical Society, 1887), 201.

26. Hardin B. Littlepage, "The Career of the *Merrimac-Virginia*: With Some Personal History," in *Voices of the Civil War: The Peninsula*, ed. Paul Mathless (Alexandria, Va.: Time-Life Books, 1997) (hereafter cited as Littlepage, "Career of *Merrimac-Virginia*"), 44.

27. William H. Parker, *Recollections of a Naval Officer, 1841–1865* (New York: Charles Scribner's Sons, 1883), 252.

28. John Taylor Wood, "The First Fight of the Ironclads: March 9, 1862," *Battles and Leaders of the Civil War*, ed. Robert Underwood Johnson and Clarence Clough Buel (New York: Century, 1887), 1:696.

29. Norris, 206.

30. Littlepage, "Career of *Merrimac-Virginia*," 44.

31. Norris, 206.

32. *ORN*, 1, 672.

33. William N. Still, *Iron Afloat: The Story of the Confederate Armourclad* (Nashville: Vanderbilt University Press, 1971), 29.

34. Henry Reaney, "How the Gun-Boat *Zouave* Sided the Congress," *Battles and Leaders of the Civil War*, ed. Robert Underwood Johnson and Clarence Clough Buel (New York: Century, 1887), 1:174–75.

35. John M. Kell, *Recollections of a Naval Life* (Washington, D.C.: Neale, 1900), 283.

36. Norris, 221.

37. *OR*, 4, 1:980.

38. John Taylor Wood Papers, Southern Historical Collection, Louis Round Wilson Library, University of North Carolina, Chapel Hill.

39. Franklin Buchanan Letterbook, 1861–1863, Southern Historical Collection, Louis Round Wilson Library, University of North Carolina, Chapel Hill.

40. *OR*, 1, 4:27.

41. *OR*, 1, 11, part 1:8.

42. "Facts About the Merrimac," *Scientific American*, June 6, 1862, 73.

43. Parker, 272.

44. *ORN*, 1, 7:757.

45. *ORN*, 1, 7:764–765.

46. Norris, 212.

47. *ORN*, 1, 7:764.

48. Robert Chester Foute, "Echoes from Hampton Roads," *Southern Historical Society Papers* 19 (1891): 246.

49. Norris, 212.

50. *ORN*, 1, 7:219.

51. Robert W. Daly, ed., *Aboard the U.S.S. Monitor, 1862: The Letters of Acting Paymaster William Frederick Keeler* (Annapolis, Md.: United States Naval Institute Press, 1964), 73.

52. Wood Papers.

53. Henry Ashton Ramsay, "The Most Famous of Sea Duels, The Story of the *Merrimac*'s Engagement with the *Monitor*, and the Events That Preceded and Followed the Fight, Told by a Survivor," *Harper's Weekly*, February 10, 1912, 12.

54. Ibid.

55. Richard Curtis, *History of the Famous Battle Between the Iron-clad Merrimac, CSN, and the Iron-Clad Monitor and the Cumberland and Congress of the U.S. Navy, March the 8th and 9th 1862, As Seen by a Man at the Gun* (repr. Hampton, Va.: Houston Print and Publishing, 1957), 17.

56. Stephen R. Mallory Diary, Library of Congress, Washington, D.C.

57. Brooke, *John M. Brooke*, 258.

58. S. R. Franklin, *Memoirs of a Rear Admiral* (New York: Harper & Brothers, 1892), 182–83.

5. Believe Only Half of What You Read about the Battle of Hampton Roads
MABRY TYSON

1. G. V. Fox to C. a R. Jones, August 13, 1874, Eleanor S. Brockenbrough Library, Museum of the Confederacy, Richmond, Va.

2. *Official Records of the Union and Confederate Navies in the War of the Rebellion. (ORN)*, 1, 7:762.

3. William Tindall, "The True Story of the *Virginia* and the *Monitor*: The Account of an Eye Witness," *Virginia Magazine of History and Biography* 31 (January and April 1923): 1–38, 89–139.

4. Gertrude Tartt Jones to Col. William Norris, April 1 [1891, year determined from the age of the daughter mentioned]. Eleanor S. Brockenbrough Library, The Museum of the Confederacy, Richmond, Virginia.

5. E. A. Jack, *Memoirs* (from an unpublished typewritten manuscript), undated. Published in Alan B. Flanders and Capt. Neal O. Westfall, eds., *Memoirs of E. A. Jack: Steam Engineer, CSS Virginia* (White Stone, Va.: Brandylane Publishers, 1998), 17 (Brandylane edition).

6. E. V. White, "Merrimac and Monitor," *Norfolk Virginian*, March 23, 1891.

7. Richard F. Fuller, *Chaplain Fuller: Being a Life Sketch of a New England Clergyman and Army Chaplain* (Boston: Walke, Wise, 1863), 213–45.

8. J. T. Headly, *Farragut and our Naval Commanders* (New York: E. B. Treat, 1867), 520.

9. Charles Morris, *Historical Tales, American* (New York: R. H. Whitten, 1893), 277.

10. H. Ashton Ramsay, "Most Famous of Sea Duels: The *Merrimac* and *Monitor*," *Harpers Weekly*, February 10, 1912, 11–12.

11. E. A. Jack, *Memoirs*, 17.

12. In John V. Quarstein, G. Richard Hoffeditz Jr., and J. Michael Moore, *C.S.S. Virginia: Mistress of Hampton Roads* (Appomattox, Va.: H. E. Howard, 2000), the coal consumption is stated as 2,880 pounds per hour. Based on the published tonnage of the *Merrimac* and the relative drafts of the *Merrimac* and *Virginia*, it seems likely that the tonnage of the *Virginia* was around 2,500–3,000 tons. Therefore the ship became about 1 percent lighter and so would lift by about one percent (less, because the shape of the hull) of her draft.

13. Captain Catesby ap Roger Jones, "Services of the *Virginia (Merrimac)*," *Southern Historical Society Papers* 11 (February–March, 1883): 72. Previously published in the *SHSP* in 1874.

14. William Norris, "The Story of the Confederate States Ship (once *Merrimac*). Her Victory over the Monitor Born March 7th, Died May 10th, 1862," *Southern Historical Society Papers* n.s. 42 (October 4, 1917): 204–33.

15. There are too many discrepancies in the descriptions for this position to be considered definitive.

16. William Tindall, "The True Story of the *Virginia* and the *Monitor*," 100.

17. G. V. Fox to G. Welles, March 9, 1862, *ORN*, 1, 7:6.
18. Ibid.
19. John Taylor Wood, "The First Fight of Iron-Clads," *Century Illustrated Monthly Magazine* 29 (March 1885): 738–54.
20. Roy P. Basler, ed., *The Collected Works of Abraham Lincoln*, 8 vols. (New Brunswick, N.J.: Rutgers University Press, 1953–55), 5:154.
21. *Report of the Joint Committee on the Conduct of the War, 37th Congress, Third Session*, March 19, 1862 (Washington, D.C.: Government Printing Office, 1863), 418.
22. *ORN*, 1, 7:12.
23. *ORN*, 1, 7:25.
24. J. Ericsson, "The Working of the '*Monitor*' ", *Scientific American* 7 (March 29, 1862): 194.
25. Lydia Minturn Post, ed., *Soldiers' Letters from Camps, Battle-Field and Prison* (New York: Bunce & Huntington, 1865). Retrieved August 19, 2005, from http:name.umdl.umich.edu/acp4775.
26. J. L. Worden, et al, *The Monitor and the Merrimac: Both Sides of the Story, Told by Lieut. J. L. Worden, U.S.N., Lieut. Greene, U.S.N., of the Monitor and H. Ashton Ramsay, C.S.N., Chief Engineer of the Merrimac* (New York: Harper & Brothers, 1912), 17–18.
27. William Tindall, "The True Story of the *Virginia* and the *Monitor*," 143.
28. U.S. House of Representatives, Committee on Naval Affairs, *Relief of the Officers and Crew of the United States Steamer Monitor Who Participated in the Action with the Rebel Iron-Clad Merrimac, on the 9th day of March, 1862*. 48th Congress, 1st Session, H. Rept. 1725, 1883–1884. This is also published in *SHSP* 13 (1885): 90.
29. Samuel Dana Greene, "In the Monitor Turret," *Century Illustrated Monthly Magazine* 29 (March 1885): 754–63.
30. *ORN*, 1, 7:410.
31. G. V. Fox to C. a R. Jones, September 13, 1874. Eleanor S. Brockenbrough Library, The Museum of the Confederacy, Richmond, Virginia.
32. G. V. Fox to C. a R. Jones, August 13, 1874. Eleanor S. Brockenbrough Library, The Museum of the Confederacy, Richmond, Virginia.
33. G. V. Fox to C. a R. Jones, December 2, 1874. Eleanor S. Brockenbrough Library, The Museum of the Confederacy, Richmond, Virginia.
34. J. Ericsson to G. V. Fox, November 24, 1874. This letter can be found in the previously mentioned 1923 Tindall article, 143, or in W. S. Mabry's *Brief Sketch of the Career of Captain Catesby ap R. Jones* (Selma, Ala.: 1912), n.p.

35. Samuel Howard to E. A. Jack, July 23, 1891, Portsmouth Public Library, Portsmouth, Va..

6. Victory Without Glory? The Battle of Hampton Roads in Art
HAROLD HOLZER

1. John D. Hayes, ed., *Samuel Francis DuPont: A Selection from His Civil War Letters*, 3 vols. (Ithaca: Cornell University Press, 1969), 2:317.

2. For Homer's early work on wartime sketches for prints, see Nicolai Cikovsky, Jr., and Franklin Kelly, *Winslow Homer* (New Haven: Yale University Press, 1993), 393; and Lloyd Goodrich, *The Graphic Art of Winslow Homer* (New York: Museum of Graphic Art, 1969), 10.

3. David D. Porter, *The Naval History of the Civil War* (New York: Sherman Publishing Co., 1886), iv, quoted in Harold Holzer and Mark E. Neely Jr., *Mine Eyes Have Seen the Glory: The Civil War in Art* (New York: Orion Books, 1990), 94–95 (Smith quote, 105). Much of the research in this chapter was conducted by the author and his colleague, Professor Neely, for this book and their subsequent effort, *The Union Image: Popular Prints of the Civil War North* (Chapel Hill: University of North Carolina Press, 2000), esp. 109–28.

4. Nathaniel Hawthorne, "Chiefly about War Matters by a Peaceable Man," *Atlantic Monthly* 10 (1862): 57–59.

5. The 1883 painting by William Heysham Overend, *An August Morning with Farragut: The Battle of Mobile Bay, August 5, 1864*, is in the collection of the Wadsworth Athenaeum in Hartford, Connecticut. For a reproduction see Holzer and Neely, *Mine Eyes Have Seen the Glory*, 117.

6. For reproductions see Holzer and Neely, *Mine Eyes Have Seen the Glory*, 87, 93, 90.

7. Yet another of Currier & Ives's *Monitor-Merrimac* prints claimed the Confederate vessel had not 10, but 11 guns, and yet another included a caption that boasted: "...the *Merrimac* was crippled, and the whole Rebel fleet driven back to Norfolk." The ambitious print did include scenes of nearby Fortress Monroe and several "Rebel steamers." See *Currier & Ives: A Catalogue Raisonné*, 2 vols. (Detroit: Gale, 1984), 2:655.

8. By 1862, Confederate printmaking had virtually ceased to exist, not for lack of patriotism but for lack of manpower and supplies. See Mark E. Neely, Jr., Harold Holzer, and Gabor S. Boritt, *The Confederate Image: Prints of the Lost Cause* (Chapel Hill: University of North Carolina Press, 1987), 3–10.

9. Torgerson's 1881 canvas, *Confederate Blockade Runners in Harbor, Civil War*, is in the West Point Museum, U.S. Military Academy.

10. David McNeely Stauffer, *American Engravers Upon Copper and Steel*, 2 parts (New York: Grolier Club, 1907), 1:208. Pelton produced portraits of Civil War General Ambrose E. Burnside, and two of Lincoln's cabinet officers, Secretary of State William H. Seward and Secretary of War Edwin M. Stanton, among others; see Stauffer 2:410–420.

11. Prang's artist J. D. Davidson based his watercolor of the clash on interviews with surviving crewmembers, recollections by inventor John Ericsson, and discussions with one of the *Virginia's* designer-builders, John L. Porter. Davidson further acknowledged his indebtedness to marine artist Francis A. Silva, who claimed to have witnessed and sketched the battle from the Virginia shoreline. See Louis Prang, *Text to Prang's War Pictures* (Boston: L. Prang, 1886), in Harold Holzer, *Prang's Civil War Pictures: The Complete Battle Chromos of Louis Prang* (New York: Fordham University Press, 2001), 123.

12. Harry T. Peters, *America On Stone: The Other Printmakers to the American People* (New York: Doubleday, 1931), 176–79. Peters hints that much of the firm's best work was produced by artist Charles Parsons, best known for his long association with New York rivals Currier & Ives.

13. S. D. Greene, "Inside the Monitor Turret," *Century Magazine*, March 1885, republished on The Mariners' Museum web site, www.mariner.org, consulted May 9, 2005.

14. See, for example, composer E. Mack's *Monitor Grand March*, illustrated by a lithograph showing the Union ironclad all but ramming her Confederate rival, published by Lee & Walker of Philadelphia in 1862. Original in the sheet music collection of the Library of Congress, published in Neely and Holzer, *The Union Image*, 119.

15. Smith's 1869 canvas, *Engagement Between the U. S. Ericson* [sic] *Battery Monitor and Confederate States Ram Virginia or Merrimac in Hampton Roads, Virginia, Morning of March 9, 1862*, is in the art collection of the Union League Club of Philadelphia; Torgerson's *Battle of Monitor and Merrimac* is in the Chicago Historical Society; and the Stewart image is in The Mariners' Museum collection.

16. Hawthorne, "Chiefly About War-Matters," 58.

17. The undated original gouache on paper, *United States Monitors Riding Out a Gale during the Blockade of Charleston, S.C.*, made the warships look like toys. The original is in the New-York Historical Society.

18. Francis Butts, *My First Cruise at Sea and the Loss of the Iron-Clad Monitor*, personal narrative, privately printed in Providence, Rhode Island, in 1878.

19. Advertising brochure for Endicott & Co. in the Harry T. Peters Collection, Museum of the City of New York.

20. The print, *Battle of Shiloh—April 6th, 1862*, an original of which is in the Chicago Historical Society, is illustrated and discussed in Holzer and Neely, *Mine Eyes Have Seen the Glory*, 182.

7. "This Country Now Occupies the Vantage Ground": Union Monitors vs. the British Navy
HOWARD J. FULLER

1. The *Monitor*'s turret also contains dents from the subsequent, unsuccessful attack against the batteries of Drewry's Bluff, May 15, 1862. Inside the turret are two 11-inch Dahlgren smoothbores. The contents of the guns themselves were described by Francis R. Butts in his account of the sinking of the *Monitor* in a heavy gale off Cape Hatteras on the night of December 29, 1862: "I took off my coat—one that I had received from home only a few days before (I could not feel that our noble little ship was yet lost)—and, rolling it up with my boots, drew the tompion from one of the guns, placed them inside, and replaced the tompion. A black cat was sitting on the breech of one of the guns, howling one of those hoarse and solemn tunes which no one can appreciate who is not filled with the superstitions which I had been taught by the sailors, who are always afraid to kill a cat. I would almost as soon have touched a ghost, but I caught her, and, placing her in another gun, replaced the wad and tompion; but I could still hear that distressing howl." From "The Loss of the *Monitor*," in *Battles and Leaders of the Civil War*, 4 vols., Robert Underwood Johnson and Clarence Clough Buel, eds. (New York: Castle Books, 1887; reprint, 1956), 1:746.

2. See the weighty *Report of the Secretary of the Navy in Relation to Armored Vessels* (Washington, D.C.: U.S. Government Printing Office, 1864) for a full record of monitor reports, pro and con.

3. Quoted from John Ericsson, *Contributions to the Centennial Exhibition* (New York: Nation Press, 1876), 465–6.

4. Kenneth Bourne sees the *Trent* Crisis as "the most dangerous single incident of the Civil War and perhaps in the whole course of Anglo-American relations since 1815," in *Great Britain and the Balance of Power in North America 1815–1908* (London: Longmans, Green, 1967), 251. See also Norman. B. Ferris, *The Trent Affair* (Knoxville: University of Tennessee Press, 1977).

5. *New York Herald*, December 29, 1861.

6. John G. Nicolay and John Hay, *Abraham Lincoln: A History*, 10 vols. (New

York: The Century Co., 1917), 5:35–9. For British preparations for war against the North see the British Public Record Office, Kew (hereafter "P.R.O."), ADM 3/269 (Special Minutes from Board); ADM 128/56 (Correspondence arising out of the Civil War, 1860–65); ADM 1/5766 (from Admiralty, July–December, 1861); ADM 1/5787 (from Admirals 'P', Jamaica 1-592, 1862; W.O. (War Office) 33/11, 1862; and the National Maritime Museum, Greenwich, Milne Papers Collection, MLN/125/1 "Memorandum relative to the Civil War in America"; also Kenneth Bourne, "British Preparations for War with the North, 1861–1862," *English Historical Review* 76 (October 1961): 600–32. "There is a story, derived apparently from the prime minister's private secretary, that Palmerston had opened [cabinet] business by throwing down his hat upon the table, and bluntly telling his colleagues, 'I don't know whether you are going to stand this, but I'll be damned if I do!'" True or not, the story is a good clue to the atmosphere of the occasion. Bourne, *Great Britain*, 219.

7. 23-6-1861, Palmerston to Somerset, Somerset Papers Collection, Aylesbury, Buckinghamshire Record Office, D/RA/A/2A/37, Letters from Viscount Palmerston, 1861.

8. *Congressional Globe*, 37th Congress, 2d Session, Series No. 14, 7-1-1862, 210.

9. "The Defence of Canada," *Blackwood's Edinburgh Magazine*, 91 no. 556 (February 1862): 228. One Congressman was particularly enraged; "every time this *Trent* affair comes up ... I am made to renew the horrible grief which I suffered when the news of the surrender of Mason and Slidell came. I acknowledge it, I literally wept tears of vexation. I hate it; and I hate the British Government. I have never shared in the traditionary hostility of many of my countrymen against England. But I now here publicly avow and record my inextinguishable hatred of that Government. I mean to cherish it while I live, and to bequeath it as a legacy to my children when I die ... Sir, I trust in God that the time is not far distant when we shall have suppressed this rebellion, and be prepared to avenge and wipe out this insult that we have received. We will then stir up Ireland; we will appeal to the Chartists of England; we will go to the old French *habitans* of Canada; we will join hands with France and Russia to take away the eastern possessions of that proud empire, and will darken every jewel that glitters in her diadem," *Congressional Globe*, 37th Congress, 2d Session, Series No. 21, January 14, 1862, 333.

10. James Tertius DeKay, *Monitor: The Story of the Legendary Civil War Ironclad and the Man Whose Invention Changed the Course of History* (Pimlico, London: Random House, 1999), 73. John Murray Forbes also noted to Fox his "original

idea with which I have bored you so much & which I broached to the President in *April 61* that the sea belongs to us, & ought to be made our chief dependence for putting down the Rebels & keeping the foreign bull dogs peaceable," November 19, 1862, Forbes to Fox, Gustavus Vasa Fox Papers, New-York Historical Society Library Manuscripts, New York, N.Y., Box 3: Letters received, 1862, A–K.

11. London *Times*, January 4, 1862.

12. *Hansard's Parliamentary Debates*, vol. 166 (London: Cornelius Buck, 1862), March 31, 1862, "Iron-Plated Ships—Observations," 263; April 3,1862, "Iron-Plated Ships," 433-4; June 11, 1862, Palmerston to Somerset, Somerset Papers; *Hansard*, vol. 166, April 4, 1862, "Iron-Plated Ships and Land Fortifications," 608.

13. March 31,1862, Russell to Palmerston, Palmerston Papers, University of Southampton, MS 62, GC/RU/691–716, January to June, 1862.

14. Worthington Chauncey Ford, ed., *A Cycle of Adams Letters, 1861–1865*, 2 vols. (Boston: Houghton Mifflin, 1920), 1:123.

15. April 23, 1862, Ericsson to Seward, John Ericsson Papers, American Swedish Museum, Philadelphia.

16. By August 11, 1862, Gideon Welles was writing in his diary that "we are not, it is true, in a condition for war with Great Britain just at this time, but England is in scarcely a better condition for a war with us," Howard K. Beale, ed., *Diary of Gideon Welles: Secretary of the Navy under Lincoln and Johnson*, 3 vols. (New York: Norton, 1960), 1:79.

17. See Howard Jones, *Union in Peril: The Crisis over British Intervention in the Civil War* (Chapel Hill and London: University of North Carolina Press, 1992), and his essay "History and Mythology: The Crisis over British Intervention in the Civil War," in Robert E. May, ed., *The Union, the Confederacy, and the Atlantic Rim* (West Lafayette, Ind.: Purdue University Press, 1995), 29–67.

18. P.R.O., WO 33/12 (nos. 186 to 212, 1863), November 7, 1862, "Printed for the distribution of the Cabinet," Confidential, *Recognition of the Independence of the Southern States of the North American Union*, Secretary of War Sir George C. Lewis, 2.

19. Quote from Regis. A. Courtemanche, *No Need of Glory: The British Navy in American Waters 1860–64* (Annapolis: Naval Institute Press, 1977), 153.

20. P.R.O., ADM 1/5840 (From Surveyor, January–April, 1863), January 30, 1863, "American Iron clad Vessel—Statements of the *New York Herald* forwarded by Adm. Sir A. Milne," no. 215. See also *Scientific American*'s two-page feature on "English and American Iron-Clad Ships of War," vol. 9, no. 15, October 10, 1863, 229–30.

21. See for example the *Joint Resolution Relative to Lake and River Defences of Pennsylvania* and the privately printed *Defences of Maine, 31-1-1862*, both found in the Abraham Lincoln Papers, Library of Congress, Manuscript Division, Washington D.C.; also 37th Congress, 2d Session, House of Representatives, Executive Document No. 14, *Fortification of the Sea-Coast and Lakes—Message from the President of the United States, 19-12-1861;* Report of the Board of Fortifications, *Congressional Globe*, 37th Congress, 2d Session, Series No. 162, 5-6-1862, 2589-2592; and *Congressional Globe*, 37th Congress, 2d Session, Series No. 47, 11-2-1862, 739-50.

22. "The enlargement of the Illinois and Michigan canal has, by the conduct of Great Britain, been rendered a clear, absolute, military necessity. A failure on our part to construct it would now be sheer stupidity. England has, by her canals, made the lakes as free to her navy as the ocean.... The paw of the British lion is rather too plainly in sight on these peaceful lakes," *Congressional Globe*, 37th Congress, 2d Session, Series No. 189, June 6, 1862, 3026–7; see also *Ship Canal to Connect Mississippi River and Lake Michigan—Report from Committee on Military Affairs*, 37th Congress, 2d Session, House of Representatives, Report No. 37; and "Defence of the Upper Lakes—Memorandum for the President," by Major-General Joseph Gilbert Totten, Engineers Department, Lincoln Papers, Library of Congress. See March 17, 1862, Richard P. Morgan to Ericsson, and April 14, 1862, Ericsson to Samuel B. Ruggles, Chairman of the Lake Defense Committee, New York Chamber of Commerce (Ericsson Papers, Philadelphia), on proposed specifications for a Great Lakes monitor drawing 8 feet fully loaded; 6 feet, 6 inches without stores, ammunition or ballast for canals.

23. *Congressional Globe*, 37th Congress, 2d Session, Series No. 168, June 13, 1862, 2675–80. See also the London *Times*, September 9, 1862. The *Passaic*-class monitor USS *Camanche* was dispatched (manufactured but unassembled) to San Francisco to provide added security; see Donald L. Canney, *The Old Steam Navy, Volume Two: The Ironclads, 1842–1885* (Annapolis, Md.: Naval Institute Press, 1993), 77–78.

24. See Allen Salisbury, *The Civil War and the American System: America's Battle with Britain, 1860–1876* (New York: Campaigner Publications, Inc., 1978), for an argument that Britain's economic motives for intervention were far more insidious than simply resuming the cotton trade.

25. Entry dated December 6, 1861, in *William Howard Russell's Civil War: Private Diaries and Letters, 1861–1862*, ed. Martin Crawford (Athens: University of Georgia Press, 1992), 198.

26. See, for example, the *New York Herald*, June 27, 1862. "You hardly cannot

mean to say," Russell defensively replied to Somerset, "that if the American merchants in Japan did what the Liverpool Merchants have been doing with impunity we should be obliged to go to war with America, for this would be urging that we are at this moment giving America just cause of War. This of course would be a strong condemnation of ourselves, and one which we could never admit," August 21, 1863, Russell to Somerset, Somerset Papers, D/RA/A/2A/52, Letters from Lord John Russell, 1863. Within two weeks the foreign secretary wrote Palmerston that he had ordered the detainment of the Laird Rams under private construction at Birkenhead—undeniably for Confederate service—though this was against British common law. "We shall thus test the law, and if we have to pay damages, we have satisfied the opinion which prevails here, as well as in America, that this kind of neutral hostility should not be allowed to go on without some attempt to stop it," September 3, 1863, Russell to Palmerston, MS 62, Palmerston Papers, GC/RU.

27. Charles B. Boynton, *The History of the Navy during the Rebellion*, 2 vols. (New York: D. Appleton, 1868), 1:6.

28. Stephen R. Wise, *Lifeline of the Confederacy: Blockade Running During the Civil War* (Columbia: University of South Carolina Press, 1991), 3–18, 27, 221–6. Wise notes that the South did not have a merchant marine, and initially assumed "King Cotton" diplomacy would force England to break the Northern blockade for its cotton supply.

29. Letter dated March 16, 1863, from Beverly Wilson Palmer, ed., *The Selected Letters of Charles Sumner*, 2 vols. (Boston: Northeastern University Press, 1990), 2:150.

30. May 15, 1862, Fox to A. A. Harwood, U.S. National Archives, Record Group (hereafter "N.A., R.G.") 74, Records of the Bureau of Ordnance, Entry 16, "Letters Received from the Secretary of the Navy and Navy Department Bureaus," Box 4, September 1861 to December 1866 (Letterbook), 46, emphasis mine.

31. N.A., R.G. 74, Bureau of Ordnance, Entry 98, "Reports Concerning Target Practice on Iron Plates, 1862–64," 2 vols., 2: 27, 45–46.

32. September 26, 1863, Ericsson to Fox (Fox Papers), quoted from James Phinney Baxter, *The Introduction of the Ironclad Warship* (Cambridge: Harvard University Press, 1933), 329, footnote 1.

33. April 28, 1862, Ericsson to Fox, John Ericsson Papers, Library of Congress, Manuscript Division, Washington, D.C. "Whatever success may attend the large and costly armored ships of the Warrior class, which are being constructed by some of the maritime Powers of Europe, cruising in deep waters, they can

scarcely cause alarm here, for we have within the United States few harbors that are accessible to them, and for those few the Government can always be prepared whenever a foreign war is imminent. It has been deemed advisable, however, that we should have a few large-sized armed cruisers, of great speed, for ocean service, as well as of the class of smaller vessels for coastwise and defensive operations," *Congressional Globe*, 37th Congress, 3d Session, *Appendix, Report of the Secretary of the Navy*, December 1, 1862, 18. See the contemporary description of this monitor, U.S.S. *Dictator*, in *Scientific American* 7, no. 7 (August 16, 1862), 106, which also quotes Ericsson's claim that the reinforced iron structure of the ship's prow "will split an iceberg."

34. April 28, 1862, Ericsson to Fox, John Ericsson Papers, Library of Congress.

35. *Congressional Globe*, 37th Congress, 3d Session, *Appendix, Report of the Secretary of the Navy*, December 1, 1862, 18–19.

36. *Congressional Globe*, 38th Congress, 1st Session, *Appendix, Report of the Secretary of the Navy*, December 7, 1863, 16–17. Welles makes the point in his journal entry of December 26, 1863 that "a few strong, powerful vessels will conduce to economy because they will deter commercial nations from troubling us, and if not troubled, we need no large and expensive navy," *Diary*, 1:496.

37. P.R.O., ADM 1/5879, From Captains A–G, 1864, "Report on Ships of United States Navy 1864, Capt. J. G. Goodenough, R.N., received in 'M' Dept. 21 October, 1864." Goodenough's enclosed report to Lyons is dated Washington, April 12, 1864. See also Richard M. Basoco, William E. Geoghegan, and Frank J. Merli, eds., "A British View of the Union Navy, 1864: A Report Addressed to Her Majesty's Minister at Washington," *American Neptune* 27 (January 1967): 30–45.

38. Horace Porter, *Campaigning with Grant* (1897, reprint, New York: Da Capo Press, 1986), 407–8. Another account, possibly legend, quotes Lincoln thus: "I remember when I was a lad, there were two fields behind our house separated by a fence. In each field there was a big bulldog, and these dogs spent the whole day racing up and down, snarling and yelping at each other through that fence. One day they both came at the same moment to a hole in it, big enough to let either of them through. Well, gentlemen, what do you think they did? They just turned tail and scampered away as fast as they could in opposite directions. Now England and America are like those bulldogs," from Emanuel Hertz, ed., *Lincoln Talks: A Biography in Anecdote* (New York: Viking Press, 1939), 356–7.

39. December 23, 1861, Ericsson to Welles, quoted from Baxter, *Introduction*, "Appendix G", 358–59. See also Baxter's groundbreaking exposition of the

Navy Department's own turret ironclad scheme, particularly chapter 13, "The North Seeks a Solution," 238–84, also 305–6.

40. April 28, 1862, Ericsson to Welles, Ericsson Papers, Philadelphia.

41. February 7, 1862, Welles to Senator John P. Hale, Chairman of the Naval Committee, N.A., R.G. 45, entry 5, "Letters to Congress," Letterbook 13: 457–58.

42. On the other hand, Charleston's batteries might have accomplished more with fewer though heavier guns. *ORN*, 1, 14: 111–14; also Johnson and Buel, eds., *Battles and Leaders*, 4: 32–47. See particularly Alvah F. Hunter (ed. and Introduction by Craig L. Symonds), *A Year on a Monitor and the Destruction of Fort Sumter* (Columbia: University of South Carolina Press, 1987), 33–37, 47–61.

43. April 8, 1863, USS *Passaic*, *ORN*, 1, 14: 9–11.

44. December 2, 1863, Welles to Commander Thomas Craven, Gideon Welles Papers, Library of Congress, Manuscript Division, Washington, D.C., "Correspondence, October–December, 1863."

45. *ORN* Series I, 14: 265–8 (CSS *Atlanta*); 417–20, 425–8, and 21: 494–6, 531–3 (CSS *Tennessee*); 11: 658 (CSS *Virginia II*); Johnson and Buel, eds., *Battles and Leaders*, 4: 27–31; 379–406; 705–7, respectively. See also the vivid account of the capture of the *Atlanta* in Hunter, *A Year on a Monitor*, 73–86.

46. As also noticed by the *New York Herald*, see November 3, 1864.

47. *Scientific American*, 11, no. 26 (December 24, 1864), 402.

48. London *Times*, November 1, 1865.

49. See Spencer Tucker, *The Jeffersonian Gunboat Navy* (Columbia: South Carolina University Press, 1993), also his article "The Jeffersonian Gunboats in Service, 1804–1825," *American Neptune* 55 (spring 1995): 97–110; Gene Allen Smith, "A Means to an End: Gunboats and Thomas Jefferson's Theory of Defense," *American Neptune* 55 (spring 1995): 111–21; Samuel J. Watson, "Knowledge, Interest, and the Limits of Military Professionalism: The Discourse on American Coastal Defence, 1815–1860," *War in History* 5 (1998): 3:280–307; and Gene Allen Smith, "The Ruinous Folly of a Navy: A History of the Jeffersonian Gunboat Program" (Ph.D. diss., Auburn University, 1991).

Contributors

HAROLD HOLZER, coeditor, is cochairman of the U.S. Lincoln Bicentennial Commission and senior vice president for external affairs at The Metropolitan Museum of Art in New York. His twenty-three books on Lincoln and the Civil War include *Prang's Civil War Pictures, State of the Union: New York and the Civil War; The Confederate Image* (coauthored with Mark E. Neely Jr. and Gabor Boritt); and *The Union Image* and *Mine Eyes Have Seen the Glory: The Civil War in Art* (both coauthored with Neely). He has won many awards for his books, including a Lincoln Prize in 2004.

TIM MULLIGAN, coeditor, is director of external affairs for The Bard Graduate Center for Studies in the Decorative Arts, Design, and Culture in New York City. He is the author of three books: *The Traveler's Guide to the Hudson River Valley; Virginia: A History and Guide,* and *The Traveler's Guide to Western New England and the Connecticut River Valley.* He has also written for many of the major magazines in this country.

WILLIAM C. DAVIS is director of programs for the Virginia Center for Civil War Studies at Virginia Tech, where he also serves as professor of history. He is the author or editor of more than forty books in the fields of Civil War and Southern history, as well as numerous documentary screenplays. Davis was on-camera senior consultant for fifty-two episodes of the History Channel series, *Civil War Journal*.

HOWARD J. FULLER is a senior lecturer in war studies at the School of Humanities, Languages, and Social Studies at the University of Wolverhampton in Great Britain. A specialist in the American Civil War, particularly naval technology and strategy, he has lectured widely and written for many scholarly journals, and serves as associate editor for the *International Journal of Naval History*. He is at work on books about Civil War naval history and early American and British ironclad development.

JOSEPH A. GUTIERREZ JR. is senior director for museum operations and education at the Jamestown-Yorktown Foundation in Williamsburg, Virginia. He has published articles in *Museum News* and other professional journals and served as an adjunct faculty member at Hampton University, Old Dominion University, the College of William and Mary, the University of Virginia, and Virginia Commonwealth University.

JEFF JOHNSTON has served as a research assistant and program specialist with the National Oceanic and Atmospheric Association's (NOAA) *Monitor* National Marine Sanctuary since 1995, and as one of the NOAA team leaders on *Monitor* expeditions since 1998. As part of NOAA's archaeology team, he was instrumental in the successful recoveries from the ocean floor of both the ship's unique steam engine and its iconic gun turret.

DAVID A. MINDELL is Dibner Associate Professor of the History of Engineering and Manufacturing in the Program in Science, Technology, and Society at the Massachusetts Institute of Technology (MIT). He has degrees in electrical engineering and literature from

Yale University, and holds the Ph.D. in the history of technology from MIT.

JOHN V. QUARSTEIN is director of the Virginia War Museum and administrator of historical services and museums for the city of Newport News, Virginia. He serves as adjunct professor at the College of William and Mary, the University of Virginia, and Virginia Commonwealth University. Quarstein's seven books include *The Battle of the Ironclads*, and he has lectured on the *Monitor-Virginia* duel nationwide.

CRAIG L. SYMONDS, who retired in 2005 after nearly thirty years as professor of history at the U.S. Naval Academy at Annapolis, where he taught Civil War and naval history, recently became chief historian of the Monitor Center at The Mariners' Museum. His many books include *Confederate Admiral: The Life and Wars of Franklin Buchanan* and the *Naval Institute Historical Atlas of the U.S. Navy*.

MABRY TYSON is the great-grandson of Catesby Jones, commander of the CSS *Virginia*, and is the creator if the web site CSSVirginia.org. He has spoken often on the Battle of Hampton Roads.

Index

Adams, Charles Francis, 129
Anderson, Hans, 104
Armor, 2
    of *Monitor,* 143; salvage of, 163–65
    of *Virginia,* 25–26, 67–68, 76, 141
Armstrong, William, 135
Army and Navy Journal, 52
Aroostoock (USS), 80
Atlanta (CSS), 136–37
Atwater, Norman K., 169
Austria, 144
Auxiliary steamers, 20

Baker Wrecking Company, 62
Baltimore Riot, 70
Bard, James and John, 190
Barnard, John G., 75, 144
Barnard principle, 144
Battlefield artists, land-based, 112
Baxter, J. P., 134
Beaufort (CSS), 72
Black Prince (HMS), 2
Blockade, 21–22
Bolts, 21, 66, 75
    Brooke, 142, 144
    of *Monitor,* 13
Boot, salvaged, 168
Britain
    Ericsson on, 126, 136
    and ironclads, xiii, 1–2, 23, 88, 125–39
    Proclamation of Neutrality, 132
    Union responses to, 134–36
Broadwater, John, 159
Brooke, John Mercer, 75–76, 82
    background of, 65
    and *Virginia* designs, 24–25, 64–67, 188
Brooke bolts, 142, 144
Brooke rifles, 67, 142, 144
Browning, Robert, 190
Buchanan, Franklin
    background of, 70
    at battle of Hampton Roads, 4, 57, 71, 73, 87, 145–46
    and *Monitor,* 74
    and *Virginia,* 58, 82
Bushnell, Cornelius, 27–28, 128
Buttersworth, James, 190
Buttre, John Chester, 187
Butts, Francis, 42, 51, 168–69
Byrd, Richard, 190

Calvert Lithography Company, 121
Campbell, Albert B., 40–41
    in art, 187
Canal network, 132
Cape Charles lighthouse, 190
Cape Hatteras, 155, 164
Century Illustrated Magazine, 46, 103
Chesapeake Bay, Mariners' Museum collection on, 190
Chickasaw (USS), 138

Chittenden, Lucius E., 101–2
Church, William Conant, 52
Coal, 20
  and salvage, 165
Cobden, Richard, 133
Colorado (USS), 58
Communications, on *Monitor*, 7, 44–45
Confederacy
  and art, 116–17
  on battle of Hampton Roads, 88, 95
  industrial weakness of, 21, 23, 25, 63, 141
  plan to capture *Monitor*, 77–78
Congress (USS), 3, 35, 73
  in art, 114–15
Continental (Shipbuilding) Works, 118
Crabtree, August F., 191
Crankshafts, 20
Cumberland (USS), 3, 35, 61, 69, 73
  in art, 115
Currier & Ives, 115–16
Curtis, Richard, 69, 82
Cyclorama, 91–92, 119

Dahlgren guns, 30, 51, 66–67, 134, 142–44
  in museum collection, 175
Davidson, Hunter, 4, 69
Davidson, Julian Oliver, 119
Davis, Jefferson, 63, 69
Dawson, Montague, 190
Debate on *Monitor* versus *Virginia*, 14, 74, 141–54
  facts agreed upon by both sides, 86–88
  facts disputed, 88–89
Delaware (USS), 59
Demologos, 23
Diamond Shoals, 157
Draft
  of *Monitor*, 8, 145
  of *Virginia*, 25, 81, 145
Dragon (USS), 148
Drake, Francis, 142
Drayton, Percival, 51, 53, 137
Drewry's Bluff, 47–48
Duke University, 157
Du Pont, Samuel F., 111

Edgerton, Doc, 157

Eggleston, George, 4
Eggleston, John Randolph, 70, 72, 80
18-pound guns, 20
Electrolysis, reverse, 161
11-inch guns, 21, 30, 143–44, 162
Enamel spoons, 118
Endicott & Co., 118–19
Engine(s)
  of *Monitor*, 8; in museum collection, 173–74; salvage of, 161–62
  steam, 2, 19–20; and blockade, 22
  of *Virginia*, 25, 64–65, 67–68
Engineers
  art and, 113–14, 120
  viewpoint of, 46, 54
Ericsson, George Fred, 169
Ericsson, John
  in art, 120
  Gutierrez on, 143
  and living conditions, 41–43, 50
  and monitor designs, 27–29
  and name of *Monitor*, 126
  on naval power, 129–31, 136
  reputation of, 28, 45–46, 52–54, 92, 105–7
  and screw propeller, 59
  and sea trial, 31
Explosive shells, 21

Farragut, David Glasgow, 114
15-inch guns, 21, 134
The First Encounter of Iron-Clads, 121
The First Naval Conflict Between Iron Clad Vessels, 120
5-inch guns, 20
Flye, William, 187
Forks, salvaged, 184
Forrest, French, 62–63, 65
Fort Calhoun, 60
Fort Monroe, 60
Fort Morgan, 22
Fort Norfolk, 60–61
Fort Sumter, 22
Foute, R. C., 77–78
Fox, Gustavus Vasa, 86, 92, 98–99, 105–6, 126, 134
France, and ironclads, 2, 23
Franklin, Benjamin, 85
Franklin, S. R., 82

Fuller, A. B., 93
Fulton, Robert, 23

Galena (USS), 47, 80, 132
Geer, George, 39, 42
Germantown (USS), 59, 62–63
Gettysburg, battle of, in art, 117–18
Gloire, 2, 23
Glory, technology and, 122
Goldsborough, Louis, 47, 75, 80
Goodenough, James G., 135
Gosport Navy Yard, 23–24, 59–63
Graveyard of the Atlantic, 157
The Great Fight Between the "Merrimac" & "Monitor," 116
Greene, Richard, 9
Greene, Samuel Dana
  accounts of battle, 100–104
  in art, 187
  background of, 32
  at battle of Hampton Roads, 6–8, 10, 12, 14, 88
  on communications, 45
  death of, 89
  Ericsson and, 100, 106
  Fox and, 98
  on living conditions, 40, 48
  reputation of, 45–46
Griswold, Albert, 69
Grog, 3
Guns
  ironclad-killing, 134
  of *Monitor*, 10, 30–31, 51, 78, 143–44; in museum collection, 175; salvage of, 162, 168
  navy and, 20–21
  proofing, 31
  shell gun, 2
  of *Virginia*, 9, 25, 66–67, 142, 144

Hampton Roads, battle of, 1–17, 73–74. *See also* Debate
  in art, 111–23
  effects of, xiii, 15–17
  historiography of, 85–109
  lead-up to, 34–35
  map of, 97
  misconceptions about, sources of, 92–95
  observers on, 14–15
  participant accounts of, 89–95
  ship positions at, 95–98
  significance of setting, 60
Harper's Weekly, 51, 118
Hartford (USS), 114
Hasker, Charles, 69
Hawthorne, Nathaniel, on *Monitor*, 39–40, 43–44, 113–14, 119
Headley, J. T., 93–94
Heth, Henry, 61
HH (artist), 114
Holloway, Anna, 141–54
Hot shot guns, 66–67, 142, 144
Howard, Samuel, 109
Hudnut, J. M., 187
Huger, Benjamin, 69, 80
Hunley, 21
Huntington, Archer M., 189
Huntington, Collis P., 189

Infernal machines, 21
Ironclad(s)
  appropriations for, 131–32
  in art, 120
  and Britain, xiii, 1–2, 23, 125–39
  building, 19–35; cost of, 29
  history of, 1–2, 19–20
Ironclad Board, 26, 28–29
Ironclad-killing ironclad, 137
Ironclad-killing weapons, 134
Iron coffin, term, 44
Isherwood, Benjamin Franklin, 60

Jack, E. A., 91, 94, 107
Jacobsen, Antonio, 190
Jamestown (CSS), 4, 78, 148
Jeffers, William, 47–50, 105
Jefferson, Thomas, 139
Johnson, Joseph Eggleston, 79
Jones, Catesby ap Roger
  account of battle, 89, 105–7
  after battle, 80
  and armor, 67
  in art, 118
  background of, 68
  at battle of Hampton Roads, 4, 8, 12–14, 74, 87, 94
  on casemate, 72

Jones, Catesby ap Roger, cont.
  and command decisions, 146
  and name of *Virginia,* 58
  and scuttling, 82
Jones, Gertrude Tartt, 89–91
Jones, John Pembroke, 81

Keeler, William
  in art, 187
  at battle of Hampton Roads, 6–7, 9–10, 12–13
  on guard duty, 79
  on living conditions, 37–39, 41–43, 48–49
  and uniform, 32
Kevill, Thomas, 70
Kurz & Allison, 117

Lane, Fitz Hugh, 190
Last of the Wooden Navy, 114
League Island dockyard, 135
Lee, Robert E., 62, 77
Lee, Sidney Smith, 68
Lenthall, John, 57
Lewis, B. A., 187
Lewis, George, 130
Lewis, Samuel Augee, 169
Lighting, of *Monitor,* 32–33, 38, 180–81
Lincoln, Abraham
  and ironclads, 26
  and *Monitor,* 28, 101
  and *Trent* Affair, 126, 135–36
  and war, 59, 80
  and Worden, 99
Lincoln Forum, xiv
Lissa, battle of, 144
Lithographers, 117, 121
Littlepage, Hardin, 4, 8, 72–73
Long, John Collins, 59
Lynch, William, 69
Lyons, Richard, 135

Magruder, John Bankhead, 69, 71, 77
Mahone, William, 61
Mallory, Stephen Russell, 22–23, 63–65, 71, 82
Manhattan (USS), 138
Mansfield, Joseph King Fenno, 80

Marine artists, 111–23
  female, 116
  in museum collection, 190
Mariners' Museum, 115, 189–91
  Monitor Center, xiii–xiv
  and salvaging of *Monitor,* 158–59
Marston, John, 147
Mason, James, 126
Matthews, W. B., 114
McCauley, Charles Stewart, 23, 59–60
McClellan, George B., 47, 75–76, 148
McCormick Harvester, 121, 123
McKay, Donald, 2
Mechanics' Magazine, 138
Media, on battle of Hampton Roads, 88, 92–95
Melville, Herman, 122
Merrimack on the brain. See Ram fever
Merrimack (USS). *See also Virginia*
  condition of, 25, 58, 62
  early history of, 59
  name, 57–59
  raising of, 62–63
  scuttling of, 60–61
Milne, Alexander, 130
Mines, 21
Minnesota (USS), 3–8, 35, 58, 73, 148
  position of, 97–98
Minor, Robert Dabney, 69, 74
Monitor (USS). *See also* Debate; Hampton Roads
  after battle, 16, 47–51, 78, 80
  armor, 143; salvage of, 163–65
  at battle of Hampton Roads, 3–17
  Berth Deck, 118
  blower belts, 40, 49
  blower engine, 51
  bolts, 13
  British reaction to, 128–29
  building of, timeframe, 29–30, 68, 86
  and Civil War, 153
  combat record of, 148–49
  command decisions of, 147
  condition of, 98
  crew, 30, 32, 41–42, 167; in art, 187
  design of, 142–43
  diagonal braces, salvage of, 167–68
  draft of, 8, 145

engine, 8; in museum collection, 173–74; salvage of, 161–62
fighting capability of, 144–45; living conditions and, 44, 50
freeboard, 143
guns, 10, 30–31, 51, 78, 143–44; in museum collection, 175; salvage of, 162, 168
importance of, 125
leaks, 33, 40
legacy of, 153–54
lighting, 32–33, 38, 180–81
living conditions, 9–11, 32–33, 37–55
name, 126
objects in museum collection, 173–88
observers on, 4–5
overhaul of, 50–51, 161
and Peninsula Campaign, 151
port stoppers, 10
propeller: in museum collection, 178; salvage of, 160–61
salvage of, 125, 155–69; funding for, 159–61, 166
sea trial of, 31–34, 40–41
sinking of, 51, 155–56; in art, 119–20
speaking tube, 7, 44–45
steering, 31
technological impact of, 151–52
turret, 44, 48, 143–45; in art, 118; in museum collection, 173; salvage of, 125, 160, 162–63, 165–67; seal of, 33, 53
ventilation, 33–34, 38–41, 49–50, 143
victory claims, 149
Monroe Doctrine, 132
Morris, Charles, 94
Mosquito Fleet, 69
Murray, Christopher, 160

Napoleon Bonaparte, 108
Napoleon III, 132
National Oceanic and Atmospheric Association (NOAA), xiii, xiv, 125, 158–59, 190
Naugatuck (USS), 78, 80
Nautilus, 40
Naval Affairs Committee, 103–4
Naval power, Ericsson on, 129–31, 136

Navy, U.S.
and Ericsson, 28
and ironclads, 52–53
Mariners' Museum collection on, 191
Mobile Diving and Salvage Unit 2, 160
and steam engines, 20
New Ironsides (USS), 131–32
Newman, F., 116
Newton, Isaac, 6, 52
New York Herald, 126–27
Niagara (USS), 58
Nichols, Jacob, 169
9-inch guns, 21, 66, 142, 144
Norris, William, 58–59, 90, 95
North Carolina Division of Archives and History, 157
North Carolina (USS), 39

Oliver, Charles, 69
Onondaga (USS), 138
Oriental, 156

Pacific Squadron, 59
Paddlewheels, 20
Palmer, Flora Bond (Fanny), 116
Palmerston, Henry Temple, Viscount, 127, 129
Parker, William, 72
Parrott rifle, 78
Passaic-class monitors, 134, 137
Passaic (USS), 51, 137
Patrick Henry (CSS), 4
Pawnee (USS), 61
Pegram, Robert, 62
Pelton, Oliver, 117
Peninsula Campaign, 47, 148
influences on, 150–51
Pennsylvania (USS), 59
Perry, Matthew C., 70
Philadelphia Union League, 119
Phillips, Dinwiddie, 3, 72
Pierce, Franklin, 58
Pivot guns, 67
Playing cards, 118–19
Plymouth (USS), 62–63
Pook, Samuel, 27
Porter, David Dixon, 112
Porter, John Luke, 65, 24–25, 64–65, 68–69, 188

Porter, W. M., 180
Port Royal (USS), 80
Prang, Louis, 117, 119
Princeton (USS), 28
Printmakers, 115, 119–20
   Confederate, 116–17
Prize money claims, 89, 103–4
Proclamation of Neutrality, Britain, 132
Propeller, 20, 59
   of *Monitor:* in museum collection, 178; salvage of, 160–61

Railroads
   Confederate, and *Virginia,* 25
   transcontinental, 132
Raleigh, Charles Sidney, 114
Raleigh (CSS), 72
Ram fever, 16, 75, 150
Rammer head, salvaged, 167
Ramsey, Henry Ashton, 11–12, 58, 65, 68–69, 94
Reserves and Sanctuaries Marine Estuarial Act, 158
Reverse electrolysis, 161
Rhode Island (USS), 155
   logbook of, 156–57
Rifling, 21, 66
Roanoke (USS), 3, 15, 58, 73
Robinson, Robert Spencer, 130–31
Rochelle, James, 4–5
Rodman guns, 134
Rogers, John, 53
Russell, John, 129
Russell, William Howard, 132–33
Russia, and shell guns, 2

St. Lawrence (USS), 3, 73, 148
Salmon, Robert, 178
San Jacinto (USS), 80
Scientific American, 77, 138
Screw propeller, 20, 59
Scrimshaw, 118
Selfridge, Thomas O., 98, 100
Sepoy Mutiny, 130
7-inch guns, 21, 67, 142
Seward, William H., 28, 129
Sheet music covers, 119
Shell gun, 2
Shells, 66

Shot, 75
Shot ladle, salvaged, 167
Silver
   salvaged, 168, 184
   spoons, 118
Simms, Charles Carroll, 69
Skinner, Thomas C., 119
Slidell, John, 126
Smith, commodore, 29–30
Smith, John, 178
Smith, Xanthus Russell, 111–12, 119
Smokestacks, 20
Solid shot, 21
Somerset, Edward Seymour, Duke of, 129
Southern Historical Society Papers, 106
Spain, and ironclads, 1
Speaking tube, of *Monitor,* 7, 44–45
Spoons, 118
   salvaged, 169, 184
Steam engines, 2, 19–20
   and blockade, 22
Steering
   of *Monitor,* 31
   of *Virginia,* 11, 72–73
Stevens Battery, 23
Stimers, Alban, 6, 9–10, 13, 68, 101
   background of, 32
   Fox on, 98
   and sea trial, 33–34
Stockton, Robert, 28
Stodder, Louis Napoleon, 6–7, 13
   in art, 187
Stuart, Alexander Charles, 114–15, 119
Submarines, 21, 40
Sumner, Charles, 133
Sunstrom, Mark, 187
Super-*Alabamas,* 135
Susquehanna (USS), 70, 80
Symonds, Craig L., xiv

Taliaferro, William Booth, 61
Tattnall, Josiah, 76–81, 146–47
Taylor, Zachary, 69
Teaser (CSS), 4
Technology
   and art, 113, 115, 121–22
   and battle of Hampton Roads, 1, 19
   Ericsson and, 46, 54

and glory, 122
and living conditions, 41–42, 44
Monitor and, 151–52
Virginia and, 152
Tennessee (CSS), 138
Terrific Combat Between Monitor 2 Guns and Merrimac 10 Guns, 116
Tiffany & Co., 118
Times (London), 128, 138, 154
Tindall, William, 97
Toffey, Daniel, 45
  in art, 187
Torgerson, William, 117, 119
Torpedoes, underwater, 21
Tredegar Iron Works, 25, 41, 64, 66
Trent Affair, 128, 135
Trent's Reach, 138
Trescott, William, 7
Turret, of *Monitor,* 44, 48, 143–45
  in art, 118
  in museum collection, 173
  salvage of, 125, 160, 162–63, 165–67
  seal of, 33, 53
Turtle boat, 1
12-pound guns, 20
20-inch guns, 21, 134

Union
  on battle of Hampton Roads, 88, 92–95, 97–108
  and foreign intervention, 125–39; response to, 134–36
  industrial advantage of, 21; and art, 114
  losses at Hampton Roads, 74
  and *Virginia* destruction, 82

Van Brunt, Henry Gershon Jacques, 73–74, 99, 147
Vanderbilt, Cornelius, 77
Ventilation
  Ericsson on, 41, 43, 50
  of *Monitor,* 33–34, 38–41, 49–50, 143
Verne, Jules, 40
Victoria, Queen, 132
Victory claims, 85, 105
  for *Monitor,* 149
  for *Virginia,* 74, 108, 149–50
Vikings, 1

Virginia (CSS), 57–83. *See also* Debate; Hampton Roads; *Merrimack*
  after battle, 15–16, 75, 79–80, 91–92
  armor, 25–26, 68, 76, 141
  at battle of Hampton Roads, 4–17, 73–74
  building of, 24–26, 64–70; cost of, 65; credit for, 24, 65; design, 141–42, 188; timeframe, 26, 68, 86
  casemate, 24–25, 64, 66, 72, 141, 144
  and Civil War, 152–53
  combat record of, 148
  command decisions of, 145–47
  commissioning of, 31, 70–71
  crew, 69–70, 91
  draft of, 25, 81, 145
  engine, 25, 64–65, 67–68
  fighting capability of, 143–44
  guns, 9, 25, 66–67, 142, 144
  legacy of, 154
  living conditions, 11
  name, 58–59
  observers on, 74
  officers, 69–70
  and Peninsula Campaign, 150–51
  ram, 12, 67, 76, 142–43
  scuttling of, 82, 146–47; in art, 120
  shutters, 76
  smokestack, 11
  steering, 11, 72–73
  technological impact of, 152
  victory claims, 74, 108, 149–50
  web site for, 91
Virginia II (CSS), 138

Wabash (USS), 58, 111
Warrior (HMS), 2, 23, 127, 129
Watters, John III, 187
Watts, Gordon, 157
Weehawken (USS), 137–38
Welles, Gideon
  and Buchanan, 70
  and ironclads, 26–27, 29, 52, 135–37
  and living conditions, 42
  and *Merrimack,* 60–61
White, E. V., 91
Williams, Frank, xiv
Williams, Peter, 6

Williamson, William P., 24–25, 65, 67–68
Wood, John Taylor, 5, 69, 72–73, 82, 148
   on *Monitor*, 74, 149
Wool, John Ellis, 80
Worden, John L.
   account of battle, 102
   in art, 118, 187
   background of, 30
   at battle of Hampton Roads, 6–7, 12–14, 34, 147
   Fox and, 98
   on living conditions, 42–44
   and sea trial, 31, 33

Yi, Admiral, 1

Zouave (USS), 148

www.ingramcontent.com/pod-product-compliance
Lightning Source LLC
Chambersburg PA
CBHW031240290426
44109CB00012B/376